A Poets' War:

British Poets and the
Spanish Civil War

A Poets' War:
British Poets and the
Spanish Civil War

by

Hugh D. Ford

Philadelphia

UNIVERSITY OF PENNSYLVANIA PRESS

LONDON: OXFORD UNIVERSITY PRESS

1965

For James and Theodosia Ford,
Therese, and Nancy

7484

Printed in the United States of America

Preface

BOOKS ABOUT THE SPANISH CIVIL WAR CONTINUE TO APPEAR. The publication in the past few years of four historical studies, several volumes of literary criticism, each containing sizable sections on the writing of the war, and a spate of biographies, memoirs, and social commentaries—many by participants— suggests that the Spanish war is well on the way to becoming one of the most thoroughly investigated conflicts of the twentieth century.

My own contribution to this burgeoning literature is modest. In scope, it covers only a few years in the 1930s. Geographically, it is confined almost entirely to England. The *dramatis personae* are the British poets who, for a variety of reasons, became involved in the Spanish struggle, either as participants or as supporters of one of the warring factions. It is the story of their response to the Spanish war as recorded in their poetry and lives that I have endeavored to set down here.

In the process of gathering material for this book in the United States, England, Ireland, France, and Spain, I consulted many of the writers discussed in the following pages. All generously permitted me to question them at length, even when such questioning must have revived memories that might better have remained undisturbed. And what became apparent in nearly every discussion was that these writers were talking about a war which they consider unfinished, despite the fact that Generalissimo Francisco Franco announced the end of the civil war on April 1, 1939. With this thought in mind, I must add that my own study is necessarily incomplete.

My acknowledgments are many. First, for the material of Chapter 1, I must note the considerable assistance I received from the following books: Alison Peers' *The Spanish Tragedy* (London, 1936), William Rust's *Britons in Spain* (London, 1939), *Book of the XVth International Brigade* (Madrid, 1939), Julio Álvarez del Vayo's *Freedom's Battle* (New York, 1940), David Cattell's two excellent studies, *Communism and the Spanish Civil War* (Berkeley, 1955), and *Soviet Diplomacy and the Spanish Civil War* (Berkeley, 1957), Salvador de Madariaga's *Spain: A Modern History* (New York, 1958), and Hugh Thomas' *The Spanish Civil War* (London, 1961).

For assistance in gathering the material found in later chapters, I wish to thank William Alexander, of the Communist Party of Great Britain; Countess Azobel, who generously agreed to speak for the Spanish Nationalists; Alvah Bessie; Len Crome; Alec Digges, secretary of the International Brigades Association, whose assistance in locating people and materials was most valuable; Charles Duff, who provided so much useful information about his own publications; Frank Edwards; Louis Fischer; Moe Fishman, secretary of the Veterans of the Abraham Lincoln Brigade; Victor Gollancz; Mrs. Kathleen Hoagland, who helped in reconstructing the activities of Charles Donnelly and Ewart Milne; James Hughes; John Langdon-Davies, whose vast knowledge of the war in Catalonia aided me greatly; Sean Nolan; Thomas O'Brian; Brian O'Neill, of the *Irish Press,* who knows as much about the Irish participation in the Spanish war as anyone I have met; V. S. Pritchett; Kenneth Rexroth, whose opinions on the war were helpful; and Richard Turner.

My thanks go also to the following authors for their generous assistance: W. H. Auden; Austin Clarke; Miss Nancy Cunard, who turned over her entire collection of Spanish war materials to me and patiently answered innumerable questions; Leslie Daiken, whose thoughtfulness and help I deeply value; John Dos Passos; Eric Edney; Miss Margot Heinemann; Rayner Heppenstall; Miss Josephine Herbst; Laurie Lee; John Lehmann, who made several valuable suggestions; C. Day Lewis, whose enthusiastic encouragement of this project I greatly appreciated; Jack Lindsay, who showed me several unpublished poems of the period and who made the rare items of his own library available to me; Peader O'Donnell, whose suggestions were well-chosen and fruitful; Paul Potts; Edgell Rickword, former editor of *Left Review,* who answered numerous inquiries; Stephen Spender; Randall Swingler; and Miles Tomalin, who permitted me to read his poems written while he was serving as a member of the International Brigades.

Finally, I should like to thank the librarians at the British Museum, Marx House, the National Library, Dublin, Princeton University, the University of Pennsylvania, and, especially, Miss Joyce Brodowski, of the Roscoe L. West Library, Trenton State College, for their help in locating books and periodicals. For assistance of another kind, I am especially indebted to Mr. and Mrs. James C. Ford, without whose help this study would be far less complete than it is; to Professor Mark Longaker, for his kindly and sage advice and encouragement; and to my wife, Therese Ford, whose many sacrifices, large and small, during the past few years have made steady concentration on this project possible.

HUGH D. FORD

Acknowledgments

CURTIS BROWN, LTD. for excerpts from *Flowering Rifle*, "The Carmelites of Toledo," "A Letter from the San Mateo Front," "The Hoopoe," "Talking Bronco," "La Mancha in Wartime," "Monologue," "Dawn on the Sierra of Gredos," copyright 1957 by Roy Campbell, reprinted from *Collected Poems* of Roy Campbell, by permission of Curtis Brown, Ltd.

CHARLES DUFF for "Incident 1938" by Dennis Birch, "To A Free People" by John Gawsworth, "In Remembrance of a Son of Wales" by T. E. Nicholas, "To a Certain Priest" by Stanley Richardson, all of which appeared in *Voice of Spain*.

FABER AND FABER, LTD. for excerpts from "Calamiterror" and "Elegy on Spain," copyright 1957 by George Barker, reprinted from *Collected Poems* by George Barker, by permission of Faber and Faber, Ltd., excerpt from *Autumn Journal*, copyright 1939 by Louis MacNeice, reprinted from *Autumn Journal*, by permission of Faber and Faber, Ltd.

LAURIE LEE for his poem "A Moment of War."

JOHN LEHMANN for excerpts from "San Pedro" by Clive Branson, "Heart of the Heartless World" and "As Our Might Lessens" by John Cornford, "For R.J.C." and "Grieve in a New Way for New Losses" by Margot Heinemann, all of which appeared in *New Writing;* "Eyes," "Retrospect" by David Marshall, "Battle of Jarama 1937" by John Lepper, "Jarama Front" by T. A. R. Hyndman, "Full Moon at Tierz" by John Cornford, "Tolerance of Crows" by Charles Donnelly, "Guadalajara" and "Death of Garcia Lorca" by J. Bronowski, "The

Tourist Looks at Spain" by Rex Warner, "This New Offensive" by Margot Heinemann, "The Calpe Hunt" by S. Richardson, "The Madrid Defenders" by Richard Church, "For Those with Investments in Spain" by Brian Howard, "Lorca" by Geoffrey Parsons, "Spain" and "The Future Is Near Us" by H. B. Mallalieu, all of which appeared in *Poems for Spain,* edited by John Lehmann and Stephen Spender, London, 1939.

JACK LINDSAY for excerpts from "Looking at a Map of Spain on the Devon Coast," "On Guard for Spain," "Requiem Mass."

HUGH MACDIARMID for excerpts from "Fascists, You Have Killed My Comrades" and "Postscript."

EWART MILNE for excerpts from "Thinking of Artolas" and "The Hour Glass (1)."

NEW DIRECTIONS for excerpts from "A Song for the Spanish Anarchists," "Bombing Casualties," and "The Heart Conscripted," copyright 1951 by Herbert Read, reprinted from *Collected Poems* of Herbert Read, by permission of New Directions.

NEW STATESMAN for excerpts from "Analogy in Madrid" by Elizabeth Cluer and "They Got What They Wanted" by Sagittarius.

PEADAR O'DONNELL for excerpt from "Off to Salamanca."

OXFORD UNIVERSITY PRESS, INC. for excerpts from "Bombers," "The Volunteers" and "The Nabara," copyright 1945, by C. Day Lewis, reprinted from *Short Is the Time; Poems 1936-43,* by permission of Oxford University Press, Inc.

RANDOM HOUSE, INC. for excerpts from "Spain 1937," copyright 1940 by W. H. Auden, reprinted from *The Collected Poetry of W. H. Auden,* by permission of Random House, Inc.; excerpts from "Ultima Ratio Regum," "The Coward," "Two Armies," "Fall of a City" and "Port Bou," copyright 1942 by Stephen Spender, reprinted from *Collected Poems 1928-1953,* by Stephen Spender, by permission of Random House, Inc.

EDGELL RICKWORD for excerpts from "To the Wife of Any Non-Intervention Statesman."

KITTY WINTRINGHAM for excerpts from "Granen," "Barcelona Nerves" and "Monument : A Poem from the Spanish Front" by Tom Wintringham.

Contents

A Poets' War:
British Poets and the
Spanish Civil War

Introduction

The Mood of Protest and Spain

WE NOW KNOW THAT THE GROUP OF POETS LED BY W. H. Auden was considerably less cohesive than it was thought to be in the 1930s. Since that decade, when they rather suddenly came into prominence and when their poetry seemed the only important poetry being written, Auden, Spender, and Day Lewis have repeatedly exhibited their exclusiveness from one another. But the homogeneity that prompted critics like Michael Roberts to "collectivize" them into the Audenites, or the Movement Poets, was not wholly illusory. Indeed, at the time a common morality, or ideology, bound them together. Roberts called it social communism, and contended it was really no less than an "extension of personality and consciousness which comes to a group of men when they are working together from some common purpose."[1]

The common purpose early in the decade consisted primarily of searching for the causes of England's moral and social disintegration, and of castigating those responsible for it, and of advocating ways to improve the situation. The previous generation ("death to the old gang," Auden recommended) they accused of having no social conscience and, even worse, of attempting to foster a social and cultural detachment at a time of appalling poverty and misery. They maintained that

17

the traditions that had once unified English society had worn out, and that a new and revitalized tradition that would end the country's problems must replace them.

The first step toward revitalizing tradition was to achieve "solidarity with others," mainly with the common people, the working classes who, either by parliamentary action or—as seemed more probable at the time—by revolutionary upheaval, would eventually supersede the bourgeoisie as the dominant class. As the word revolution suggests, they believed the way to create a revitalized tradition was to emulate the Marxist "social experiment" which had already begun to transform Czarist Russia into a workers' paradise. To left-wing poets the Marxist solution hardly seemed too radical a remedy for England's ills. And its promise of a new era of human progress and potentiality was something they might help to effect in England. Their poetry began hinting of socialist utopias and equality and the general happiness. The sense of purpose in their most socially conscious poems was strong. Day Lewis has recently recollected that the "sense of engagement," of living and writing at a time when "it seemed possible to hope, to choose, to act, as individuals but for a common end," lent urgency to everything they did. They looked across the bridge that spanned "the old romantic chasm between the artist and the man of action, the poet and the ordinary man,"[2] and they prepared to cross over.

In a sense Auden, Spender, and Day Lewis never quite made that crossing. But a great many other poets did. The former were only the most prominent of the dozens of poets who comprised the left-wing literary movement, and though their work has been accorded more attention than that by less renowned poets of the period, it is certainly not, a priori, the only or perhaps even the best index to the thought of the time. The poets who crossed the bridge, or at least got closer to the opposite end than the Audenites, poets like Hugh Mac-Diarmid, John Cornford, Christopher Caudwell, Charles Madge, and Charles Donnelly—to name only a few—represent, perhaps, the mainstream of the left-wing poetry. Their popular verse—unsophisticated, inclined toward bluntness and slogan-making, shrill and rough—was capable, notwithstanding all its violations of accepted poetic standards, of reaching a new and expanding audience. Their work cannot so easily be written off as propaganda either, because as Day Lewis explained at the time, "there is no reason why poetry should not also be propaganda." The single requirement Day Lewis demanded of the revolutionary poet (and it is the one I should say these poets violated, but less often than is commonly appreciated) was that "propaganda verse is to be condemned when the didactic is achieved at the expense of the poetic."[3]

One reason the Audenites did not cross over the bridge is implicit in Day Lewis' statement about propaganda. The quarrel he waged with himself—and Spender and Auden had much the same quarrel—arose out of the difficulty of determining whether he had responded to political ideas, which presupposed that the artist would and could become "the man of action" as well as "the ordinary man," first as a man, or whether he had merely experienced a rhetorical feeling about them. The really undesirable situation, he felt, was for the poet to have "dealings with political ideas as a poet without first having feelings about them as a man: for direct contact between the poetic function and abstract ideas can give birth only to rhetoric."[4]

By 1936, what could only be described as a formidable proletarian movement in British literature, especially the poetry, was well-established and flourishing. The successful launching of the *Left Review*, in 1934, and of *New Writing* and the Left Book Club, in 1936, assured not only the Audenites but all the left-wing poets, representing all poetical-political positions, of a bigger audience. Indeed, it seemed as though the union beween poet and public, heretofore generally regarded as more theoretical than actual, was about to take place. How complete this union might have become if the Spanish Civil War had not provided the impetus that actually brought it into being for a while, is hard to say. But there seems little doubt now that the war that broke out in Spanish Morocco in July 1936 provided a cause to which both poet and reader eagerly responded, and in which the poet found materials for a new common symbolism. The common ground between poet and reader had never before been so great, or so fertile. If poets were ever to draw closer to their audience, in a unity based upon shared experience, the Spanish war seemed made for the occasion.

If the socially conscious writing of the early 1930s had lacked a central force, a cohesive symbol of some sort, that was no longer the case. After July, the Spanish war became the rallying point for all the writers of the Left. Moreover, it exerted an extraordinary pull upon many others to whom politics can scarcely said to have existed prior to the outbreak of war in Spain. On these nonpolitical writers, as well as the Leftists themselves, the war acted as a catalyst, bringing to the surface their half-formulated political theories and humanitarian hopes. Most saw the war as a counteraction which could possibly resolve the most pressing problem of their time : the advance of fascism, both in Europe and at home. For all its incoherence, the fight of the Spanish Republic against the rebels and their foreign supporters became symbolic of the struggle against fascism. Many in England believed that the future of Europe would be decided in Spain. Rex Warner pronounced that Spain had "torn the veil of Europe,"[5] and the novelist John Sommerfield likened what was happening there to the "fighting on the plains of Tours and Poitiers when the army of Charles Martel drove back the invading Moors and turned the tide that was submerging Europe."[6] Also at stake in Spain was the existence of progressive or liberal ideas. It was generally assumed that if the Republic lost, an irreparable blow would be dealt liberal thought, which had already suffered setbacks in Germany, Austria, and Italy.

The excitement created among writers by the Spanish war was mirrored in the response of the entire intelligentsia. The whole intellectual world, wrote one commentator, if not already in Spain, had begun "talking about or writing about or thinking about that gruesome, threatening, yet in its way inspiring theme." It filled the air, and pressed "into our thoughts to the constant exclusion of other ideas."[7] Most Leftists defined it as a clear-cut issue between the defenders and destroyers of democracy, between the Spanish people and a reactionary group of aristocrats, priests, and generals— between freedom and repression. While public opinion in general favored the Republican government, the Insurgents, or rebels, soon began attracting sympathizers to their side, who defended their choice by declaring that the attack had been necessary to prevent Spain from being overrun by communism. Most Rightists viewed the struggle as between the Church and a godless Marxism rather than between fascism and antifascism. Hilaire Belloc, one of Franco's staunchest supporters, spoke for many of his compeers when he said that the struggle was "between those who would stamp out the Catholic religion . . . and those who are determined to defend it."[8] Indeed, it was not long before the intelligentsia had transformed the Spanish war into an allegory in which the major conflicts of the decade appeared as the principal adversaries. So great was their response, in fact, that Robert Graves and Alan Hodge have concluded that "never since the French

Revolution had there been a foreign question that so divided intelligent British opinion."[9]

What kind of writing did so heart-stirring an event produce? Not surprisingly, a considerabe amount of it was amateurish and bad even by journalistic standards. Of the pamphlets which poured from the news bureaus of both sides, few pretended to be more than propaganda. The same was true of most of the hastily conceived eyewitness accounts and memoirs. Polemical and inclined to exacerbate rather than explain, they sought first to arouse and mold public opinion. A few later ones, however, most notably George Orwell's *Homage to Catalonia* (1938), combined astute observation with writing of high quality. Their chief value, however, is historical rather than literary.

There have been surprisingly few novels about the Spanish struggle by British writers. By the time the war ended in 1939, only five, all of very mediocre quality, had been published. Since then the number has grown by fewer than a dozen. Both the paucity and their generally low literary caliber tend to make them dubious candidates for serious critical attention.

Before discusing my reasons for limiting this study to the British poetry of the Spanish war, I want to say a word about the first two chapters. Because it is impossible to understand the poetry of the Spanish war without at least being acquainted with the major outlines of the conflict, I decided to make Chapter I a concise survey of the war. It is intended to introduce the reader to the complicated origins of the struggle, as well as to the international meanings it came to embody. It will also suggest the enormity of the major military engagements, which partisans on both sides followed so closely. Finally, I felt it was necessary to discuss in some detail the part Russia played in the Spanish war, since the conduct of the Soviets in some way influenced most of the poets discussed in this study. Although so brief a survey runs the unavoidable risk of being misleading, or of irritating sympathizers on both sides, or both, I have tried to be catholic in selecting my sources and dispassionate in writing the survey, though I must add that preserving a neutrality toward the Spanish Civil War, even for one too young to remember more than a few vague headlines, is all but impossible. Detachment appears to be the first piece of critical appartus the critic loses when he begins investigating the labyrinthine meanings of the conflict.

Chapter 2 surveys the response to the war of the major political parties in England, as well as of a few smaller groups like the Communists and pacifists. Since nearly every party had a theory on how best to cope with the Spanish situation, and since there existed considerable disagreement with the policy the government had decided upon, the chapter will assist us in seeing where poets stood in relation to public policies. Also, because its influence upon the population as well as upon the poets themselves was enormous, I have discussed the not too distinguished record of the press in England. Lastly, I have tried to show how journals of opinion and literary magazines functioned as both shapers of thought and outlets for war literature. The influence of newspapers and journals upon the poetry of the war cannot be underestimated, since all but a few poets remained in England during the war, and depended therefore upon these media for the raw material of their verse.

Enough has been said thus far to suggest the crucial position that the Spanish war occupies in the literary life of England. The question that now confronts us is, where can we find the most accurate reflection of the impact which the war made upon the literary imagination of Britain? In my opinion, the reflection we seek, in all its variety, can be found in the mass of poetry produced during the war. Such a consideration,

however, will demand that we examine more than just the
work of good poets. We must consider as well some poetry
for which even the most charitable critic would find the term
rueful. At best, it can be called verse journalism. Its extraliterary functions are today so evident that whatever artistry
this verse might one time have been generously granted is now
almost completely annulled. But aesthetic disappointment must
not blind us to the contribution that this verse makes to the
response we seek. It is perhaps hardly necessary to mention
that the very adaptability of poetic forms makes verse the
most convenient medium for expressing the immediate. Verse
has always accompanied war, and, in large measure, verse
written during a struggle has always been preoccupied with
whatever is at hand, with immediate, topical matters rather
than deeper experiences. In contrast, the novelist can never
really capture the immediacy of war. Nor can he expect to re-
create completely the feelings that existed during a struggle.
The span between observation and creation, being of necessity
long, allows him time to formulate a comprehensive view
before he begins writing. When he starts, say, after hostilities
have ended, he knows the outcome of the struggle, a factor
which will unquestionably influence his entire presentation.
Not so the poet. In wartime, we expect him to sharpen our
emotional life and to intensify our reactions. We expect him to
celebrate the victories of our side, to exhort us to make sacrifices, to inspirit us when our firmness wanes. If some of his
verse sounds a bit shrill after the battlefields have emptied,
perhaps we ought to temper our objections, remembering that
it is likely that our voice was one that the poet tried to echo.
Not all poets, of course, wrote just occasional war verse. Some
eschewed it altogether and tried to create at a deeper level,
to synthesize their own feelings about war with those of society;

and responding to heavier demands, they often revealed more about the forces at work.

It is perhaps not an overstatement to say that, to the poets discussed in this book, the Spanish Civil War was the intellectual and emotional climax of the 1930s, and to a few of them it became the turning point of their lives. In the first place, the excitement and drama of the struggle compelled them to act, either according to the "line" promulgated by political groups like the Communist Party, or, individually, as writers and private citizens. Whatever they did required that they first decide how they could be most useful to the side they supported. For most, it was a fairly easy matter to lend their names to partisan organizations, to participate in their demonstrations, or even to make donations. Signing protests and petitions and answering questionnaires certainly would not jeopardize their careers. After all, why should such things be resisted? But even if they went this far in supporting one of the Spanish contestants—and most did—there remained the agonizing question of whether they had done enough. Did the crisis demand that they go beyond just being nominal supporters? Should they consider placing their art at the service of the cause? These and other questions could not be so easily answered. If they went all-out for one side, was there a danger that their work might be relegated to the level of propaganda? On the other hand, was not verse which compared the "virtues" of one side with the "corruption" of the other precisely what was needed under the circumstances? Could a poet, really, avoid extremes, mute his anger or indignation, and yet write effectively about the struggle? Ultimately, the problem of deciding how and what to write involved a consideration of ends and means, and the decision these poets made depended to a large extent upon how fervently they believed in the Spanish Republic, or in General

Franco's campaign against that government, and in the part they thought they could play in bringing about the victory and survival of one or the other.

It is, then, to three large questions that I have addressed myself. First, what was the response of a large number of British poets to the demands of the Spanish war? Second, how did their response affect the nature of, and their attitude toward, their work? Third, what aesthetic, social, or historical importance does this poetry of the Spanish Civil War have in the pattern of recent British literature?

Chapter 1 : Background and War

Left-wing Politics Before Spain

THE ATTACK UPON THE SPANISH REPUBLICAN GOVERNMENT
gave the Left what it widely acclaimed was a "pure" cause :
defending democracy against fascism. Left-wing poets had, in
fact, warned repeatedly that the rise of Hitler and Mussolini
posed the most serious threat to the future of liberalism. In
Vienna (1935), for example, Stephen Spender had excoriated
Dollfuss for suppressing the Austrian workers' movement at the
request of Mussolini. Even as early as 1931 Spender had been
so moved by the division of bourgeoisie and proletariat and so
strongly in sympathy with the oppressed that he concluded
that revolution could not—indeed, should not—be avoided.
Developments in Austria and Germany had a similar effect on
John Lehmann, to whom the elimination of all liberal and
social reforming parties in Germany and the crushing of
Vienna's democratic government by reactionaries pointed to
one conclusion : "that capitalism would stop at nothing to
turn back the wheels of democratic progress and social justice."
What had happened in central Europe seemed part of "an
international conspiracy in which all capitalist countries acted
in secret concert."[1] W. H. Auden came to nearly the same
conclusion in *Dance of Death* (1933), where Europe's sickness
is contrasted with Russia's health. This is "a picture of the

decline of a class," the announcer says at the opening of the play. "Its members dream of a new life, but secretly desire the old, for there is death inside them."[2] Similar warnings and incitements resounded in Christopher Isherwood's Berlin stories, Rex Warner's novels and poems, and Edward Upward's short stories.

A move toward a fuller political commitment had begun among these poets long before war broke out in Spain. In most cases, the adoption of a revolutionary point of view—sometimes as a Communist—was due to the concern over the spread of fascism on the continent and the abysmal conditions in England, which Baldwin's government seemed powerless to correct. Simultaneously, any artistic isolation became increasingly more difficult to justify. The feeling that all who cared about what happened (especially writers) had to act became persistently stronger. Prior to the Spanish war, action usually took one of two forms: either joining in a public demonstration against the government, in which case one at least had the feeling of having done something; or expressing a private protest of some sort in writing. But in a sense neither was entirely satisfactory, if only because protesting seemed to make so little difference. Baldwin's policies, or lack of them, had endeared him to the average voter. To oppose the status quo was simple enough. But to change it was not. Protesting against unemployment and the deplorable conditions of the British workers, or against the spread of fascism, generated far less interest among most Britons than the question of whether Edward VIII should or should not marry a woman who had been married twice before. What the Spanish war succeeded in doing was not only pumping new life into the Left movement at a critical time in its existence by providing it with a focal point for its energies, but awakening a large segment of the population to the dangers that Hitler and Mussolini represented.

Spender has rightly called the Spanish war a "poet's war." But obviously it was also a war in which politics figured prominently. Few of the British poets who were to become involved in it had, however, followed the fortunes of the Second Spanish Republic since its establishment in 1931. If they had they would have known, in 1936, that it had developed along liberal lines, except for the interval between November 1933 and December 1935 when a Right-Center coalition government halted the process and attempted to undo what had already been done. But at the outset of the conflict very few on the Left understood the background of the Spanish war. Thus, the majority of left-wing poets understandably responded not so much to the fact that a liberal government had been attacked—though, of course, this fact was by no means overlooked—as to the ideological implications that the contest posed. It was a lot easier to take sides when the choice was between fascism and democracy than between rival Spanish factions that few outside Spain had ever heard of.

In fairness, it should be said here that many English poets did not make the mistake of assuming that an ideological war would somehow be different from any other war. They understood that the general ideological significance that had attached itself to the civil war did not alter the fact that the war itself was the reality. Politics may have drawn them into the fray, but politics did not preoccupy them so much that an emotional response was impossible. They reacted to the humane side of the battle as well. The outcome of the ideological struggle was, of course, paramount, but this consideration did not blind them to the fact that the most terrible kind of war—

a civil war—was plundering Spain of its material and human
wealth.

With the political attractiveness of the Spanish war in mind,
it is necessary, before investigating the British response in more
detail, to see what actually happened in Spain. It is not a
matter of implying that these poets were overly ingenuous, or
that left-wing periodicals in Britain showed more enthusiasm
than common sense in viewing the Spanish war. Neither
implication could be made short of distorting the record.
Rather, it is important to suggest just how complicated the
struggle was—how many unfamiliar political strands comprised its fabric—in order to show why it was almost necessary
for these poets to accept a simplified version of the war. Let me
quickly add that it is not my intention to excuse or defend
political immaturity or naïveté. And I am not interested in
exonerating any group. My main purpose is to show that the
war was a lot more complicated than most of the British
poets ever imagined, and that commitment to the Loyalist
cause involved a good deal more than belonging to a party,
supporting its platform, and writing about its aims. For many
on the Left, the Spanish war was, first of all, a rather shatter-
ing object lesson in politics.

Prologue to War

Spain's political pendulum which, beginning in 1931, had
swung from right to left and left to right swung left again in
1936. The results of the February elections surprised even the
victors who, under the direction of Manuel Azaña, had
formed a Popular Front in an all-out effort to overthrow the
Rightist National Front. With the votes tallied, the Popular
Front discovered it had won 256 seats in the Cortes, the

Spanish Assembly, to the Right's 165. Azaña, whose popularity had never been so high—and was never to be again—accepted the premiership for his part in the victory.[3]

On February 17, the second Leftist government of the decade stood on the threshold of a tragically short and turbulent existence. Jubilant victory celebrations, instead of gradually subsiding, degenerated into savage anti-Rightist demonstrations, riots, and mob attacks on churches, convents, and estates. Extremists clamored for the immediate release of prisoners held since the October 1934 revolts. Hopeful that by meeting their demands he might end the disorder, Azaña ordered thousands of embittered prisoners set free. They lost no time venting their passions upon their traditional enemies, particularly the Church. In the next four months hundreds of convents and church schools were partially wrecked or razed completely. Rightist newspapers and the homes and property of monarchists, agrarians, and traditionalists became targets for incendiarists. Though concentrated mainly in the large cities, the disorders nevertheless spread to a few provinces, notably Badajoz, where peasants, tired of waiting for the government to expropriate the great ducal estates, seized the land and divided it up among themselves.

At first the new government took only perfunctory steps to quell the lawlessness, but when the rioters showed no signs of self-discipline Azaña imposed a strict press censorship and declared a state of alarm which lasted until the outbreak of war. Although aware of the seriousness of prolonged unrest and of the propaganda advantage it gave their opponents, the administration, probably fearful of antagonizing the masses and hopeful that the terrorism would eventually subside, dealt leniently with the rioters, sometimes even granting their demands, as in the case of the Badajoz peasants. But the government found it difficult to parry the charges of the

Opposition that they lacked even the strength to control their own dissatisfied groups. Azaña's frantic appeals for calm had gone practically unheeded.[4]

Not unexpectedly, in a coalition government, squabbling soon became the rule. One clash, oddly enough involving only Socialists, resulted in the sudden deposition of President Zamora. The protagonist of this drama was Indalecio Prieto, leader of the center group of the Socialist Party, who saw a chance to best his party rival, left-wing Socialist Caballero, by maneuvering into the presidency Manual Azaña, whose views on a united nonrevolutionary Popular Front government agreed with his own and would counteract Caballero's ambitions for a dictatorship of the proletariat.[5] Prieto also had the support of most of the Popular Front delegation, who feared that Zamora's conservatism might someday obstruct their program. Elected president on May 10, 1936, by a large majority, Azaña ordered the Cortes to work at once on long-delayed church and agricultural reforms. At the same time Rightists Gil Robles and Calvo Sotelo attacked him for having allowed the economy to collapse into anarchy. In the first four months of the Popular Front, 113 general strikes and 218 partial strikes, many of them organized by Caballero's powerful UGT (General Union of Workers), had nearly reduced the business life of the country to stagnation, a condition Azaña could only ruefully admit to.[6]

The administration, however, left no doubts about their hostility toward extreme Rightists, notably the Falangists, who, pessimistic about rule by the Left and perhaps heartened by fascist accomplishments in Italy and Germany, had split off from their more lymphatic colleagues after the Popular Front victory and had succeeded in swelling their ranks with dissatisfied army officers. In the weeks just prior to war, the feelings between Right and Left extremists reached inflammatory proportions, as the prime minister made clear in a speech to the Cortes in May 1936 :

There is one thing which I wish to make clear with regard to the Government's attitude to Fascism. . . . The purpose of the Fascist groups is to attack the fundamental principles of the democratic Republic. Here the Government cannot maintain an attitude of neutrality. In its relations with Fascism, the Government is a belligerent.[7]

With the arrests of alleged Fascists multiplying daily, with the revolutionary Left still harassing the government by organizing strikes and demonstrations, and with the administration hard put to do anything about either extreme, an event occurred in Madrid which exacerbated the division between Right and Left and plunged the country into civil war. On July 12, José Castillo, a lieutenant in the Assault Guards, was shot dead by fascists on a street near his home. A few hours later, Calvo Sotelo, a militant Monarchist, disappeared. His body later turned up in a Madrid mortuary, presumably the victim of leftist vengeance. The twin murders were the Sarajevo of the Spanish war.[8] Five days later, on July 18, Madrid listened, with considerable disbelief, to news of a military revolt in Spanish Morocco. Ironically, the reports of the Moroccan uprising failed to excite the government, which refused to issue arms to the workers in the rather naïve belief that the revolt could be contained to the African colony. But to the more discerning the rumblings from Morocco signaled new efforts to reverse the course of Spain's restless political pendulum.

Revolt and War

Despite the risks and problems involved in trying to assign responsibility for an event as important as the Spanish Civil

War, I think it can be safely affirmed now that Generals Sanjurjo, Franco, and Mola set in motion a carefully planned attack against the legal government of Spain.[9] Also, it now seems clear that the war was indigenous to Spain and grew out of the long-standing antipathy between the extreme Right and Left. It was not a plot conceived in Berlin or Rome to destroy "democracy" in Spain and then in Europe,[10] nor was it, as Insurgent apologists tried to maintain, a "Red" conspiracy to communize Spain.[11] The Right revolted because Azaña had threatened to abolish their traditional privileges and powers. Needless to say, their apprehensions were justified. Landowners anticipated agrarian reforms more stringent than those of 1931; the Church, on which extremists had already vented their feelings, expected its prerogatives to be drastically curtailed; and the army, the bulwark of the Right and the only force capable of defending its privileges, had vowed to subvert Azaña's plan to depopulate the officer corps. Although the murders of Sotelo and Castillo had precipitated the war, the Insurgents must have been preparing their coup long before their death, since so complex an operation could hardly have been organized in the four days between July 12, the day of the shootings, and the opening revolts. Furthermore, rumors of an uprising had been rife in Spain for at least a month before, but complacency or optimism had apparently lulled Azaña into a false security, which vanished only when the revolts spread across the Mediterranean to the mainland.

On July 17 the army in the Spanish zone of Morocco rose and occupied Ceuta and Melilla.[12] The following day troops reached the mainland, occupied Algeciras and Cadiz, and headed north to Seville, which fell without a fight. Simultaneously, garrisons were revolting successfully in Saragossa and Pamplona. But in Barcelona, Madrid, Toledo, Bilbao, and

Valencia rebels met unexpected opposition and were defeated. By the end of the week, however, the Insurgents claimed half of Spain as theirs. They controlled the northern area of the country, from the Bay of Biscay south to the Guadarrama mountains, except for small areas along the Basque and Asturian coast; all the area along the Portuguese border; the whole southern basin from Granada to Huelva; and in the east a line extending from Huesca to Saragossa to Teruel. The government still held all the east coast, Estremadura, Mancha, New Castile, and the great plateau around Madrid, as well as the capital itself. Encouraged by their early victories, Generals Mola and Cabanellas, in the north, and Franco, in the south, drove their armies straight for Madrid, hoping to seize the capital before the government could muster a resistance force.

It soon became apparent that most of the 12,000 officers and 85 generals of the army, as well as about two-thirds of the conscript soldiers, had joined the conspiracy. To this number were added 34,000 Civil Guards, 11,000 well-trained Moors, and 5,000 Foreign Legionnaires. The almost total desertion of the army left the government with 25 staff and 500 professional officers and 6,500 shock troops.[13] In broad terms, the government could count on the loyalty of the huge unionized labor force, the parties of the Popular Front, farm laborers and peasants, moderates who felt obligated to support the government, and a few professors and intellectuals. The ancient strongholds of the Right stood solidly behind the Insurgents : landed aristocrats of the south and central provinces, industrialists like Juan March, the army, and the Church. After July, two Spains existed, a Right and a Left. For the majority of Spaniards there was no middle ground; they either fought for the government or against it, a decision

that was often shaped by their whereabouts when the war
started and the outcome of the initial uprisings.[14]

Intervention: Germany and Italy

Signs that the war would not remain peculiarly Spanish
began appearing before the end of the month. By July 29,
Franco's troops were being ferried from Morocco to Cadiz in
German Junkers transports, and on July 30 the world got
irrefutable proof of Italian intervention when three of the
Duce's Spanish-bound Savoia-Marchetti bomber-transports
made a forced landing in French Morocco. In August, William L. Shirer, in Berlin, reported seeing large shipments of
German planes dispatched to Spain,[15] and the same month
Arthur Koestler mingled with Nazi pilots in Seville's Hotel
Christina.[16] Fearful that contravention of the international law
which forbade supplying insurgents might create unwelcome
international tensions, both Hitler and Mussolini tried to conceal their intervention, perhaps hoping that Franco would
seize control before their participation could be confirmed.
Stalin's intervention on the side of the Republic put some of
their fears to rest, however. Hitler, always more reticent than
Mussolini about aiding Franco, sent no more than 20,000 men
to Spain, most of them Luftwaffe personnel.[17] Italian intervention, quantatively much greater but probably less important than Germany's, reached a peak by early 1937 when
nearly 70,000 troops were fighting in Spain. Mussolini supplied Franco with approximately 100,000 soldiers, who outnumbered the nationals of all other countries combined, and
were about two and one half times the total enlistment of the
International Brigades.[18]

The success of Franco's entire campaign can be attributed
to the aid he received from the Fascist dictators. But their

generosity threatened to abrogate much that it allowed him to win. Besides raiding Spanish mineral deposits to feed burgeoning war industries at home, both Hitler and Mussolini hoped to capitalize on Spain's strategic location in the event of a general European war. Annoyed by the Franco-Russian Alliance of May 1935, Hitler saw a chance to isolate France by gaining an ally in Spain, and even if Franco should demur at becoming embroiled in a European struggle he would at least make an inhospitable neighbor to the south of France. Mussolini's aspiration centered on achieving hegemony in the Mediterranean. To this end, Italy, with German assistance, occupied Majorca and the strategically valuable seaports of Cadiz and Malaga. In return for military assistance, Franco had to go beyond permitting the dictators to use Spain as a proving ground for war (it was "better than maneuvers," a German remarked to Nora Waln) and to exploit her raw materials : it meant offering them a chance to control the western basin of the Mediterranean, from which they might neutralize the power of the British bastion at Gibraltar and harass the French.

Nonintervention: England and France

What action, if any, would the democracies take? On July 23, a bewildered Léon Blum flew to London to confer with heads of Baldwin's government. Socialist Blum, who had just been elected Prime Minister by a Popular Front alliance, had already been asked by Giral, the new Prime Minister of the Spanish Republic, for help, and, although Blum had hoped to proceed with reforms at home, he felt that he could not ignore the needs of a sister republic. Within a few hours, however, London and Paris announced a policy of strict neutrality and nonintervention, which Republican sympathizers in both countries at once scorned as a vote of confidence for Franco, if not actually a maneuver to deny the Spanish Republic the right to purchase arms abroad. The decision satisfied the British desire for peace, however. Conservatives backed nonintervention, maintaining it would help contain the war to Spain by dissuading countries sympathetic with either side from intervening. Churchill saw no reason why England should get involved in a war which was to decide "whether Nazi dictators or Bolshevist dictators" were to triumph.[19] Among the Opposition, Major Attlee expressed sympathy for the Spanish workers and pledged "all practicable support."[20] But the Labour Party actually condoned nonintervention until July of the following year, by which time its ineffectiveness had often been demonstrated. The decision not to intervene forced Blum to compromise. His pacifism warred with his desire to send aid to the Republic. French Rightists of course bitterly opposed even the thought of intervening in the Spanish war. Most of his cabinet, on the other hand, favored assisting the Republic as much as he. During his absence, Pierre Cot, the Air Minister, had arranged to sell a shipment of airplanes to the Loyalists. When Blum returned, the contracts lay on his desk awaiting his signature. At least for the moment he saw a way out of the dilemma. André Malraux would act as buyer for the Republic and the shipment would be "effected through Mexico."[21]

Munitions agents, buyers from Spain, spies, counterspies, people of all nationalities jammed the Spanish Embassy in Paris offering arms, munitions, and aircraft at all prices. But whatever the Republic purchased had somehow to reach Spain, a problem that kept a small army of agents busy devising a multitude of cat-and-mouse smuggling operations. After the formation of a Nonintervention Committee (London

Committee) in September 1936, to which 27 nations including Italy, Germany, and Russia pledged support, Blum found that turning a blind eye while supplies for the Republic crossed the border meant jeopardizing not only England's friendship but risking internal discord as well. Yet Hitler, Mussolini, and Stalin had no intention of respecting a nonintervention agreement that prohibited sending arms and men to Spain. Knowing that the Committee lacked powers of enforcement, they reasoned that an agreement based on the quixotic assumption that subscribers would out of "good faith" support its regulations hardly posed a threat to freedom of action. While simultaneously accusing one another of violating the agreement, they went right on pouring supplies into Spain, and with each nation anxious to hide its contraventions Committee meetings often degenerated into virulent exchanges of charges and countercharges, giving all alike ample opportunity to delay or otherwise obstruct proposals that threatened to curtail their violations.

In the spring of 1937, the Committee issued a revised agreement designed to reduce the amount of aid that had been surreptitiously reaching both sides. It stationed neutral observers at the principal border crossings, and put a sea patrol comprised of ships from each member nation in the waters along the Spanish coasts. Made effective in April, after Germany, Italy, and Russia had already shipped a large part of their aid, the new regulations were only moderately effective. In July, for example, France demanded that the neutral observers along the Franco-Spanish border be replaced by French observers, whereupon it was reported that war material began reaching the Republicans again. When Loyalists bombed the German patrol ships *Deutschland* and *Leipsig,* their commanders retaliated by shelling Almeria, and then requested permission to shoot again if they were attacked. The Committee rejected the request and Hitler and Mussolini promptly withdrew their ships. By October, England and France had also ended their part in the sea patrol, and even earlier the observing systems had collapsed.

But England, still hopeful that the Committee could serve as a "deterrent," kept it alive. In November 1938, it arranged for the removal of all volunteers from Spain, but Franco, still uncertain of victory, delayed the withdrawal for several months. Irate Loyalists, who rightly believed they had much to gain from immediate removal of so-called German and Italian volunteers, petitioned the League of Nations to dissolve the Nonintervention Committee if nothing was accomplished. But the request was unnecessary. When Franco refused a second time to comply with the Committee's request, its existence ended amidst charges of favoritism, appeasement, and irresponsibility.[22]

The Republic Reorganizes

Although the government had managed to put down risings in Madrid, Valencia, Barcelona, and some other large cities, its situation remained desperate. Without an army, Azaña's only recourse was to arm as rapidly as possible the militias of the Popular Front parties and unions. Men who had never before held a gun and who had only the simplest knowledge of warfare became overnight the backbone of the Republican army. They were led by political or union leaders who in most cases had assumed military rank because they were popular among the men. There was no time for training or instruction, for the rebels, aware that the outcome of their rebellion depended on moving swiftly against the government, had by the end of July plunged deep into the interior of the country.

And unless these advancements could be arrested at once the Republic might well succumb within a month. Each union and party took charge of organizing its own militia, commandeered everything from bicycles to trucks, and, returning the shouts of encouragement that announced their departure, sallied forth to engage the advancing rebels.

Losses in the first battles were staggering. Woefully inexperienced militiamen made easy targets for Franco's trained riflemen. Moreover, superior Insurgent artillery inflicted heavy damage on makeshift Loyalist equipment. In the first two important encounters of the war, at Alto de León and Somosierra Pass, both main approaches to Madrid, each side fought savagely, bombing each other and refusing to take prisoners. Rebel equipment proved decisive, however, and the militias fell back. In the south, Insurgent General Queipo de Llano had rapidly extended the territory dominated by his capital city of Seville, and in the north Loyalists had steadily lost ground in Navarre. Only in Aragón, where Durruti's columns of Anarchists sped toward Saragossa and Huesca, could the government take courage from seeing the enemy on the defensive.

Soviet Intervention

The decision to seek aid abroad came only shortly after Franco had sought the assistance of Hitler and Mussolini. The help that Blum could send, at least after he had agreed to a policy of neutrality, would hardly be sufficient to keep an army in the field; and Mexican aid, though dependable, was limited and probably could never be increased substantially. Therefore, it was to Stalin that Azaña directed his appeal. But Stalin hesitated, apparently uncertain just how to respond to

Azaña's request. For at least two months he deliberated, presumably waiting to see how Baldwin and Blum would react. Meanwhile, besides moral support, Russia sent the Loyalists food and some raw materials, for which Russian workers and peasants were assessed a small amount each month.[23] When the announcement came that France and England had decided on nonintervention, despite the fact that Germany and Italy had already begun supplying the Insurgents, Stalin made up his mind. No Russian soldiers would be permitted to fight in Spain, but technicians and material would be sent and Comintern officials were ordered to begin recruiting volunteers for the International Brigades. Stalin's decision not to send Azaña Soviet troops, according to Franz Borkenau, was prompted by fear that a Russian force in Spain might effect a "rapprochement between Britain and Germany, and between France and Italy, against Russia."[24] To keep the fact of Soviet intervention as quiet as possible, Stalin ordered the few Russian technicians and military experts to "stay out of range of artillery fire."[25] If Russia could remain a silent partner, furnishing the Republic with munitions but not becoming involved in the struggle herself, it might be possible to allay any suspicions the democracies might have about Russian intentions in Spain and at the same time reduce the threat of a German attack on Russia by keeping Hitler busy in Spain. The Führer's ominous rise to power and the accompanying recrudescence of German militarism had led to the signing of the Franco-Soviet Security Pact in 1935. In Spain, Stalin might have seen a chance to frustrate any plans the dictator had for aggression in the East, by involving him in a war of attrition on the Iberian peninsula. Besides, there was even the possibility that England and France might eventually join Russia to subvert German imperialism. For Stalin the whole war might have been merely a delaying affair which granted him time to prepare for a Nazi attack if and when it came.[26]

International Brigades

Regardless of his motives, Stalin brought a resurgence of hope to the Loyalists, which did not abate even after they learned that a full staff of Comintern officials had descended on Madrid to supervise the distribution of Soviet supplies and munitions. Nor did they balk when they heard that most of the Spanish gold supply had been dispatched to Russia, partly in payment for supplies received and promised and partly to assure its safety.[27] The confidence that the presence of Soviet personnel and material inspired seemed worth the price. About the same time as Communist parties in Europe and England began recruiting volunteers for the Republic, a Soviet military command headed by General Goriev arrived in Madrid to begin building an army out of the polyglot collection of militiamen. Political commissars filtered out through the troops, seeking to "coordinate political and military decisions."[28]

But the major project was the formation of the International Brigades, at Albacete, where the first recruits began arriving in October. Commander of the base was the French Communist André Marty, who had known a brief moment of international glory in 1919 when he had led a mutiny of the French Black Sea Fleet against orders to aid the White Russian armies. Assisting him at Albacete were two Italians, Luigi Longo and Guiseppe de Vittorio, both of them seasoned organizers. For a while the American journalist Louis Fischer served as a quartermaster officer.[29] Three experienced revolutionaries— Emilio Kléber (whose real name was Lazar Stern), a veteran of the Russian Civil War; Hans Kahle, an ex-Prussian officer;

and the Hungarian writer Mata Zalka, who had also been in the Red Army—became the commanders of the brigades.[30]

Training with inferior equipment multiplied the problems already created by the sudden mixing of men from many lands. But after having stayed at Albacete less than a month, the XIth International Brigade arrived in Madrid on November 8, just as many Madrileños had assumed the capital lost. In the Casa de Campo, an abandoned hunting grounds at the edge of the city, the Insurgents under General Varela had been dug in for two days. Artillery pounded away at the city, and it seemed certain that the enemy would soon push into the main squares. Adding to the gloom was the fact that the government had already fled to Valencia, leaving the city in the hands of José Miaja, who had been brought out of retirement for this unrewarding task. But the sight of the straight files of internationals, uniformed and wearing steel helmets, marching down the Gran Via toward the Casa de Campo, inspired a populace that had all but accepted defeat. Cheers and cries of "Long Live the Russians" accompanied their march. Solidarity gripped the city as Madrileños rededicated themselves to the battle. What had happened "seemed like a miracle," wrote *New York Times* correspondent Herbert Matthews.[31] Varela's troops made no new gains. The old incisions were gradually closed. Four days later, on November 12, the XIIth International Brigade marched into Madrid. With it came the German writer Gustav Regler, who was the Brigade commissar; two other Germans—the novelist Ludwig Renn and the Bavarian Communist Hans Beimler; Italians Randolfo Pacciardi and Pietro Nenni, leaders of the Garibaldi Battalion; and Esmond Romilly, nephew of Winston Churchill.[32]

In the weeks that followed one of the mightiest contests, certainly the most symbolic, of the war took place. Some observers contended that the internationals had "saved the military situation."[33] Regler has since written that these "heroes" were the "saviours" who stopped Franco's Moors from "perpetrating unthinkable atrocities in the naïve, unarmed and daydreaming city of Madrid."[34] Matthews, while admiring their "courage, freshness, and zeal born of idealism," noted that the internationals numbered only about two thousand. "If Madrid and, indeed, Spain itself was to be saved, only Spaniards could do it, not foreigners."[35] But whether the Brigades saved Madrid or not is less important than the effect their presence in Spain had upon the Spanish enlistees, especially during the desperate first months of the conflict. To say the least, their arrival in Madrid at a time when its collapse seemed imminent was auspicious. It greatly raised the morale, not to mention the firepower, of troops whose position was desperate. Moreover, it verified, at a crucial moment, stories of growing international solidarity behind the Spanish Republic. Henceforward, Republicans might look forward to greater foreign support.

The battle for the capital continued through the winter of 1936–37. Meanwhile the base at Albacete began refilling with additional volunteers. By Christmas two more brigades were ready; and early in 1937 the XVth Brigade, which included the majority of English-speaking volunteers organized into the British Battalion, the Abraham Lincoln and George Washington Brigades and the Canadian Mackenzie-Papineau Battalion, was formed. Though the prospects for an early Loyalist victory could hardly be called bright, the situation at the close of 1936 was far from hopeless. Azaña had reason to be confident. Madrid had withstood Franco's heaviest onslaught. Russian supplies were flowing into Spain. The formation of an International Brigade had been realized and had already influenced the military situation. There was reason to believe that world opinion would swing even more fully behind the Republic. And finally, the Russian cadre had started transforming the rag-tag assemblage of workers into an organized People's Army modeled after the Brigades. Azaña could look forward to 1937 with the expectation that the Loyalists might at least meet the Insurgents on something close to an equal footing.

Warring Ideologies

To a world ignorant of the internecine struggle between the Spanish Right and Left which had precipitated the uprising, the Spanish war seemed less concerned with issues indigenous to Spain than with world-wide problems. Propagandists for both sides succeeded in giving the war an international character by calling the belligerents Communists, or "Reds," and Fascists, and by reducing the issues to such simple but misleading appellations as "communism and anticommunism," "order and anarchy," "liberalism and ultraconservatism." And when it became known that Italy and Germany had intervened on the side of the Nationalists and that Russia had begun to supply the Loyalists, little doubt remained that Spain had become the international battleground of opposing ideologies.

If the war had multiple meanings outside the country, to a good many Spaniards it was the latest episode in the long and tragic chronicle of domestic strife in Spain. This fact was, of course, partly evident in the composition of the belligerents. But the division between the Right and Left merely beclouded the fact that within the opposing camps some sharp divisions existed, particularly on the Left. For instance, in the opening months of the war President Azaña, alarmed by the centrifugal forces that threatened to destroy what little authority the

government had managed to retain, only just restrained
extremist activity—largely left-wing Socialist and Anarchist—
by deliberately appointing one of the chief instigators of the
unrest, Largo Caballero, to the post of Prime Minister. Formed
in September 1936, with moderate as well as revolutionary
elements represented, as Azaña had hoped, the Caballero
Cabinet contained a majority of Socialists (six) and Communists (two). Only after the crucial May Days in Barcelona,
which finally broke the Anarchist resistance to the government,
did Anarchists deign to cooperate with Azaña.

In the reorganized Popular Front the Spanish Communists,
though they represented an expanding but certainly far from
large electorate, adroitly sought to exploit the power they
derived by virtue of Russian succor. With Russia the only
major nation supporting the Republic, the Spanish Communist Party grew to 249,000 in March 1937, and from a
minority faction (in 1931 the Party had the unimpressive total
of 1,000 members), with almost no voice in the government, it
assumed the role, if never the distinction, of a major decision-
making party. The Communists (and I include here the Soviet
cadre and members of the Comintern with whom the Spanish
Communists collaborated closely), using the fact of Soviet aid
as a lever for exerting pressure on the government to grant
their demands, even went so far as to decrease or stop supplies
altogether when the government proved intractable.[36] Employing this bargaining mechanism, they were able to pressure
Caballero to disband the workers' militias in favor of a People's
Army, which they intended to control, and for which the
Communist-organized International Brigades would serve as
models. But the prospect of integrating all divergent groups
into a People's Army was especially repugnant to the Anarchists, who since the start of the war had opposed the Communists' "reactionary" view that the defeat of fascism must

precede the social revolution. Anarchists, most notably in
Catalonia, long the center of Spanish anarchism, had begun
an extensive program of collectivism, which they feared would
collapse if it were not conducted simultaneously with the war
against Franco. To the Anarchists, then, Communists seemed
to have deserted the principles of revolution, to have degenerated into right-wing reactionaries as dangerous as the Fascists
themselves. Beneath the Communist campaign for "order and
discipline," the Anarchists thought they detected the first step
toward totalitarian regimentation.[37]

One Year of War

Despite the delivery of Soviet supplies and the assistance of
the International Brigades and the Russian military command,
the Loyalists lost ground the first year to a well-equipped, professional Nationalist force. However, Madrid, which the Republicans realized had deep symbolic meanings for Spaniards
as well as for international observers, was kept well fortified
and remained in government hands. But in February, 1937,
Málaga had fallen to the Italians, who rejoiced over the results
of an experiment involving the coordinated use of tanks,
planes, and infantry. This blitzkrieg method failed them a
month later at Guadalajara, however, where the Loyalists won
their first significant battle of the war. With Madrid a stale-
mate, Insurgent General Mola began a campaign to subdue
northern Spain. Commencing in June, his troops swept along
the frontier, capturing, at two-month intervals, Bilbao, San-
tander, and Gijón. It was during Mola's campaign that German bombers demolished the Basque town of Guernica, killing
1,654 and wounding 889. Nationalists tried to blame fanatical
Basques for deliberately destroying their town before retreat-

ing, but more reliable evidence pointed to a planned aerial bombardment which became the first blitz of the Second World War.[38]

May Days : Barcelona, 1937

On May 3 a handful of CNT (National Confederation of Labor : Anarchist) workers in the Barcelona Telefonica thought that the presence of the Chief of Police at their head-quarters signaled the long expected government take-over of the telephone exchange. They opened fire, and before the end of the day all the political organizations in Barcelona had uncovered their caches and stood ready for battle. The PSUC (Socialist Party of Catalonia), along with the Catalan government, controlled half the city, the Anarchists controlled the other half, and the CNT occupied the suburbs. Sporadic gun-fire kept the combatants alert and civilians tense. While the Catalan government and the Anarchists conducted nego-tiations, the POUM (Party of Marxist Unification), the Youth Group of the FAI (Union of Spanish Anarchists), and an extreme Anarchist group that called itself the Friends of Durruti, after the Italian Anarchist whose column was not far from Barcelona at the time, formed a junta and announced that all responsible (i.e., the government officials) "for the attack on the Telefonica would be shot."[39] The next few days brought no cessation to the "civil war" within a civil war. However, on May 6, four thousand Assault Guards arrived in Barcelona from Valencia. The CNT issued a plea for a cease-fire. POUMists objected, but they stood no chance against the Asaltos. Extinguished on May 9, the "Barcelona Revolt," according to the Soviets, clearly showed the perils of tolerating opposition elements; the treachery of the POUM had finally been exposed. Within a few months OGPU agents rounded up members of the POUM and its leader Andrés Nin. In most cases they were either imprisoned or liquidated.[40]

The Republic Reorganizes Again

Shortly before the Barcelona incident the Communists precipitated a Cabinet crisis designed to force Caballero out of office. Often at variance with the Soviets on matters of military strategy and clearly opposed to their efforts to eliminate intransigents, Caballero had become increasingly meddlesome, if not outrightly antagonistic. Fearful lest he become openly hostile, the Soviets inveigled Republicans and Right Socialists to join them in walking out of a Cabinet meeting. This caused the immediate collapse of the government and forced Caballero, despite strong Anarchist support, to resign. The new government, headed by moderate Socialist Juan Negrín, took office on May 17 and lasted, with relatively few changes, until the final days of the war. Cooperative but by no means a Communist puppet, Negín opposed a Soviet campaign to unify the Socialist and Communist parties, and permitted Defense Minister Prieto to draw up and put into effect a plan to reduce the large force of Soviet military commissars. Prieto's plan, almost the duplicate of a scheme once devised by Caballero, threatened seriously to weaken the Communist grip on the People's Army. Again, as in the case of the POUM, a military crisis came to the aid of the Communists. By using the defeats at the front as "evidence" of Prieto's incompetence, the Soviets were able to agitate for his immediate dismissal.[41] And, as usual, Soviet supplies began to dwindle. Worried lest Russia stop supporting the Loyalists altogether, Negrín complied with Communist demands and accepted Prieto's resignation.

Second Year of War

The year 1938 began hopefully for the Republicans with the capture of Teruel; however, on February 22, Nationalists recaptured the city and, except for the Loyalist counterdrive along the Ebro in the summer and early fall, steadily reduced the size of government-held territory. On March 9, the Nationalists opened the Aragón offensive, with attacks upon Lérida and Caspe, both of which fell in April, and then encountered strong Loyalist opposition at Castellón and Valencia. But Franco's troops captured Castellón on June 15, and stood on the shores of the Mediterranean. North, along the Ebro, the Republicans surprised the Insurgents by taking the offensive. Evidently not alarmed by these developments, Franco spent the summer organizing what turned out to be the final offensive of the war, an all-out attack on Catalonia, now the chief producer of Loyalist war material and the center of the only formidable government opposition. In December he was ready. By the third week of January, 1939, Franco had captured Artesa, Tarragona, Igualada and was completely in control of Barcelona, which had fallen after thirty-four days.

The End : Revolt in Madrid

Several bitter arguments and a revolt were to occur before the war came to an official close. Since the Republic still controlled a large part of central Spain, including Madrid, and several hundred thousand troops, some members of the government, mostly Communists, Premier Negrín and Madrid defender Miaja, favored continuing the fight. Opposed were the other members of the Popular Front who considered further opposition futile and urged immediate surrender.

Precisely why Negrín wished to continue resistance is a mystery. It is possible, however, that he thought a general European war—surely not far off in February, 1939—would save the Republic and perhaps even bring English and French aid. It is possible, too, that he wanted time to negotiate with Franco on such matters as reprisals, prisoner exchanges, and amnesty. On February 1, in the cellar of the ancient fortress at Figueras, he outlined his peace terms before a much depleted Cortes. Franco ignored them. On February 28, both England and France officially recognized Franco's regime. President Azaña resigned and left for France to join Companys, Aguirre, and Barrio, who had already fled. But Negrín, determined to carry on the war, tried replacing unenthusiastic commanders with Communists who supported his policy. This action, however, touched off a revolt led by General Casado in Madrid that wrenched the fate of Spain from his hands and sent him and the remainder of the government into exile in Algiers.⁴² Casado, with popular Leftist Besteiro, set up a National Defense Council, which opened peace negotiations with Franco and ended the war on March 26, 1939.

Chapter 2 : England and the Spanish Civil War

Conservatives and Nonintervention

CONSERVATIVE REACTION TO THE SPANISH CIVIL WAR WAS inextricably bound up with the government's Nonintervention Committee, which hoped to contain the war to Spain, to forestall a general European conflagration as long as possible by dissuading countries sympathetic with either side from intervening, and to provide a common meeting place for discussions and proposals which might lead to a settlement. As we have seen, the committee failed to achieve most of its purposes. However, despite the fact that the policy was violated by members of the committee itself, right up to its demise in 1939, many besides conservatives continued to support the policy because they felt that it at least would minimize England's chances of becoming involved in the Spanish war. It was not difficult to convince a public plainly interested in preserving peace as long as possible that neutrality was the best means to deter war, especially when France, which stood to lose even more than England in the event of a Franco victory, had agreed to support the same policy. The Opposition, of course, decried the government's nonintervention pact as not only discriminatory but detrimental to British interests in Spain and

the entire Mediterranean area. They scorned conservatives for
the unfairness of a policy which obstructed the efforts of the
legal government of Spain to purchase arms and supplies to
defend itself against attack, while the rebels easily procured all
the supplies they needed. If Conservatives recognized an element of truth in this charge, they never admitted it. Instead
they offered in rebuttal the one clearly undeniable fact, that
England and most of Europe enjoyed peace. It formed part of
Chamberlain's defense of his party's policy in July, 1937, a
defense which also implied that the opposition consisted of
warmongers :

The task we had been asked to undertake was one of great
difficulty and delicacy, but in the interests of general peace we
undertook it . . .There was only one objector and that was His
Majesty's Opposition . . . As soon as they saw these proposals they
rushed in to move the adjournment of the House, to call upon
the Government to withdraw them, to abandon the policy of
Non-Intervention, and to intervene on the side of the Spanish
Government. I can hardly imagine a more deplorable exhibition
of reckless irresponsibility than that.[1]

Before the dissolution of the Nonintervention Committee,
its conservative defenders contended that, if it had failed to
realize all that it had set out to do, it at least had kept England
from actively espousing the cause of one of the Spanish factions, which in all likelihood would have divided Europe into
two rival camps, with the democracies and Russia opposing
Germany and Italy. They admitted that committee meetings
had often degenerated into an exchange of patent insincerities,
but they pointed to the value of keeping open the channels of
communication between nations whose territorial aspirations
and suspicions of one another were barely concealed. Moreover, they conceded that the committee's recommendations
and policies had more often than not died quiet deaths in the
protracted negotiations, and that those that did survive the

weeks of obstructionism and were translated into action had often been silently ignored by their very creators. But they denied that nonintervention had been a delusion, or that it had been maintained at the expense of appeasing Italy. However, that such finally became the opinion of Foreign Minister Anthony Eden could hardly be ignored. His resignation in April, 1938, following Chamberlain's agreement with the Duce, whereby England recognized Italy's conquest of Ethiopia and Mussolini promised to withdraw his "volunteers" from Spain as soon as the war ended, came as a result of what the Foreign Secretary clearly labeled "appeasement" in his resignation speech :

I do not believe that we can make progress in European appeasement if we allow the impression to gain currency abroad that we yield to constant pressure . . . I am certain in my own mind that progress depends above all on the temper of the nation, and that temper must find expression in a firm spirit. That spirit I am confident is there. Not to give voice to it is I believe fair neither to this country nor to the world.[2]

What seemed the most deplorable example of the government's ostrich-like behavior concerning the Spanish struggle was its apparent obliviousness to the threat which the Caesarian aspirations of Mussolini imposed upon British hegemony in the Mediterranean. Were Conservatives unable to see that Britain's lifeline to the Middle East and India, as well as Gibraltar itself, would be seriously imperiled if Mussolini and Hitler secured a foothold in Spain? Although the government had relied on its neutral policy in refusing to guarantee that private investments in Spain would be protected, could it justifiably use the same argument to ignore the interests of the Empire? In a document entitled the "British Manifesto," issued by several M. P.'s and signed by J. M. Keynes, Harold Nicolson, Gilbert Murray, and other notables, the government was challenged to face up to the threat to the safety as well as the economy of the country :

The open invasion of an independent European country to prevent an expression of its people's wishes brings us to the very brink of disaster. One more such victory for international bullying will create a situation in which, apart from anything else, it will become strategically impossible to preserve the independence or even the narrowest economic interests of this country. . . . In view of the vital strategic importance of Spain, unless we can immediately secure the positive discontinuance of all outside support by the use of our naval preeminence the policy of Non-Intervention should be abandoned.[3]

The answer as to why the government seemed to be taking only minimal precautions to protect the Empire's "rights" in Spain and the Mediterranean was less a matter of putting peace even ahead of national welfare, or of relying on the non-intervention Committee to remind Italian and German representatives of England's right to Gibraltar and certain other areas in the Mediterranean, than simply the fact that the government lacked the military strength to protect the Empire's holdings. When Germany and Italy started constructing air bases on the Balearic Islands and gave every indication they would soon entrench themselves on the mainland, Robert Graves, long a resident of Majorca and scarcely a Loyalist sympathizer, reported the situation to Churchill, making it clear that while he decried intervening in "the pretended ideological struggle in Spain," British interests should somehow be safeguarded. Churchill's reply that England was too weak to do anything about British interests was hardly comforting.[4] What seems apparent now is that the Conservatives were marking time, hopeful that the dictators could be contained, perhaps even to Spain, until Britain's defensives could be strengthened.

Among Conservatives there was just enough mistrust of

political radicalism to sustain the fear that the emergence of a second leftist government in Spain (there was already one in France) might encourage Leftists in Britain to step up their antigovernment attacks, which had grown in volume and bitterness since the outbreak of the war in Spain. Conservatives suspected (in many cases rightly) that left-wing organizations were being used as "fronts" for the propagation of Marxism, despite the fact that there were many prominent Englishmen who either belonged to these groups or supported them. They became especially suspicious of the euphemistic slogans and mottoes that Leftists had adopted after the start of the war. What did Leftists mean when they said they were dedicated to the principles of "liberty" and "democracy"? Why had the British Communists adopted the names "antifascists" and "defenders of peace"? Why did Leftists decide to defend "bourgeois democracy," which for so long they had castigated, and support national unity against fascism? The introduction of this new vocabulary, the fraternizing between the Left and the middle classes in the Popular Front, and the confusing political situation in Spain itself caused most Conservatives to assume an extremely cautious attitude toward the Spanish struggle.

All political and national interests aside, however, some Conservatives were drawn to Franco because he seemed to imply respectability, order, and stability, while Republicans were a "clear revelation of the anti-Christ, working to overthrow religion, order and civilization."[5] They felt that Franco would follow the examples of Hitler and Mussolini and eventually restore order in Spain, drive the Communists out of the country or underground, and replace the defeated Republican government with a mild dictatorship on the order of that of Primo de Rivera. Franco seemed the lesser of two evils. In the early months of the conflict Churchill, for instance, showed

a willingness to accept Franco as the better choice, largely
because he feared that Azaña had opened the door to communism in Europe.[6] The same fear haunted Catholics who
acclaimed Franco a "Christian gentleman" leading a crusade
to rid Spain of foreign "heretics" and restore the order of the
Church. They feared that behind the Spanish government
moved the specter of Russia, whose presence represented a
"threat to civilized ideals." In the event of a Franco victory
that threat would diminish, and if Churchill's prediction that
Germany and Italy would quit Spain after the war turned
out to be accurate, then Britain could cash in with reconstruc-
tion loans and win back Spanish favor.[7]

Labour's Quandary

The British Labour Party, traditionally pacifist and opposed
to Baldwin's rearmament program, incurred considerable
abuse when it recommended that the government adopt a
strong "antifascist policy" toward the Spanish conflict. Irked
by Labour's denouncements of their rearmament policies, Conservatives retaliated by charging that Labourites clearly had a
"divided mind." How could they advocate an aggressive
foreign policy, particularly one that would deter the dictators,
when they themselves obstructed the build-up of military
strength required to back such a policy? Furthermore, to go
as far as to recommend sending aid to the Loyalists while
simultaneously preaching disarmament seemed so contradictory as to render Labour's recommendations slightly absurd.

Only a few Labourites, however, actually advocated sending
supplies to the Spanish government. The majority of the
Labour Party stopped short of proposing direct intervention
and, up until June, 1937, did little more than recognize that

the legal government of Spain was being attacked by disloyal Spanish officers in league with Italy, Germany, and Portugal, and that the Nonintervention Agreement, which the National Council of Labour (representing the L.P., the Parliamentary L.P., and the T.U.C.) reluctantly agreed to support on September 9, 1936, had, in fact, given the Insurgents belligerent status. Thus, Labour's early position on Spain consisted of no more than a guarded statement of sympathy with the Spanish people.

Although Bevin and Citrine and other defenders of nonintervention within the Labour Party spoke for most of their colleagues, their opponents—particularly Morrison and Attlee —pressed party leaders for an agreement whereby Labour would withdraw its support of nonintervention if breaches of the agreement became known. Following an interview between the Prime Minister and Attlee and Greenwood on alleged violations of the Pact, party heads agreed to reverse their stand if infractions of the Pact could be proved. Meanwhile the party attempted to salve its conscience by organizing relief projects for the Spanish Republic and publishing pamphlets which, though purporting to be truthful explanations of the origin and opening events of the war, were actually class-conscious interpretations of the conflict. Then, beginning in 1937, while the bombing of Guernica, the enforcement of the Foreign Enlistment Act, which tried to prevent British volunteers from joining the Loyalist forces, the shelling of the Republican seacoast town of Almería by the German cruiser *Deutschland,* and the open and extensive use of Italian troops in Spain clearly revealed the ineffectiveness of the nonintervention system, Labour gradually began to review its stand. In July, the National Council officially withdrew its support, primarily because the agreement had failed to prevent intervention. In addition, the Council asked the League of

Nations "to draw up measures to put an end to the Fascist intervention in Spain." Included among Labour's other new policies were giving "moral and humanitarian aid to Valencia," selling arms to the legal government of Spain, and being prepared "to resist force with force" should the "Fascist Powers persist in armed aggression."[8]

Hoping to repair their damaged prestige, particularly among the Left, many Labourites, headed usually by Attlee and Morrison, sponsored showy Republican demonstrations in Trafalgar Square and elsewhere to publicize Labour's more vigorous support of the Loyalists and its opposition to nonintervention. By far the most outspoken Loyalist partisan was Attlee, whose recommendations went beyond advocating that the Spanish government should have the right to purchase arms wherever it pleased and that the League should be given complete responsibility for investigating the conduct of both sides, to recommending that Britain herself should intervene on a unilateral basis and ship arms to Spain. His brief but well-publicized visits to Spain undoubtedly helped to restore confidence in Labour's leadership in the workers' cause.[9]

Labour's opposition to nonintervention and its strong antifascist line, however, only made more glaring the anomaly of advocating a forthright foreign policy while refusing to support rearmament. Realizing, finally, the untenability of such a position, despite the tremendous efforts of Bevin to prevent any change of policy, the National Council, with the support of most of the members, announced in September, 1937, that Labour would henceforth favor rearmament, since the conduct of the Fascist nations clearly threatened all of Europe. Thus the last trace of Labour's pacifist tradition finally disappeared.

The Independent Labour Party, part of the labor movement but not represented in the National Council, never found

itself involved in the same quandary from which the Labour
Party so painfully extricated itself. But it had other problems.
Under the direction of James Maxton, Fenner Brockway, and
others, the I.L.P. collaborated with the Communist Party to
the extent of accepting the slogan "Against War and Fascism,"
but opposed the policy by which it was expressed and sought
to extend it. "The policy advocated by the Labour Party and
the Communist Party," wrote Brockway, "was a military
alliance between Britain, France and Russia against Germany
and Italy." The I.L.P. adopted the view that

This division of Europe into antagonistic groups would provoke
rather than prevent war. We sought to extend the slogan by
including 'against Imperialism.' We held that the liquidation of
British Imperialism was essential to peace.

This did not mean that we underestimated the evil of Fascism
in Italy or of Nazism in Germany. . . . But we could not identify
ourselves with our own ruling class in their imperialist rivalry
with Italy and Germany. Such surrender of the class struggle
would in our view be an invitation to Fascism to penetrate Britain,
for we held that Fascism was at bottom the political and economic
structure of national unity in a class state. We believed that our
best service against War and Fascism was to intensify the struggle
against Capitalism and Imperialism in Britain, whilst assisting
our comrades in the Fascist countries in every possible way.[10]

What collaboration existed between the I.L.P. and the
Communists before May, 1937, stopped abruptly after the
"Barcelona Revolt" in that month, when, according to the
I.L.P., the Communists successfully liquidated their Spanish
counterpart, the so-called Trotskyite organization POUM. In
a spate of pamphlets by Brockway and others, Communists
were denigrated as enemies of the working classes, whose first
and only loyalty was to the Comintern and whose conception
of an enemy was anyone the slightest bit critical of Russia.
The investigation of the "Barcelona Revolt" convinced mem-

bers of the I.L.P. that the POUM had been destroyed because it opposed the attempts of Communists to take control of the militias in Catalonia.[11]

The Communist Machine

The Communist Party of Great Britain, which attracted recruits from all classes to its ranks in the 1930s, had an inconspicuous beginning at the Cannon Street Hotel, in London, on July 31, 1920. Actually a fusion of several small Marxist groups, it united the British Socialist Party, Socialist Labour Party, and the South Wales Socialist Society. During the twenties it remained small, but as the depression worsened, as the capitalist system seemed less and less capable of rectifying its own weaknesses, and as the Russian "experiment" continued to be hailed as a successful venture into cooperative living, party membership increased. Although still small in 1930, the party was nevertheless able to raise enough money to launch the *Daily Worker*. Moreover, it could claim to have made converts of Rex Warner and Edward Upward, who by 1930 had joined the party, and fellow travelers of G. B. Shaw, Lady Astor, and Hewlett Johnson, who, having visited Russia as Stalin's distinguished guests, loudly praised Soviet progress. At British universities, young Communists formed Leftist clubs, such as the October Club at Cambridge, in honor of the Bolshevist Revolution, and the much larger Federation of Student Societies and University Labour Federation, which united over 2,000 students from several colleges.

But the magnetic attraction of communism that students, liberals, and members of the professional classes felt exerted almost no pull upon most trade unionists, nor in general upon the laboring masses. In 1933, the Communists, acting on a manifesto from the Comintern, endeavored to organize a United Front against Fascism, and asked the Labour Party, the Trades Union Congress, the Co-operative Party and the Independent Labour Party to join in forming a coalition. In reply, both the L.P. and the T.U.C. condemned Communist and Nazi dictatorships in a manifesto of their own called "Democracy versus Dictatorship," and dissuaded members from having contact with Communists.[12] It was apparent that most Labourites wished to avoid fraternization with the extreme Left, especially with Marxists.

But despite the bellicosity of Labourites and Conservatives, the Communist Party continued to flourish. Not all turned down the idea of a United Front. The I.L.P. joined the Communists in forming a Joint Committee for Antifascist Action, which, when war broke out in Ethiopia and later in Spain, helped consolidate the party's antifascist role. Between 1935 and 1939, the heyday of the Popular Front, membership in the party reached its highest total, near 11,000 in 1937,[13] and enjoyed the support of such prominent people as the Webbs, whose two-volume study, *Soviet Communism, A New Civilization* (1935), did much to make a belief in Russia respectable. In 1937, the Duchess of Atholl, Eleanor Rathbone, the Dean of Canterbury, and the economist G. D. H. Cole addressed the Second National Congress of Peace and Friendship with the U.S.S.R. The same year appeared *The Mind In Chains,* subtitled "Socialism and the Cultural Revolution" (edited by Communist C. Day Lewis), which tried to show that culture under capitalism was at a standstill since capitalism itself, as Rex Warner, one of the contributors wrote, had "no further use for culture."[14]

At the outbreak of the Spanish Civil War the Communist Party's antifascist slogans and its Popular Front policy had attracted a heterogeneous group of stray M.P.'s, far-Left

Labourites, liberals, and Socialists, who maintained that inter-party quarreling encouraged the Fascists to increase their aggressive actions, and that only a formidable United Front movement could firmly oppose fascism and prevent a war. Hopeful that what had been done in France and Spain would also occur in England, they welcomed help from all quarters and "sought to cooperate with prominent personalities and speakers of all political parties and points of view who would address meetings and collect money."[15]

Besides a string of "volunteers" on leave from the Spanish front, whose talks at Popular Front rallies inevitably combined a plea for abolishment of nonintervention with vivid accounts of the heroic struggle of the Spanish people against inter-national fascism, such well-known personages as the Duchess of Atholl, Clement Attlee, Eleanor Rathbone, Gilbert Murray, and G. D. H. Cole made strong appeals for the Loyalist cause on the same program with avowed Communists like Harry Pollitt and C. Day Lewis. Many of these people also served, along with Philip Noel-Baker, Lord Faringdon, and Professor Trend, as distinguished members of one or more of the numerous Republican organizations, which included the Lon-don Committee for Spanish Medical Aid, the National Joint Committee for Spanish Relief, the Basque Children's Com-mittee, and, most popular of all, the Friends of Spain.[16] As the party's ranks began to increase, so did its output of publica-tions. Up to September 30, 1936, it had published and sold eight pamphlets on peace problems, totaling 140,000; three on Spain, totaling 225,000; and three on affiliation, totaling 80,000—altogether half a million pamphlets.[17] In addition, the *Daily Worker* had doubled its circulation, and *Challenge*, a Communist weekly, claimed at least 20,000 readers.

As party secretary, Harry Pollitt spoke officially for the C.P.G.B. Though slightly more emotional than many of his colleagues, he nonetheless succeeded in presenting a reasonably clear picture of the Communist attitude toward Spain and related matters. First on Pollitt's list of complaints was the government's nonintervention policy:

The National Government [he wrote] by its refusal to provide fuel and food supplies for the ships and aeroplanes of the legal Spanish Government, by the courtesy visits of its naval officers to Spanish fascist warships, by permitting unparalleled lying and provocation, has struck dastardly blows at the Spanish people.[18]

The struggle has removed "the mask from the face of the Tory Party." The Tories' "open support of the Spanish fascists is a grave warning of what lies in store for the British people as the struggle develops to maintain democratic institutions against the growing tendencies towards fascist dictatorship." Calling the charge that the Spanish people fought "to establish Soviets, or the proletarian dictatorship" the work of "downright lying scoundrels, or misguided self-styled Leftists," he, of course, made no reference to Russian involvement in Spain, declaring that the war had been forced on the Spanish people "in the attempt to restore feudal, monarchist and clerical reactionaries to power and crush the people." Therefore, it was a "struggle for the maintenance of democracy and a free constitution in a country whose economy is still backward . . . and whose institutions until recently were autocratic and feudal in character." The rebellion, however, was meant to have repercussions outside Spain—in France, for example—and "to stem the rising tide of unity and the demand for a people's front in every country where democracy still persists." Finally, Pollitt declared, the rebellion was "part of the fight for fascist war preparations which can only be carried through successfully if all those people who stand for democracy and peace are crushed by a bloody fascist dictatorship."[19]

Soon one of the main responsibilities of the party became

the recruiting of "volunteers" for the International Brigades. Before the League of Nations supervised the removal of all foreigners fighting for the Republic, in December, 1938, two thousand British volunteers had gone to Spain to join the XV Brigade, the British unit of the International Brigades. Of this number, 500 were killed, including writers John Cornford, Charles Donnelly, Ralph Fox, Christopher Caudwell, Julian Bell, and David Guest; 1,200 were wounded; and at the time of withdrawal only 800 were still in the ranks.[20] Volunteers at first arose spontaneously, and by the end of 1936 there were enough in Spain to form a British battalion. But early in 1937, it became more difficult for Harry Pollitt, who was also the party's principal recruiting officer, to fill his quota of volunteers, which was based on the party's "membership manpower and its sympathizers."[21] Eventually, pressure from the Comintern forced Pollitt to abandon plans to take only unmarried men under twenty-one and to include "married comrades and the youth of the Young Communist League."[22] At the same time, the government declared the party's recruiting operation illegal, and in an effort to check the flow of volunteers going to Republican Spain revived the Foreign Enlistment Act of 1870, which threatened to levy fines and impose prison terms upon any British nationals who left England to serve in a foreign army. While it never seriously inhibited Pollitt's activities, it nevertheless necessitated taking certain precautions, such as providing volunteers with credentials and other papers to satisfy the government agents who were stationed at Southampton and Newhaven.[23]

Most of the volunteers were workers. Many of them, according to Charlotte Haldane, who served as a receptionist in the Paris headquarters of the Brigades, were unemployed miners who were forced into enlistment by "years of depression and the dole."[24] But some volunteers were middle-class intellectuals, and a few were university men of "rather vague progressive views, who were not connected with the working-class movement . . . [but] were most anxious to prove their integrity and ability."[25] All but a handful were Communists. The exceptions held moderate or liberal views, or had no political opinions at all. A few had had previous military training, but most of them had had none, and some had even been pacifists.

From England, the volunteers went to Brigade headquarters in Paris, where the political background of each man was thoroughly investigated before he was sent on to Spain. For even though the party had enthusiastically endorsed the Popular Front, which presupposed a spirit of cooperation among all its members, it nevertheless attempted to restrict the composition of the Brigades primarily to Communists. In accordance with Soviet strategy, the International Brigades would eventually form the core of the new People's Army, which Communists in Spain were attempting to organize in spite of the strong opposition of Anarchists and Socialists, who rightly feared that a struggle for power within the Republican camp would dangerously weaken its fighting potential. Before the decisive struggle with the POUM at Barcelona, which assured the Soviets virtual control of the military, they were making certain that no would-be recalcitrants slipped into the ranks of the Brigades to frustrate their intentions.

Pacifist Turnabout

The first signs of what by 1935 had become a vigorous pacifist movement began appearing early in the decade. In 1932 delegates from twenty-seven countries gathered at an Anti-war Congress in Amsterdam and decided that imperialistic rivalry had caused World War I and that the fate of

Europe now "lay at the mercy of diplomatic disagreements, political crimes, and frontier incidents."[26] The same year, at the Disarmament Conference in Geneva, Arthur Henderson failed to win agreement for a program that would limit the type and use of weapons Europeans would be permitted to own. The breakdown of the Conference did not, however, discourage those who believed that peace could be made to prevail in Europe and that the League of Nations was the means to secure it. In November, 1934, a group of League sympathizers began conducting a poll (later named the Peace Ballot) on specific matters relating to international peace. They asked such questions as : "Should Britain remain a member of the League? Are you in favour of an all-round reduction in armaments by international agreement? Are you in favour of an all-round abolition of national military and naval aircraft by international agreement? Should the private manufacture and sale of arms be prohibited by international agreement? Do you consider that, if a nation insists on attacking another, the other nations should combine to compel it to stop by (a) Economic and non-military measures? (b) If necessary, military measures?"[27] Conservatives in the House of Commons attacked the poll, but when the results were announced in June, 1935, they were sufficiently impressed to build their forthcoming campaign around what appeared to be a nation-wide wish for peace. To all questions, the majority of eleven and a half million voters, representing 37.9 per cent of the electorate, answered yes. Over eleven million answered "yes to the first question, around ten million to the others. To the last question, 5(b), 6,784,368 voted yes, 2,351,981 (20 per cent) no."[28] Such clear-cut support of the League gave Baldwin a ready-made campaign platform. By advocating peace and promising to support the League, he not only deprived the Labour Party of its chief plank, but at the same time capitalized on the electorate's desire for peace.

The movement toward pacifism manifested itself in other ways in 1935. Several organizations which supported the League, "collective security," or disarmament built up large memberships and enlisted eminent men to speak for their cause. The Peace Society, the Oxford Union, the League of Nations Union all opposed rearmament. Canon "Dick" Sheppard, of St. Martin-in-the-Fields, an ardent and long-time pacifist, spoke for those who blamed politicians for supporting rearmament. To show how the people actually felt, he asked his congregations and others to send him a post card saying that they subscribed to the following peace pledge: "I renounce war and never again will I support or sanction another, and I will do all in my power to persuade others to do the same."[29] This was the beginning of the Peace Pledge Union, which by 1937 had 130,000 members, including Vera Brittain, Rose Macaulay, Lord Ponsonby and Aldous Huxley.[30]

In spite of Baldwin's willingness to support the League and to limit rearmament, England surreptitiously began to strengthen its military power after the 1935 election. Labourites only mildly objected to the government's defense spending, perhaps partly because it had become obvious that Germany and Italy had begun serious rearmament since the abandonment of the Disarmament Conference, and also partly because rearmament created work and wages. More than anything else, however, it was Mussolini's attack on Ethiopia that disspelled the hopes for peace and made rearmament seem imperative. As the Italian dictator persisted in his invasion and remained impervious to the protests of the League, certain that no nation would risk war to stop him—not even England—it became apparent that the League and "collective security" had failed and that in the future smaller nations could not expect to be protected from the Fascist dictators. Sir Samuel Hoare's peace settlement, made in conjunction with Pierre Laval, by which Ethiopia was to cede to Italy "some 60,000 square miles along

the borders of Italian Somaliland and Eritrea in return for a
corridor of about 3,000 square miles connecting Ethiopia with
the port of Assab in Eritrea," [31] created so much bitterness in
England that Baldwin was forced to replace Hoare with
Anthony Eden. Pacifists of all kinds joined in declaring that the
Baldwin government had betrayed the people, the League, and
Ethiopia. Without a strong League, they reasoned, there would
be no way to stop fascist aggression short of war itself. If
Baldwin was anxious to stay on good terms with Italy and
Germany in order to preserve the status quo, he was not only
encouraging the dictators to attempt additional annexations,
but denying the League the support of England which it so
obviously needed.

As the situation in Spain approached the conflagration
point, the mood of pacifists in England became more militant.
The dangers of fascism had been demonstrated in Ethiopia and
Germany. Pacifists blamed Conservatives for mollycoddling
the dictators, while Stalin forthrightly condemned their aggressive
actions and urged a quick and peaceful settlement in
Ethiopia. But when Mussolini and Hitler struck at the "democratically
elected" liberal government of Spain, nearly all
pacifists abandoned their faith. To remain a pacifist while a
democratic government was under attack by the combined
forces of fascist dictators was tantamount to being profascist.
They quickly discarded their antiwar policy, gave up any ideas
that pacifism could prevent another war, and bitterly ridiculed
nonintervention as appeasement of the dictators. While the
pacifist Left moved from opposition to outright advocacy of
war, the normally belligerent Right paradoxically took up the
policy the Left had discarded—pacifism and above all nonintervention. [32]
To old-time liberals such as Philip Gibbs, Leftists
were guilty of allowing partisanship to dominate the philosophical
mind:

They were traditional pacifists. Now these very same leaders
. . . are scornful of that terrified pacifism, . . . which prevents G. B.
from striking a blow anywhere on behalf of liberty or against
the enemies of Democracy. The intellectual leaders, like Professor
Gilbert Murray, Sir Norman Angell, Mr. Noel-Baker and Mr.
Attlee, have now changed the tone of their arguments and sternly
remind their followers that there must be risks for peace, as
well as for war, that men of faith must be prepared to die
for it, and that Democracy is not worth its salt unless the true
democrat is willing to defend his liberties. . . . Meanwhile the
traditional militarists of the old school and the old-school tie
are all for dodging war . . . and "buying off the Danes" by con-
cessions. . . .[33]

Perhaps the motive behind this partisanship was generous,
Gibbs added, but to condone militarism on behalf of a system
that was at least as oppressive as Fascism was to be blind to
the "atrocious tyrannies in Russia" and to the outrages
"against liberty of opinion and the rights of conscience" committed by the Spanish Republican government. It was an
example of "false logic and false sentiment due to the necessity
of simple minds to see life in blacks and whites, and to become
fanatical partisans of this side or that. . . ."[34] Ex-pacifists
replied to charges made by men like Gibbs by saying that
pacifism was simply inapplicable to the state of things in 1936.
The aggression of fascist nations made a strong counterattack
in Spain imperative. If fascism was ever to be halted, Spain
offered perhaps the final opportunity. Thus pacifism seemed
inadequate in view of the pressing obligations of liberals everywhere.[35]

However, not all members of the Peace Movement abruptly
deserted pacifism for militarism. Those who did not declared
themselves "pure" pacifists and contended that, although war
was inevitable, they would have nothing to do with it, regardless of the issues involved. They reasoned that in wartime all

governments became increasingly fascist and that, therefore, there would be no real purpose in fighting. They formed the Peace Pledge Union and appealed "to young men and women" to withdraw "from active participation in politics and to concentrate their attention upon the discipline of self-improvement." Their appeal was religious rather than political; it aimed at the "preservation of individual integrity in the face of war rather than the prevention of war."[36] To the "pure" pacifist, like C. E. M. Joad, the recruiting slogans used by volunteers on leave from the Spanish front sounded ominously like the exhortations of the minutemen in 1914. And there was considerable acumen in Joad's belief that this "Holy War" might conclude on a similar note of despair.

Editors Take Sides

Before the Spanish Civil War had entered the second month, even before some newspapers in England were sure of who was fighting whom or how to classify the conflict, people began choosing sides. Exactly how they decided which side to support is uncertain. But in view of what gradually became clear their decisions appear to have been strongly influenced by political or religious feelings and not by any careful evaluation of the reports then trickling in from Spain. Admittedly, reporting at this time was often inaccurate or incomplete, or both, but even if it had been more reliable, the majority of people would probably have stuck to the old religious and political criteria. It was easier than sifting facts and inferences, and it gave the war a manageable and exciting simplicity.

Unfortunately, instead of enlightening public opinion much of the press in England tended to polarize it. Instead of viewing the Spanish war as the culmination of unsolved social, political and religious problems, as a phenomenon indigenously Spanish, publishers reinforced the prejudices of their readers by transforming it into a determinative struggle between rival ideologies—between fascism and communism, conservatism and liberalism, totalitarianism and democracy. Headlines in the popular press bristled with epithets like "Fascist warmongers," "Bolshevists," "forces of anti-Christ," which, while they probably aroused the complacent and no doubt delighted the partisans—and perhaps increased sales—also accomplished the perfidious function of superimposing a set of opposing beliefs upon a civil struggle. Who, after all, could ignore a headline proclaiming that in Spain the forces of fascism and communism had locked in mortal combat? With terminology that seemed to make everything explicit, why should one investigate, say, the contention between the Spanish Right and Left that had ignited the fires of civil conflict, or, for that matter, the evidence on which the terminology itself was based? As the *Spectator* pungently commented in the final month of the war, the distorting glass of deliberate propaganda through which much of the press viewed the war "magnified the illusions that they conjured up."[37]

Besides magnifying reports of atrocities or breaches of nonintervention, or even misrepresenting the actual military situation so as to praise or exonerate the side they supported, most newspapers devised a nomenclature to designate each combatant which clearly revealed their sympathies. Pro-Nationalist papers labeled the Republicans "Reds" or "Bolshevists"; pro-Republican papers called the Nationalists "Rebels" or "Fascists," while neutral papers generally used the terms "Republicans," "Nationalists," or "Insurgents." However, according to Julian Huxley, even a newspaper as term-conscious as the *Times* was not above suspicion. After watching the terms in the *Times,* first, from July 20–23 and then from July 27–31,

1936, Huxley concluded that the descriptive terminology had changed, "and changed in a way which set the Insurgents in a better, and the constituted authority, in a worse, light."[38]

But aside from the political and religious reasons, there were other reasons why the war was unreliably reported and hence generally misread in England. For instance, since the principal telephone and cable lines were in Republican-held territory, dispatches from the Republican side reached England at least forty-eight hours ahead of Nationalist news. Needless to say, the time advantage permitted pro-Loyalist newspapers like the *News Chronicle* and *Manchester Guardian* a priceless opportunity to reach the public first with their version of new developments in Spain. Moreover, the Republicans evidently became aware long before the Nationalists of the considerable influence that favorable press relations could have upon observers throughout the world, and spent lavishly on propaganda, which included providing unusually accommodating services for foreign journalists. Nationalists, on the contrary, granted few privileges to reporters behind their lines and on several occasions actually expelled journalists whose reports were deemed distortions of fact.[39] In the opinion of the *Spectator,* "their censorship was as absurd as it was damaging to their own cause."[40] Above all, since the account of the Spanish war was being read against a European background, of which England because of its propinquity and ideological ties was a part, it tended to arouse old and new fears about Britain's role in European affairs, which the press often did its utmost to exploit.

Once a newspaper had taken a stand on the Spanish war, it usually remained unchanged despite evidence that might contradict its viewpoint. For example, following the liquidation of Guernica by German bombers, pro-Nationalist papers retailed the fabrication that Basques had deliberately set fire to their town before fleeing. And, on the other side, the pro-Loyalist press avoided mentioning whenever possible the steady infiltration of Communists into Loyalist ranks.

Of the papers supporting the Nationalists, the Rothermere-owned *Daily Mail* and *Evening News* epitomized the worst excesses of the Right. Not content with the tactical advantage that the Insurgents already derived from the Anglo-French nonintervention policy, they advocated sending aid directly to Franco to bolster his "holy campaign" against the "committers of atrocities," a plan also warmly espoused by the *Catholic Herald* and *Catholic Times*. With less zeal, the *Morning Post*, the *Daily Sketch*, and the *Observer* backed the Nationalist cause.

The most nearly neutral papers were those reflecting conservative opinion, such as Lord Beaverbrook's *Evening Standard*, which stressed the need to stay out of European affairs completely; the *Daily Telegraph* and *London Times*, both of which supported nonintervention, the latter proclaiming that every people should have the right to work out their own destiny without interference; therefore, "nonintervention is best for Spain; it is necessary for Europe."[41] More liberal than the *Times* and the *Telegraph* were the *Manchester Guardian* and *News Chronicle*, especially the latter, which recommended supplying the Loyalists even at the risk of war.[42]

The *Daily Herald*, the semiofficial paper of the Labour Party, represented the view of the moderate Left. While tending to print only Republican news, it favored nonintervention, at least until the Bournemouth Conference. Not unexpectedly, the *Daily Worker* printed mostly propaganda and decried Baldwin's refusal to supply arms to the Loyalists. Almost as extreme was the *Labour Monthly*, whose main theme became the class struggle. England, it maintained, revealed its sympathy with the ruling powers in Spain when it denied the workers weapons to defend themselves against fascist imperialism.

Weeklies and Journals: Left and Right

If the British popular press had reached the nadir that some said it had, few of the weeklies could claim to be any more reliable. Most of them saw the conflict in black and white terms, even though in lengthy editorials, articles by special correspondents, and eyewitness accounts they tried to give the impression of careful analysis and scrupulous documentation. In far too many instances, however, the length and documentation were merely screens hiding some biased journalistic scholarship.

For sheer extremism, Lady Houston's *Saturday Review* had no peer among weeklies of the Right. It justified the Generalissimo's revolt by contending that the Spanish government had betrayed the country by surrendering authority to "Stalin's master-plotters."[43] To combat Communist infiltration and restore Spanish leadership to Spaniards, Franco had clearly acted on a tacit mandate from the people. The *Saturday Review* saw no contradiction in Franco's use of Moorish troops in his crusade against the forces of the anti-Christ. The Moors, F. H. Mellor wrote, fight "because they are devout Moslems, worshipping one God and believing that Mahomet is his Prophet. They realize just as much as the Catholic Spaniards that they are fighting for religion against the enemies of God."[44] He assured readers that they were as dedicated as Franco himself to the restoration of the Church, which he contended had always been non-political and devoted to the educational and spiritual welfare of the people.

Like her opponents on the Left, Lady Houston attacked the nonintervention policy, but for different reasons. First, she believed that Blum had proposed nonintervention in order to assist the Republicans to win, with the aid of Russia, which intervened first. Then when they could no longer condone the "Red menace," Italy and Germany intervened as "defenders of Christianity and civilization." Instead of cowering behind a policy of neutrality, England should have approached the other great powers with a proposal to intervene in Spain.[45] But by failing to do so England lent invaluable support to the Communist conspiracy and, should Franco lose, will have imperiled the security of the whole British Empire; "for our future most surely rests on the outcome of their [Nationalist] struggle. Their victory will mean the victory of civilization over chaos, their defeat may mean general disruption and civil war in Europe, the hoisting of the Red flag over the capitals of the world."[46]

Considerably more reliable and informative than the *Saturday Review* was the moderate, generally conservative *Spectator*. Like the *Times,* it tried at first to avoid taking sides and excoriated those who did, maintaining that supporting either side not only created dangerous divisions in England but led to deliberate distortion of truth and suppression of facts. The *Spectator* found weaknesses on both sides. Responsibility for starting the war certainly rested with Franco and his aides, but if one could view the war in the context of Spanish political history, then the revolt was clearly another pronunciamento and a very familiar part of Spanish politics. While the Republicans had a better cause, they ran the risk of falling into the hands of Marxists, who in the long run would do little to improve the conditions of the Spanish masses.

In spite of the peril to British rights in the Mediterranean, however, the *Spectator* denied that the danger was serious enough to necessitate intervention. Above all, the Spanish Civil War must be kept a civil war. Agreeing with Blum's statement that there "must be no crusade of ideals in Europe," the editors

predicted that any attempts to intervene in Spain would certainly transform the war into an international affair and
divide Europe into hostile camps. England's responsibility,
along with France, required working for the isolation of the
conflict by means of the Non-Intervention Committee and
avoiding embroilment altogether. However, with unusual
candor, the *Spectator* admitted by the end of 1936 that nonintervention had been disappointing and that Germany, Italy,
and particularly Portugal had flouted its restrictions. But still
it had "cooled the atmosphere" and contained the war to the
Iberian peninsula. No one expected the policy to halt the flow
of arms into Spain completely, but on the other hand no one
quite thought it would be used as a tool to favor the Insurgents.
When it became evident that this was what was happening and
that it "worked to the detriment of the oppressed liberals," the
Spectator withdrew its support and joined the *Manchester
Guardian* and the *New Statesman and Nation* in opposing
nonintervention and recommending sending aid to the Republicans even at the risk of war.[47]

The foremost weekly of the Left was Kingsley Martin's
New Statesman and Nation,[48] which predicated everything it
published about Spain on the premise that the Loyalist cause
was democracy's fight against the encroachment of world
fascism. Its correspondents tirelessly sought to universalize the
conflict, exclaiming that Republicans were fighting for no less
than the "ideals of liberty and democracy." Readers were
warned that should the dictators be victorious in Spain the
future of the democratic states would be seriously jeopardized,
since Spain was the vortex of an international struggle, the
outcome of which could decide between a future of "liberty
and freedom" or "repression and totalitarianism." In the
meantime, wrote Louis Fischer from Madrid, Spain was the
"scapegoat for the world's inability to solve its problems."[49]

Appalled by the government's policy on Spain, the *New*

Statesman and Nation levied its heaviest attacks at nonintervention. Asserting that nonintervention could possibly emerge
as the deciding factor if the Loyalists lost, Martin contended
that the Agreement was inadequate since the Committee
obviously could not curtail the flow of material reaching the
Nationalists. Mussolini, he contended, was allowed to intervene
in Spain because the Western powers planned to seek his
"neutrality" in the event of war.[50] As though strengthening
the Insurgent armies were not enough, the Insurgents actually
used the equipment received in defiance of nonintervention to
destroy nonmilitary towns in Loyalist-held territory. But the
Non-Intervention Committee, since it was responsible for denying Loyalists the weapons with which to defend their cities,
was really the guilty party.[51]

Besides the *New Statesman and Nation,* the Left received
support from at least three literary publications. G. Grigson's
New Verse (1933–1939), while it published poems by Leftist
poets, scrupulously avoided lining up with communism, or any
other "ism,"[52] and tried to show its political disinterestedness
by accepting poems from writers with a variety of politics and
by avoiding as much as possible political theorizing.[53] But
The Left Review, The Left Book News, and the literary
anthology, *New Writing,* were all Leftist bulwarks, especially
the first which came close to being the "unofficial" organ of
the Communist Party. Begun in 1934 under the joint editorship
of Communists Montagu Slater, A. Williams-Ellis, and T.
Wintringham, and with the help of Edgell Rickword and
Ralph Fox, the *Left Review* hoped to create the conditions in
which good proletarian art could be produced, mainly by
expanding writers' knowledge of Marxist theory and of the
"ordinary people of the world." It operated on the premise
that "literature is propaganda" and that its job, therefore, was
"to influence readers, to work a change, and to record change
both in reader and writer." It sought to bring together authors

anxious to write against imperialist war, "in defence of the Soviet Union and the struggle of the working-class towards a new form of society." In addition, it endeavored "to help working-class writers express the feelings of their class" and "to work out a Marxist line of criticism and understanding for English literature."[54]

Its contributors and reviewers were mostly Communists, although work by non-Marxists like John Lehmann and Stephen Spender also appeared occasionally. By January, 1936, when Edgell Rickword became editor, it had begun a campaign to create a People's Front based on an alliance of all groups favoring "improved conditions for workers," peace through collective security, and the "extension of civil liberties."[55] The campaign was stepped up following the outbreak of war in Spain, and those slow to back the Spanish Republic, such as the Labour Party, were severely scored. From this time on, the Spanish Republic became the *cause célèbre*. Ralph Bates, an English Communist who had lived in Spain before the war, described the psychology of the Spanish Anarchists in "Compañero Sagasta Burns a Church," Robert Westerby wrote "Militia Man"; John Cornford sent a poem, "A Letter from Aragon"; Sylvia Townsend Warner assured readers that Anarchists, not Communists, had set fire to the Barcelona churches; Tom Wintringham, who had left his editor's job for the Spanish front, praised the courageous work of the British Medical Unit; and even Spender was allowed to expand on the Loyalist "Sympathy outside Spain." Rickword's editorials harped on the idea that the Republican cause was above all the defense of culture. From Jack Lindsay, Rickword requested a recitative on Spain similar to the author's popular "not english? a Reminder for May Day," and Lindsay responded with "On Guard for Spain!" Nonintervention was satirized in Rickword's own poem, "To the Wife of Any Non-

Intervention Statesman," and more savagely in Rex Warner's "Arms in Spain." C. Day Lewis' "Bombers," Wintringham's "Monument," and Charlotte Haldane's "Pasionaria" all clearly emerged out of the Spanish conflict. And Nancy Cunard, that energetic organizer and literary jack-of-all-trades, took a particular interest in the Negro poets in Spain, including the American Langston Hughes, and translated the poems of the Chilean Pablo Neruda and Haitian Jacques Roumain.

In June, 1937, Randall Swingler, at Rickword's request, replaced him as editor, and the journal started a decline that ended with its suspension a year later. However, it did not fail because of ineptness on Swingler's part. Rather, a combination of unreasonable party control and a gradual exhaustion of funds brought about its demise. During Swingler's tenure, the party gradually assumed full control of the journal, including the purely mechanical details of size and shape, with an eye primarily on increasing its sale. It was the party's idea to expand the size of the journal as well as its circulation, but, lacking funds, neither was accomplished. In June, 1938, Swingler wrote one final editorial and went off to work full-time for the *Daily Worker*. *Left Review* was closing, he wrote, to give writers time for other matters, a "wider project, which can reach a vastly greater mass of the people." [56]

While not actually a literary journal, *The Left Book News* had, by December, 1936, when it became *The Left News* and was made available to the general public instead of just to members of the Left Book Club, burgeoned from a few pages announcing the club's selections into a sizable pamphlet containing, for example, articles on the USSR by Ivor Montagu; reports about the Spanish war by Clement Attlee, Julio Álvarez del Vayo, and John Strachey; and a number of militant editorials, mostly by Victor Gollancz, which rather monotonously forecast certain war unless swift action was taken to halt fascism in Spain. "I am obsessed by the thought," Gollancz wrote in June, 1937, "that we are all fighting against time. If War and Fascism come, every scrap of decency will vanish from the world : and the only thing which will prevent War and Fascism coming is a public opinion so educated and so determined that against it neither deception nor force can prevail."[57] In his race against time, Gollancz fathered an incredible number of schemes designed to marshal public opinion and to turn club members into "missionaries for civilization." Besides establishing the local study groups where the Club's selections could be discussed and the differences of opinion aired if not solved, he organized a Junior Left Book Club, for ages fourteen to twenty-one, financed a Unity Theatre to provide the Left with a theatrical outlet, organized a summer school for club members interested in learning more about socialism, arranged tours to Russia and Spain, and even issued a Left Song Book and club badges. Adept at setting up competitions as well, he conducted a contest for the best proletarian novel, another for the best book on unemployment, and at one time offered club members the opportunity to earn 2s. 6d. for every new member they enrolled. His greatest organizational efforts, however, were reserved for rallies and rambles, the largest of which took place at Albert Hall, where Cripps, Pollitt, Pritt, and others joined Gollancz and the board of the Left Book Club in issuing warnings about the threat of fascism. Under his auspices flourished a Readers' and Writers' Group, which heard such speakers as Rex Warner, Arthur Calder-Marshall, Edgell Rickword, and Randall Swingler discuss the Group's purpose : "to bring readers into closer contact with writers so as to enable them to discuss fully the whole question of the writer in relation to social change";[58] a Propaganda Art Group, which, under the direction of Eric Gill and others, devoted itself primarily to banner making; and a Poetry Group, probably the most popular of Gollancz's creations outside of the Club Circles and Albert Hall rallies. Its aim was to restore the "traditional link between poetry and the people . . . [to let] them hear poetry which has some connection with reality and their daily lives."[59] A poetry clinic offered constructive criticism of poems submitted by members, and an elocutionist assisted in training volunteers to recite verse at Left Book Club meetings, Co-op Guilds, League of Nations' Unions, or Aid Spain meetings. The Group issued a monthly called *Poetry and the People,* which usually contained articles and original verse by Jack Lindsay, Swingler, Miles Carpenter, and Janet Watson. It also published "broadsheets," which members sold in markets and outside factories.

Gollancz controlled the Club's policy toward the Spanish war. He recommended a series of stop-gap actions designed to have immediate results rather than to lay the foundation for a long-range political program on Spain. He immediately branded England and France for withholding the arms which would defeat "the wretched hirelings of Hitler and Mussolini,"[60] and urged members to apply "unremitting pressure . . . on the Nationalist government to compel it at least to go no further on its shameful path, at best to retrace its steps."[61] John Strachey condemned Labour's endorsement of nonintervention and commended Cripps, Attlee, and Laski for taking an opposite stand and urging their party to support the Spanish Republic.[62] As the shortcomings of the government's policies grew obvious, Gollancz's editorials became more caustic, and in May, 1938, he demanded the removal of the Government and "its supersession by a Government representative of the progressive feeling of the country" and the "immediate support of the peoples of Spain."[63]

New Writing, however, put literature before politics. In

the "Manifesto" published in the first number in the spring of
1936, John Lehmann, the founder, wrote : *"New Writing* is
first and foremost interested in literature, and though it does
not intend to open its pages to writers of reactionary or Fascist
sentiments, it is independent of any political party."[64] Lehmann
believed that *New Writing's* antifascist politics would function
as a sort of "undertone" which would not impinge on the
integrity of the art but would serve as a rallying point for
writers of his generation, those disturbed enough about the
"impasse of the 1930's" to want to do something.[65]

When the Spanish Civil War began, Lehmann promised
that *New Writing* would publish all imaginative literature
about the war, to show the tremendous wave of antifascist
idealism that was gathering momentum throughout all of
Europe, or as he wrote later, to mirror "the new life breath-
ing through the old."[66] More than any other edition, *New
Writing* #3, published in the spring of 1937, showed what
Lehmann meant. Here translated from the Spanish were
"Children of Estremadura," by C. M. Arconada; "Long Live
the Revolution," by González Tuñon; and "Against the Cold
in the Mountains," by José Herrera Peters; from the German,
Rudolf Leonhard's *El Hel,* "A Tale of the Spanish Civil
War"; from the Russian, Sergo Kldiashvili's, "The Lord of
Lashkheti" and P. Tehikvadze's, "The Road to Affluence";
and among the English contributions were John Sommerfield's
"To Madrid," James Stern's "A Stranger Among Miners,"
George Garrett's "The First Hunger March," Spender's "Two
Speeches from a Play," and Auden's "Lay Your Sleeping
Head, My Love." *New Writing* never again attained such an
apogee of political representation, but subsequent numbers
contained several reports, stories and poems about the Spanish
war.

Chapter 3 : Politics and Literature

AS NEWS OF THE SPANISH WAR BEGAN REACHING ENGLAND in the final weeks of July, there were indeed few left-wing poets who did not feel that politics had at last really encroached upon their personal life. Of those discussed in this book nearly all in the early thirties had adopted some form of radical politics. Although many factors influenced their decision, what appealed most strongly to most of them was the decisiveness with which radical programs not only analyzed what was wrong with society, but offered a plan for improving it. That the plan called for no less than the discontinuance of capitalism and the establishment of universal socialism seemed not just plausible but entirely realizable. But advancing such a plan was little more than a general protest. It did not necessarily presage political action. It is well to remember that, although their verse contained many references to the coming social revolution, it also abounded with allusions to personal shame and rebellion, which probably provided more, or at least as much, imaginative stimulation as the rather vague sort of socialism they had adopted. I am not suggesting that their political commitment was in any way spurious, or that inactivity impaired it. What I am saying is that the vitality of their verse—its energy, scrappiness, and honesty—was the result of inspiration that came from within rather than from outside. In other words, politics afforded a framework for the problems they themselves had experienced. Hence it was not a political creed that inspired them so much as it was their own observations and personal reactions to the injustices that the political creed promised to ameliorate. In short, they remained poets at a time when they might have become servants of political doctrine.

Only the work of the most politically oriented poets, such as Hugh MacDiarmid, consistently reflected Marxist dogma. The majority of left-wing poets practiced an eclecticism that infuriated hard-core Marxists like John Cornford and Christopher Caudwell. They made almost no effort to adhere to the Communist party line, with the result that their verse is politically less rigid than is commonly appreciated. Even among some Communist poets and many fellow travelers there was little apprehension over being made to feel the heavy hand of party censorship. Such tolerance was due partly to the difficulty of deciding what to do with writers who had aligned themselves with the party, and partly to the fact that the C.P.G.B. had always maintained considerable freedom from direct Russian control. Moreover, except for a few party functionaries who wrote poetry, most of the left-wing poets had only a limited grasp of Marxism, and consequently had no clear notion of what not to write in the interests of orthodoxy.

Thus, when the Spanish war broke out a fairly relaxed relationship, based on respect for each other's independence, existed between left-wing poets and politicians. It is true that Cornford, Caudwell, and Julian Bell were condemning the Auden group as too "bourgeois."[1] But this internecine feud seemed peripheral. More importantly, many poets had formed their ideas independently of a political organization. When their views harmonized with those advanced by political parties, the similarity, while not wholly accidental, was more a case of merely being in agreement with politicians than an attempt on their part to coerce poets to adopt a particular line. All that seemed to matter was that poets and politicians had become distressed by the same things and were determined to do something about them.

This tolerant relationship began to change somewhat, however, after July, 1936. With the emergence of a Popular Front that united the entire Left, except Labour, behind the Spanish Republic, there was increasing pressure upon writers to state their attitudes toward the struggle and, if possible, to persuade them to work for the Popular Front. Not all the pressure was exerted by politicians. Francis Meynell, speaking at a rally for Medical Aid to the Republic, urged the audience to "Give—give until it hurts. . . . We are five hundred miles from Spain, but only three miles from Aldgate" (where Sir Oswald Mosley's Fascists had demonstrated).[2] Noting that Portugal had sided with Franco, Louis Golding recommended that antifascists give up port wine. At the first Great London Rally, in October, 1936, Ethel Mannin joined Fenner Brockway, James Maxton, and Stafford Cripps to mobilize support for the Catalan Defense Committee. The Artists International Association started a fund for medical aid to the International Column. Cyril Connelly's impassioned dispatches from Barcelona spoke of a "new and all-pervading sense of moral elevation . . . [as] the dominating note in Catalonia."[3] In a pamphlet published soon after the start of hostilities, J. B. Priestley warned that the "fascist" views of the Rothermere papers must not go unchallenged. "It is the duty of all of us who believe in the right of people to govern themselves to answer these voices, to proclaim the truth against a thousand lies."[4] Thus from the start writers themselves exhorted their colleagues to take collective action against the common enemy.

No doubt the publication of *Authors Take Sides* climaxed the effort to mobilize the Left literati behind the Spanish Republic. Consisting of brief statements by British writers, *Authors Take Sides* sought to dispel the notion that detachment, or worse yet, isolation was still possible, as the questionnaire sent to the writers clearly implied :

It is clear to many of us throughout the whole world that now, as certainly never before, we are determined or compelled to take sides. The equivocal attitude, the ivory tower, the paradoxical, the ironic detachment, will no longer do.

We have seen murder and destruction by Fascism in Italy, in Germany—the organization there of social injustice and cultural death—and revived, imperial Rome, abetted by international treachery, has conquered her place in the Abyssinian war. The dark millions in the colonies are unavenged.

Today the struggle is in Spain. Tomorrow it may be in other countries—our own. But there are some who, despite the martyrdom of Durango and Guernica, the enduring agony of Madrid and of Bilbao, and Germany's shelling of Almeria, are still in doubt, or who aver that it is possible that Fascism may be what it proclaims it is : the saviour of civilization.

Having given definition to the Spanish war, the questionnaire went on to ask,

Are you for, or against, the legal Government and the people of Republican Spain?[5]

Of the 148 replies received, 127 answered they favored the Republic. Although mostly Leftists, some of those who replied affirmatively, such as Leonard Woolf, Havelock Ellis, and H. M. Tomlinson, were nonpolitical and reflected the interest in the cause by people attracted to it for reasons besides politics. Seventeen, including Pound, Eliot, Wells, and Alec Waugh, preferred to remain neutral. Only Eliot and Waugh, however, implied that artistic reasons had led to their decision. Eliot's is the more succinct : "I still feel convinced that it is best that at least a few men of letters should remain isolated, and take no part in these collective activities." The five who opposed the Republic (most prominent were Evelyn Waugh and Edmund Blunden) said they believed the Franco revolt would in the end profit Spain.

If the questionnaire showed that a larger number of writers favored the Loyalists, it did not indicate what, if anything, they would be willing to do to support their cause. Sympathizing with the Republic, surely not difficult for most of the signatories, was one thing. But acting in concert with this sympathy was something different. There were several questions implicit in the questionnaire which must have nagged those who replied affirmatively. Broadly speaking, they concerned a writer's relationship to his society. As writers, did they have a responsibility toward civilization, and if they believed they did, what was it? If they assumed that writers could help to change social conditions, should they interrupt their careers to fight in Spain? Or, if not that, should they steal time from their writing to work for the cause at home? And perhaps most important of all, to what extent should they use their talents for propagandistic purposes?

Questions like these, full of misgivings and doubts, of course had occurred to these writers many times before the Spanish war. But the difference lay in the situation that existed after July, 1936. Whereas beforehand there was no real need to resolve these questions, now there was. With a fascist enemy in the field, with a liberal government the intended victim, with a social revolution in the making, and with a Popular Front at home pressing for public demonstrations of loyalty, it was simply no longer possible to postpone answering such questions. Henceforward, they would demand conclusive replies. For perhaps the first time in the decade these writers were being pressed to act upon their political beliefs—no matter how elementary they might be—with the result that, for the first time also, many felt themselves caught between the demands of politics on the one hand and literature on the other. It was a dilemma that perhaps a crucible only as severe as the Spanish war could create and resolve.

The problem of whether literature should be made to serve extraliterary functions, particularly political, was exhaustively discussed long before the outbreak of the Spanish Civil War, but perhaps nowhere more satisfactorily than by C. Day Lewis in *A Hope for Poetry* (1934). Although he wrote as a member of the Communist Party, Lewis nevertheless did not insist on a poet's accepting Marxism as the only valid interpretation of life before venturing to write political poetry. Merely embracing Marxism might have nothing more behind it than the wish to demonstrate one's opposition to the government, or the desire to experience some kind of literary uplift from a seemingly dynamic system. Lewis began with the premise with which all critics of the Left started, that the poet must not secede from the world of human beings. If the poet recognized a bond of humanity with his fellows, which implied that he accepted his responsibility both as a poet and as a man toward others, he might well decide that one political program would fulfill better than others certain beliefs he had about a richer, more satisfying life. What happened, Lewis contended, was that the poet, as a man, was attracted to a certain set of political ideas. He felt their pull and power. It was his humanity that was concerned with them. When this occurred, when this intensification process involving the acceptance of a political system as a man, not primarily as a poet, took place, there would follow a merger of politics and poetry. It was the strong, human emotion—the feeling of the poet as a man —which worked on ideas, and made "them a more tractable material for poetry; the poetic faculty will, in fact, have to deal—not with an abstract idea—but with an idea suffused and moulded by emotion; and that is a common subject for poetry." If the secret of writing poetry that dealt with politics lay in this fusion of the poet's being as poet and as man, then the absence of such a fusion would presumably result in a poet's attempting to palm off the didactic, or propagandistic, at the expense of the poetic—a completely undesirable situation.

Lewis' discussion of political verse has several important implications. First, he defended the belief, so common among Marxist critics, that poetry of high quality could be written when a reconciliation took place "between the poetic self and the rest of the man," a theory which John Strachey and Edward Upward and other Marxists were saying showed that writers were finally realizing their relationship as well as their responsibility to society and turning away from the "romantic" notion that condoned the separation between the poet and the people. Second, he believed that feeling and experiencing a political idea was necessary before that idea could become the raw material of poetry. The poet first had to quarrel with himself over the matter. Third, he implied that a dogmatic, rigid doctrine like communism could provide the impetus for lasting poetry, that the materialistic world view of communism could be sustaining and productive. Although Lewis said nothing about a writer's aligning himself with the proletariat so that his work would better correspond to "reality," the idea was implicit in his argument. Fourth, Lewis' concern over the sincerity of poetic feeling—its solidly humanistic core formed by man's struggle with himself—suggested that political poetry that did not result from this struggle could not expect to receive any approval from him, despite the fact that the politics of the author might correspond to his own. The distinction he made between propaganda (that which the poet tried to convince others of without having either uncertainty or conviction himself) and genuine political poetry was sound, because it was based on the belief that poetry is poetry only when it is felt, when the emotion is the result of inner tension, when the ideas of the poem are "suffused and moulded by emotion."[6]

Several other critics, however, imposed more stringent demands upon writers. While Lewis still recognized that political poetry must have its basis in the fusion of the "inner life" and "outer life"—and the "outer life" meant the world of social facts—others seemingly forgot that anything like an "inner life" existed and urged bourgeois writers to dissociate themselves from their class, join the proletariat, and write about the class struggle. A good book, wrote Edward Upward, is one that is true to life; that is, "one that is true not merely to a temporarily existing situation but also to the future conditions which are developing within that situation." Upward believed that the trouble with so much writing was that it was done by non-Marxists who were simply incapable of writing a poem or novel that truthfully represented the surface and hidden forces at work in their society, and hence their work was not only irrelevant but untruthful. Only Marxist literature presented the changing material world of nature and human society accurately, and that literature was itself a product of this changing world.[7]

If, in 1936, there was still confusion about what Marxist critics meant by literature, the demands imposed upon writers by the Spanish war did little to end the confusion. But several left-wing critics, who characteristically seldom agreed with each other, tried to recommend ways in which the Spanish war might help clear up misunderstandings. Citing the example of Wordsworth, whose revolutionary sentiments, twice stimulated by events in France and Spain, as one who realized that the

dignity of man's desires can sometimes only find fulfillment
"by transcending themselves in action," Ralph Fox assured
writers that the demands of life in 1936 corresponded to the
"dignity and intensity of man's desires." The Spanish Civil
War, where the conflict of classes was being decided, placed
the utmost demands upon the human spirit. Writers could
ignore neither events in Spain nor the "economic slavery" and
"national decay" in England. Both belonged to the "national
vision, which in turn must colour the writer's imagination."
By participating in the life of their time, authors were bound
to be imaginatively stimulated, with the result that not only
writers of diverse tendencies, but writers and the proletariat
would be drawn together into a communion based on common
goals. In France such a unification had brought together
Malraux, Celine, Romains, and Block. While Fox believed
that revolutionary action would lead to fulfillment, he did not
necessarily mean it was the only course open to the leftist
writer. But the tone of his letters from Spain suggest that
action was for him enormously satisfying.[8]

For those who did not go to Spain, however, the only proof
of the stimulating effects of participation appeared in newspapers and journals. Writing in *Left Review,* John Lehmann
and C. Day Lewis agreed that the place of the writer was in
the Popular Front supporting the cause of democracy, and, if
possible, on the platform at rallies for the Republic. In addition, they advocated that writers pay stricter attention to the
"complex of facts and theories that make up the problem of
Fascism, war and the social revolution" so that their art might
depict more exactly the social forces at work in the world.
They should study Marxist analysis of history and society to
make their "thought structure" firmer. Unlike Lewis, however,
Lehmann avoided saying outright that writers should use their
talents to oppose fascism. Instead, he offered the rather bland

proposal that if writers accepted the Marxist map of the world, their work would automatically have a propagandistic effect against fascism. Concerning the poet, Lehmann applied the same test to political poetry that Lewis had voiced in *A Hope for Poetry*. "The test has always been whether the opinion is felt imaginatively as well as thought." In this case, "the propaganda he thus makes will in the end be far more valuable than any other kind of propaganda he could make as a journalist or committeeman." Above all, the creative artist must "never engage in any other activity, for the cause of peace and liberty he is supporting, to the extent of abandoning, or seriously curtailing for any length of time, his activity as an imaginative creator."[9]

Lehmann's recognition of the importance to writers of preserving a sense of artistic individuality and integrity (it was one of the key proposals in the Manifesto of *New Writing*) differed sharply from what C. Day Lewis began preaching after the start of the war. Lewis joined Edgell Rickword, then editor of the *Left Review*, in popularizing the belief that fascism was intent upon destroying not just the cultural achievements of Spain but the whole cultural heritage of all peoples; therefore writers, as people interested in preserving the culture of the world, must support the fight against fascism. The argument was easily expanded to include an indictment of the Nationalists on the grounds that they were collaborating with European fascists. Lewis went further and urged authors, besides joining the Popular Front, to translate contemporary problems into emotional terms so as to appeal to man's "latent idealism." Moreover, they should counter every tendency to imperialist war manifested in the press, fiction and poetry, and if possible, stir the imagination of the Labour Movement (which remained outside the People's Front), to remind it of "the greatness of its past history and convince it that the future is waiting to be moulded by its hands."[10] Lewis' plea for integrity, voiced so hopefully in *A Hope for Poetry*, all but vanished under the pressing demands of the Popular Front and the Spanish cause. He was primarily concerned now with the influence writers could have upon the intractable Labour Party, and how their work might strengthen the antifascist cause.

Assuming that the poet, whose medium could be conveniently adapted to celebrating the Republican cause, would be the first to confront the problem of what to do with his art, what alternatives were open to him? He could, of course, meet Lewis' demands and join the Popular Front and write poetry celebrating the Loyalist cause. The most obvious danger here, though, was that the poet would be preoccupied primarily with theory and doctrine, rather than with his own experience, and hence would be apt to accept only whatever concurred with the prevailing orthodoxy. Also, because of his distance from Spain, he would necessarily have to rely on the reports of participants or observers for material. In a sense, he would function as a sort of intermediary between the Popular Front and the reader, which meant that his work might meet certain political standards but fail entirely to meet many of the standards of poetry.

A second alternative was to use the Spanish war as the raw material of a poem, but to refrain from laying over the poem a veneer of dogma. That is, the poem's content would correspond to the poet's own experience and feelings and not to any political formula. If such a poem happened to conform to political standards, it would not be because the poet had conscientiously tried to meet those standards. The similarity, while perhaps not wholly coincidental, would however be unsolicited. The poet would have worked independently to his conclusions.

A third alternative was to restrict oneself to a narrative treatment of the war in the manner, say, of Tennyson's "The Charge of the Light Brigade," or Thomas Campbell's "Hohenlinden." Since the event being celebrated would already be familiar to a vast number of people, the poet's job would consist primarily of arranging the details into a dramatic unity. This kind of poetry, perhaps best represented by C. Day Lewis' *The Nabara,* made rather minimal demands on the poet's creative faculties and hardly necessitated revealing any strong political commitment. Perhaps the only other alternative was for a poet to participate in Popular Front activities to give some indication of where he stood, but to resist pressure to transform his art into a strictly political tool. But despite efforts to preserve the uses of his art, this poet, as Stephen Spender has suggested, ran the risk of drawing too heavily on his credit as a writer; that is, in making a contribution to the cause, this poet was counting on his reputation as a writer to add weight to the side he supported.[11] The danger here lay in becoming so closely identified with a partisan group, or the Popular Front, that too much time would be spent just fulfilling their demands for speeches, appearances, and meetings. Eventually, the poet would have to make a choice between poetry and politics.

The spontaneous but short-lived popularity which most of the poetry of the Spanish Civil War enjoyed in England was due in large measure to the receptive mood of a rather large audience. As we have seen, newspapers and journals regularly spread the events of the war across the front pages. Their frank partisanship generated a similar partisanship among readers, making them sensitive to criticism that tended to sully the cause in which they believed and strong supporters of those who defended it. In a sense, a kind of informal "working agreement" developed between journalists and some poets. The former, as Matthew Arnold wrote of the critic in *The Function of Criticism,* were consciously engaged in establishing an order of ideas. They provided the raw material for poetry, and, in addition, created, for some, an atmosphere which inspired them to write. Furthermore, they kept a substantial audience informed and concerned about the fate of Spain. The result was that a poem about Spain which showed the "correct" politics could depend on having a warm reception, regardless of its poetic quality. It meant that the poet, sure of the feelings of most of his audience, could rely on their emotions rather than his own to endow, say, a highly theoretical poem with some emotional content. It meant, too, that a poet who used names like Madrid, La Pasionaria and Guernica could be certain that, besides being immediately recognized, they would evoke appropriate responses. In the long run, it meant that, in a sense, the poet had a "captive audience," ready and eager to read his work, certain to praise it, and receptive to as much of it as he could provide. How much he provided and its quality depended in most cases on how successfully he withstood the temptation to capitalize on the sudden popularity of the subject, or on how well he managed to fuse his beliefs as a man and as a poet.

Chapter 4 : Poet-Volunteers

Ideals and Violence

BEFORE EXAMINING THE VERSE WRITTEN BY POETS WHO
volunteered to fight in Spain, we should note that of the
approximately forty poets who wrote about the Spanish war
only a dozen or so volunteered to fight, and all of them with
the Loyalists. The only poet who came close to bearing arms
for Franco was Roy Campbell, but he left Spain in August,
1936, along with Robert Graves and Laura Riding, and
returned sometime later as a "well-protected war correspondent."[1] The brief and somewhat regulated visits which
Spender, Auden, and a few others made to Madrid, or to one
of the quiet fronts, had propaganda value, especially in England, but gave the poets themselves hardly more than a worm's-
eye view of the war.

Those who went to Spain—to stay and fight—naturally
believed that action outweighed all other demonstrations of
solidarity. They were not by any means "fanatical revolutionaries," as Churchill called them before he changed his mind
about Franco, nor did they fit Dean Inge's scornful description
of "international gunmen."[2] Possessed with perhaps more
courage (or more foolhardiness, some would say) than their
colleagues and certainly more determined to meet fascism
head-on in Spain, they exposed themselves wholeheartedly to

the physical and emotional stresses of military life for the sake of a cause behind which the Left had thrown all its prestige.

Behind the volunteers' involvement in the Spanish war burned a bright political ideal. To vindicate it, they did more than proselytize; they fought. And by doing so they subjected that ideal to the severest possible test : war. For it is evident that a political ideal can be more easily nurtured and maintained if it is never seriously tested. However, when someone volunteers to fight to defend a political ideal, we can assume that that person has decided that safety and, perhaps, even survival, are to him less important than the preservation of the political ideal. What this person cannot know beforehand, however, is how the exigencies of war will affect him personally and, in turn, his politics. There are statements in John Cornford's verse, for example, that suggest that even the most dedicated Communist might flinch before the trials of actual combat. It would seem that for Cornford and most poet-volunteers it became necessary to accept the carnage of war as a disagreeable but necessary part of defending the political ideal that had brought them to Spain. In other words, they had to believe that the ideal justified all the slaughter, and as long as they could sustain this belief it acted as a bulwark against any revulsion which steady subjection to war might provoke and which, in turn, might erode the ideal. The cause, therefore, had the double duty of making suffering and death palatable and keeping the volunteers fortified for combat.

But what would happen if the crucible of war should become too severe? What would happen if the bulwark of political idealism should crack? Would the volunteer withdraw from the war and perhaps even from politics, made contrite by the realization that not even a political ideal could condone such inhumanity? Or would he cling to the shattered ideal, hoping to salvage at least some of its sustaining force, or anticipating that it might someday be restored completely?

When the volunteer happened to be a poet, the pressures to recognize more than the exhortatory capacity of wartime ideals increased enormously. If he was not wholly insensitive to human suffering, he had to admit, at least to himself, that war was the most bestial method ever devised to inflict indiscriminate and wholesale suffering on the mass of mankind. This he could not ignore. But he could, for the sake of an ideal in which he believed, attempt to justify war as the only means to achieve the end that the ideal promised. Or he could glorify, or romanticize, war as an activity which made public man's heroic virtues of courage and endurance. Quite understandably, these sentiments appealed to some poet volunteers, even though they may themselves have been genuinely shocked by experiences in Spain. But to record their aversion might be construed as damaging the ideal, even, in fact, betraying it. Moreover, besides reflecting unfavorably on the efficacy and authority of the crusade, such an attitude might suggest an unhealthy concern with their own individuality and fate, which, in turn, would weaken the belief that a united people were every day fearlessly and unselfishly spending themselves in the war against fascism. On the other hand, if they gave preference to political ideals in their verse, they risked alienating those who had been conditioned by experience, or who had no illusions about the "war of democracy" being different from any other war. To this audience, verse that exalted ideology instead of the realities of war would appear tendentious and falsely heroic.

Faced, then, with the dilemma of how to reconcile politics and brute force while simultaneously trying to control any personal feelings of shock, some volunteers settled for what can only be called a compromise. They could not emulate Wilfred Owen and search their own hearts for the tragedy of war and say that the poetry is in the pity of it all. Not unless they could somehow transcend the bounds of political orthodoxy, and this seemed beyond both their abilities and desires. However, they could try serving a political and poetic muse at the same time, try recording compassion alongside creed, to show that they could write convincingly about the atmosphere of war, the reactions of their comrades, and, perhaps, their own reactions to fear, or defeat, while simultaneously recognizing and fulfilling political obligations. In too many instances, however, the compromise proved fatal to the poetry. Too often the demands of politics beset the poets with insoluble problems.

The Heat of Battle

The main problem that confronted six of the volunteers, however, was not how to reconcile politics and brute force, but how to express their personal reaction to war. Though often pretentious, melodramatic and sentimental, their poems are nevertheless frequently moving and even touching. The presentation ranges from re-creating a single dramatic event —a bombing raid or a battle—to reproducing the thoughts a soldier has as he prepares for battle. The form can be as simple and rough as "Eyes," or as mannered and theatrical as "A Moment of War." The former, found scribbled on the leaf of a notebook, was written by an anonymous soldier in the International Brigade. It has all the earmarks of rapid composition : the facile observance of exact parallels and rhymes, a slightly tedious repetition. But the unaffected quality of the poem, the spontaneity, and lack of cultured diction endow it with honesty and excitement :

> Eyes of men running, falling, screaming
> Eyes of men shouting, sweating, bleeding
> The eyes of the fearful, those of the sad
> The eyes of exhaustion, and those of the mad.

Eyes of men thinking, hoping, waiting
Eyes of men loving, cursing, hating
The eyes of the wounded sodden in red
The eyes of the dying and those of the dead.

Laurie Lee's poem, "A Moment of War," dated the Spanish Frontier, 1937, fails to convey the sense of terror that "Eyes" accomplished so artlessly. The studied, sensuous imagery ("stuttering with fear," "melts with pity," "odour and kiss of final pain") and the oratorical declamations on the comparative safety of worms and fish inject an incongruity into the war setting. The beginning seems particularly stagy and stilted:

It is night like a red rag
drawn across the eyes
the flesh is bitterly pinned
to desperate vigilance
the blood is stuttering with fear.

O praise the security of worms
in cool crumbs of soil,
flatter the hidden sap
and the lost unfertilized spawn of fish!

The hands melt with weakness
into the gun's hot iron
the body melts with pity
the face is braced for wounds
the odour and the kiss of final pain.

Yet, the feeling of terror burns through in the last stanza, despite the sudden shift to the second person and the fuzziness of the final line:

But darkness opens like a knife for you
and you are marked down by your pulsing brain
and isolated

and your breathing,
your breathing is the blast, the bullet,
and the final sky.[3]

The poems of Dennis Birch and David Marshall comment
on the physical and moral effects of the devastating aerial
bombings carried out by both sides, but with particularly
brutal effectiveness by the Germans in celebrated raids on
Madrid, Barcelona, and Guernica. Prior to the massive bombings of the Second World War, the attacks on Spanish cities
were the largest and deadliest the world had yet seen. As
military experts coolly assessed the effects of the bombings,
many writers, intellectuals and artists protested against what
seemed at the time man's most homicidal weapon of destruction.[4] C. Day Lewis, Herbert Read, Nancy Cunard, and
Stephen Spender, appalled and disgusted by the barbarity of
such mass killing, expressed their feelings in poems that rose
above conventional statements of protest and achieved a synthesis of outraged sensibility and tragedy that is absent entirely
from the work of Birch and Marshall. The main difficulty
with Marshall's poem, "Retrospect," is that it comes so close
to being a piece of reportorial journalism, an actual transcript
of life, that it almost ceases to be poetry. Marshall probably
witnessed the bombing he described. But he has not transformed it into an imaginative re-creation of the event which,
besides embodying his own feelings, will give meaning to the
experience. Striving for the effect of montage, he attempted to
blend disparate images of a joyful and steady England and a
hapless and war-tense Spain. The effect is startling, but slick :

> While here
> Kids slide in the roadways
> Steadied feet thudding in the gutters :
> Ice blurs
> The red orange blue of neon lights—

> The harlot shops invite.
> But there
> The cafe lights blink and blacken
> Ribs tighten, skin grows ware—

The frantic efforts to find safety before the bombs begin falling and the bombing itself are struck off in terse, staccato
language :

> Then the bombs
> Belching earth-pits
> One two three sudden,
> Four, wait wait wait five,
> Six god that's it
> Glass smashing and one thin endless scream
> Then a dullness in the head,
> We stand over the table,
>   . . . .
> A no-sex voice from the street
> Cries Sanidad Sanidad
> —Christ let's get out of this . . .
> Ay, alli mucha de la muerto hay,
> Y aqui, que hay major.[5]

Though imparting a kind of stabbing power, "Retrospect"
merely chronicles a few agonizing moments in the lives of
some anonymous Spaniards.

On the other hand, Birch's poem, "Incident 1938," seems
spurious precisely because it lacks verisimilitude. The setting,
a peaceful Spanish town, replete with a lone gypsy, chattering
women and dozing children, and a young girl praying at the
town shrine, is too idyllic and cozy to be real. It is a cardboard
town, a prop useful in exploiting the awesome event about to
occur. After the planes have dropped their bombs and flown
off, leaving behind a rubble-filled market place, it is no

surprise to learn that the gypsy, the children, and the young
worshiper have all been killed. Their death only compounds
the bathos :

> That night
> No bell rang out for vespers,
> No painted carts set out for upland farms,
> No dancers leapt to laughter in the square,
> No song, no wine, no lovers anywhere.
> But
> Little lakes of blood still specked the stones.
> There were no fingers left to pluck the lute,
> No one could tell the gypsy's name,
> His folk or whence he came.
> Lanterns were lit beside the crater's mouth :
> A pile of stones stood where the children slept—
> They will not notice sun or shadow now.[6]

Birch's preoccupation with the loss of song and wine, absent
lovers and dancers, dead gypsies and silent church bells suggests that for the purposes of his poem, at least, he relied on
the durable legend of a gay, romantic, reverent Spain, the
eternal home of Don Juan, Don Quixote, and Saint Theresa.
Not only do we mistrust this tinsel facsimile of Spanish life,
especially since the exigencies of civil war had introduced a
stern and solemn soberness into Spanish life, but we strongly
suspect it was being used primarily to bestir interest in
the cause.

At least two volunteers wrote about the battle of Jarama,
which was a particularly disastrous engagement for the British
battalion.[7] John Lepper, in "Battle of Jarama 1937," captures
the surface excitement of the battle by selecting details that
particularize the encounter : a sun-filled valley rent with a
"metallic clang"; clouds of dust rising behind klaxoning
ambulances; the wounded and dead lying still where they

fell; flushed, "sweat-streaked" riflemen holding "their hot rifles." These carefully etched images breathe life into the panorama. Less effective, however, is the personified figure of Death, stalking "the olive trees / Picking his men." Besides being only partly visualized, the personification hardly complements the poet's more realistic view of the dead: "Men torn by shell-shards lay / Still on the ground." Even worse, however, is the lapse into the macabre in the final stanza. War hardly becomes more repellent by the addition of this gruesome detail:

> With the coming of darkness
> Deep in the wood
> A fox howled to heaven
> Smelling the blood.[8]

T. A. R. Hyndman, in "Jarama Front," uses a smaller canvas and a more personal idiom. Only twenty lines, "Jarama Front" tries to suggest much more than it says:

> I tried not to see,
> But heard his voice.
> How brown the earth
> And green the trees.
> One tree was his.
> He could not move.
> Wounded all over,
> He lay there moaning.

The admission that the "I" tried to evade the dying soldier to avoid exposing himself to danger and the sight of death, and the observation that the colors of the earth and trees seem to intensify during a crisis suggest that Hyndman had at least limited powers of selection and suggestion. The conclusion, however, is ambiguous:

> But he was dying
> And the blanket sagged.
> "God bless you, comrades,
> He will thank you."
> That was all,
> No slogan,
> No clenched fist
> Except in pain.[9]

By trying to impart a quiet dignity to the dying comrade, Hyndman becomes maudlin. "God bless you, comrades, / He will thank you," has an unconvincing sugary bravado. The reason for this, as well as for the observations which follow ("No slogan, / No clenched fist"), may be political. To disparage the notion that antifascist volunteers fanatically threw themselves into battle, waving upraised fists and shouting antifascist slogans, Hyndman has created a "comrade" whose resoluteness is tempered with Christian charitableness. But, unfortunately, the latter quality seems misplaced. Are we to assume that the inspiring ideals embodied in wartime slogans and salutes are forgotten in the agony of death? Or is Hyndman suggesting that the dying man is not a Communist, and hence that the Spanish war has attracted men of various political beliefs? In either case, the conclusion suffers from an implicit tendency toward argument, or, at best, explanation, either of which creates complications that cannot easily be resolved.

Clive Branson's sonnet, "San Pedro," the location of the camp in which he was imprisoned, catches the somnambulant unreality of the prisoner-of-war camp and the despondency of its ghostly habitants. A harmonious group of images based on light and darkness and a sense of enervation distinguish the octave:

A foreign darkness fills the air to-night.
The moon betrays this unfamiliar scene.
Strange creatures, shadow-ghosts of what had been
Live with no aim than groping through half light.
Talk dreamily, walk wandering, delight
In trivial acts that formerly would mean
Nothing. A livid memory, this lean
Ill-clad rabble of a lost dreaded might.

The sestet, however, is less impressive. Branson's anger has tricked him into condemning his captors as "idiots" and proclaiming the captives chained "giants." The exaggeration, besides disturbing the controlled passion of the octave, leaves a residue of hate and Promethean boasting:

Look longer, deeper, the accustomed eyes
Know more than quick appearances can tell.
These fools, this shoddy crowd, this dirt, are lies
Their idiot captors wantonly compel.
These men are giants chained down from the skies
To congregate an old and empty hell.[10]

Commissar Wintringham's War

What distinguishes the verse of Tom Wintringham, the oldest of the poet-volunteers, from that of the poets just discussed is the extent to which political considerations are allowed to dominate in his work. While Marshall, Lepper, Hyndman, and the others registered disturbing reactions to war in verse in which politics plays an implicit role, Wintringham manifested almost no shock at all and contentiously justified the war as one of political necessity. Not all of his grit, however, was due to any inordinate courage. A veteran of the First World War, he was undoubtedly better prepared for the strain of combat than his youthful comrades. Moreover, as a brigade commissar, he was expected to exemplify fortitude as an inspiration to others. Then, too, his commitment to communism was unquestionably firmer than that of men like Hyndman and Lepper, and therefore party interests naturally tended to prevail in his life as well as in his verse. Besides politics, however, Wintringham's whole heritage had influenced his decision to go to Spain :

Why was I here? Yes, hatred of war; trying to stamp war out as one would a forest fire, before it spreads. But more than that : all that lay behind me and, if I lived, ahead of me, led me here.

Eight or nine generations back before my birth one of my ancestors, a Nonconformist hedge preacher, had his tongue torn out by order of a royal court of justice. It was the only way to stop him "carrying subversive propaganda," as we should call it today. Something of that man's attitude to life had come through to me from my parents, the most really Liberal people I know. That hedge-doctor had sent me here. So, to a lesser extent, had the sickly child Tom who had started to read war histories at the age of ten, had loved battle-tales . . . So had the poet who had no time for poems because the miseries of a world shadowed by war "were Misery and would not let him rest"—or let him be a poet. So had the lad in prison for incitement of mutiny, sedition; twenty-seven years old, waiting for April for liberty and May's General Strike. I was here because of all I was and would be.[11]

In his verse, Wintringham sets out to instruct and inspire the volunteers who had joined the people's "war for democracy." "Barcelona Nerves" and "Granen" celebrate the new and positive commitment to life which has sprung from the determination to fight for social improvement :

Neither fools nor children any longer,
Those ways, traits, gone and away
That once made life a luck-game, death a stranger,
We're going on.

Fear of death, though formidable, must be overcome; for "life's a matter of beating this, of breaking/ By own hardness, and a held hand, out/ From fury, frustration, fear, the waiting, the shouting. . . ." Among the volunteers, "the hate of fate," the everlasting postponement of social amelioration, has made the will to alter the condition of things stronger than the dread of suffering and death. "We'll make what wrecks these others into our gaining,/ Into our choice" ("Barcelona Nerves"). And the "others," the fascists, "our enemies," are the necromaniacs; they "can praise death and adore death," while we endure and ally ourselves with the sun, with the electric torch that guides the surgeon's fingers. "We are allied with this light" ("Granen").[12]

Wintringham's black and white view of the conflict dominates both poems. The fascists are the forces of night and death; the Loyalist volunteers are allied with light and sun. Although war itself is evil, a disaster foisted upon the Spanish people by the fascists, it must be fought and won. And if it must be endured, it is comforting to know that one is on the side of Right. As verses capable of inspiriting the volunteers, "Barcelona Nerves" and "Granen" unquestionably proved useful, and, in 1936–37, when many were busily extolling the courage and idealism of all who had joined the noble crusade, there was sufficient reason to find some truth in these poems. But at the end of 1938, on the eve of the Loyalist collapse, to maintain that the cause of Right stood on the threshold of victory was fatuously wishful thinking. This, however, is precisely the boast Wintringham made in "Monument: A Poem from the Spanish Front." He begins by addressing the heroic Spanish people, who will finally win the victory alone:

Take then these metals, under the deep sky
And digging in the harsh earth,
When by words hard as bullets,

> Thoughts simple as death,
> You have won victory,
> People of Spain, You will remember the free men
>   who fought beside you,
>   enduring and dying with you, the strangers
> Whose breath was your breath.

They will commemorate their triumph by erecting a gigantic tower composed of bits of metal and earth collected from all over Spain. In describing the gathering of these ingredients, Wintringham recounts the sins perpetrated upon the Spanish people and the battles and atrocities which these injustices incited. The "enemies of the People" are besmirched in noisome imagery ("eating gangrene of wealth, the grey pus/ Of pride, the black scab of those strangers/ Who were choking your breath") or snarling epithets. When the whole assortment of material and soil has at last been amassed, an almost spiritual amalgamation occurs:

> Take then these metals, under the deep sky
> Melt them together; take these pieces of earth
> And mix them; add your bullets,
> And memories of death;
> You have won victory,
> People of Spain,
> And the tower into which your earth is built, and
>   Your blood and ours, shall state Spain's
>   Unity, happiness, strength; it shall face the breath
> Of the east, of the dawn, of the futures when
>   there will be no strangers. . . ."[13]

Not only is "Monument" false in the sense that the desperate condition of the Loyalists precluded the possibility of victory. But it is also a highly problematical vision of the future. The prophecy that "unity, happiness, strength" await a nation torn apart by civil war amounts to an inspiring but extremely

dubious hope. Wintringham tried to preserve into a disillu-
sioned era the intrepid idealism of an earlier period.

University Volunteers

With the exception of Laurie Lee and Tom Wintringham,
none of the poets discussed thus far had established a literary
reputation prior to the Spanish war. Their verse was the result
of involvement in the war. There were, however, four young
writers among the volunteers who had earned recognition, at
least in left-wing circles, as promising authors before volunteering to fight in Spain. Christopher Caudwell, Charles Donnelly,
and John Cornford were Communists. Julian Bell can best be
described as a socialist. Sometime before the outbreak of war
in Spain, Cornford and Caudwell had verified their commitment to communism by aligning themselves with the proletariat, Cornford going to live among workers in Cambridge, and
Caudwell doing the same in London's East End. When
Charles Donnelly refused to deny before Dublin University
officials that he held revolutionary views (i.e., communist), he
was expelled. Until he left for Spain, he worked for the Republican Congress Movement and wrote for *Irish Front* and
the newly established *Left Review*.[14]

While Caudwell, Cornford, and Donnelly busily attended
to party business in England—each combined a full round of
routine tasks with a good deal of political writing—Julian Bell
had gone to China to take a position at National Wuhan University. Distance did not diminish his interest in European
developments, however. As Europe moved closer to war, Bell
gradually rejected his Bloomsbury heritage with its strong
pacifist foundation, and accepted action (i.e., war) as the only
antidote against fascist aggression. From a conscientious objec-

tor he became a conscientious consenter, as his letters from China clearly reveal. When he learned of the Spanish war, he wrote to his mother (Vanessa Bell) : "Well, you may be thankful I'm safe in China, for I know in England I should be feeling that the only reasonable thing is to go and fight the fascist in Spain." In another letter (to D.E.), he wrote : "I fancy being here has salved my conscience : I know I should rather feel ashamed of myself if I'd been in England and not tried to volunteer." In December, 1936, shortly before he had definitely decided to return to England and volunteer for duty in Spain, he wrote that being in China had really not assauged his conscience at all. "It's impossible to let other people go and fight for what one believes in and refuse to risk oneself . . . I should never recover from a sense of shame if I didn't go."

Bell finally got to Spain, but not until he had successfully resisted the combined efforts of J. M. Keynes, David Garnett, as well as his parents, to dissuade him from going. In June, 1937, he joined Richard Rees and a British medical unit on the Brunete front as an ambulance driver. Six weeks later he was killed by a bomb. What he had seen of the war had, however, provided some fulfillment. "I find it perpetually entertaining and very satisfactory," he had written to Vanessa. "And though I have begun to realize what a pleasure ordinary life will be, I don't feel I've more than touched the possibilities of this . . . it's a better life than most I've led."[15]

By the time Bell arrived in Spain, Caudwell, Cornford, and Donnelly had all been killed. They had been among the first to volunteer.[16] They had no trouble deciding between different courses of action, since it was clear to them that "democracy" had to be defended wherever it was attacked. Cornford's short interlude with a POUM militia on the Aragon front shattered some of his expectations of war. Instead of order he found chaos. Boredom, rather than excitement, characterized life

along the front. Before joining the International Brigade at
Albecete in November, he recommended that the Spanish
government incorporate the Anarchist militias into a People's
army in order to guarantee its own preservation. Anarchism,
it seemed to him, would hamper the government's best efforts.
Early in December, after having suffered a head wound while
fighting in Madrid's University City, he was ordered not to
return to the front for several days. However, as Wintringham,
the company commander, observed, only "the life of the front
was real to him."[17] And Cornford rejoined his company at
Cordova and was killed almost at once, on December 28,
1936, the day after his twenty-first birthday.[18] A little over a
month later, during the battle of Jarama, Caudwell and
Donnelly went into battle for the first time. Both had been in
Spain since December. Caudwell had doubled as machine-gun
instructor and editor of the battalion newspaper, while Donnelly served as political commissar of the British section of the
Abraham Lincoln Brigade. Ironically, Caudwell lost his life
just as his brother in London had succeeded in convincing
party leaders, after showing them advance proofs of *Illusion
and Reality,* that Caudwell would be more useful as a writer
than a soldier. A cable had been dispatched recalling him to
England when he died on February 12 while covering the
retreat of his section. Two weeks later, on February 27, Donnelly died in an attack, and in the opinion of the American
poet, Edwin Rolfe, the battalion lost its "most original
talent."[19]

Only Cornford and Donnelly wrote poetry based on their
experiences in Spain. That their output is small is hardly surprising, for in their case action had superseded writing. To
their mind, being in Spain was of far greater consequence than
writing about the struggle from a distance, and therefore they
did not feel they had neglected their art for an insignificant

reason. Considering the difficulties of writing about a conflict in which one is participating physically and emotionally, we can hardly cast aspersions on their scanty offerings; and, while this consideration should not unduly influence our evaluation of their verse, it surely must have made creating at a deeper level extremely difficult.

In "Full Moon at Tierz: Before the Storming of Huesca," Cornford gives considerable metaphysical freshness to the rather well-worn point that history can be altered by changing the economic structure of society, which Cornford naturally believed the Spanish war was about:

> The past, a glacier, gripped the mountain wall,
> And Time was inches, dark was all.
> But here it scales the end of the range,
> The dialetic's point of change,
> Crashes in light and minutes to its fall.
>
> Time present is a cataract whose force
> Breaks down the banks even at its source
> And history forming in our hands
> Not plasticine but roaring sands,
> Yet we must swing it to its final course.

In speculating on "Time future," Cornford appropriately uses no image like the glacier or the cataract; "Time future" will be whatever Cornford and his comrades make it. If this were the end of the poem, and it very well could be, we might say that Cornford has simply rendered a Marxist interpretation of the war, perhaps with the intention of inspiring young Marxists to make additional sacrifices. We might argue that it is basically Communist propaganda dressed up in a few bold images. But happily the poem is grounded in more than politics, although politics motivated all Cornford's actions; it is grounded in a military experience as well, in which more than ideology was at stake. Cornford's abilities as a revolutionary were also being tested in Spain, and because he was concerned over the demands of this test the poem rises above the mere reinforcement of Communist statement. The painful recognition of his own weaknesses, and the hope that they will not betray him form the heart of the poem:

> Though Communism was my waking time,
> Always before the lights of home
> Shone clear and steady and full in view—
> Here, if you fall, there's help for you—
> Now, with my Party, I stand quite alone.
>
> Then let my private battle with my nerves,
> The fear of pain whose pain survives,
> The love that tears me by the roots,
> The loneliness that claws my guts,
> Fuse in the welded front our fight preserves.
>
> O be invincible as the strong sun,
> Hard as the metal of my gun,
> O let the mounting tempo of the train
> Sweep where my footsteps slipped in vain,
> October in the rhythm of its run.[20]

Following the poet's death, Tom Wintringham expressed surprise at the sensitivity he found in Cornford's verse. "We knew him," Wintringham said, "as a keen brain, crushing in argument; we knew how contemptuously his intelligence would have rejected the theories and rhodomontade of POUM speeches and newspapers. What we did not know . . . was that his manner was armour worn over a poet's sensitiveness, over a horror-hatred of 'this death is background to our lives.' "[21]

Wintringham's observation is borne out in at least two additional poems, "Heart of the Heartless World" and "As

Our Might Lessens," where Cornford came close to reaffirming some of Owen's attitudes toward war.[22] "As Our Might Lessens," written after Cornford had experienced his "baptism of fire" at Huesca, tries to exhort volunteers to redouble their efforts, despite fascist threats to hold them "down by murder's fears." But the fact that death forms the background of their lives overwhelms him, and he begins brooding about pain, observing that even slogans and ideals fail to assauge it. "No abstraction of the brain/Will counteract the animal pain./ The living thought must put on flesh and blood." Out of this struggle against the pain and death comes the tension of the poem. "But this fear haunts us all./ Flesh still is weak."

"Heart of the Heartless World" was addressed to Margot Heinemann, with whom, as the lyric plainly shows, Cornford had formed a close attachment.[23] In this four-stanza lyric, Cornford wrote what is probably the only love poem of the Spanish Civil War; and except for the name Huesca, it might have been written by any poet with a similar feeling in any war. The first stanza indicates the degree of his attachment:

> Heart of the heartless world,
> Dear Heart, the thought of you
> Is the pain at my side,
> The shadow that chills my view

It is both a relief and a surprise to find that the poet who had promised to fight like a Communist if not like a soldier can express affection for something besides the cause. And it is indeed remarkable to read in the next stanza that he is not only afraid to lose his love but afraid of his fear, which he hopes the spiritual presence of his love will help diminish:

> Think so kindly, dear, that I
> Sense you at my side.
> And should the encounter be his last,
> And if bad luck should lay my strength

Into the shallow grave,
Remember all the good you can;
Don't forget my love.

Except for the first two lines of the third stanza, "On the last mile to Huesca,/ The last fence for our pride," there are no allusions to Spain, and even these are too bland to be objectionable. The tender poignancy which the poet expressed as he was about to leave on an expedition which could cost him his life, and the double fear of losing his love and of being afraid of his own fear raise the poem far above the ordinary. And there is a touching levity in his use of the slangy "bad luck," instead of some other, more gallant cause for death, as though he wanted, above all, to avoid suggesting that the ideals in which he believed would justify his death. His concern over how his love might accommodate herself to the fact of his death adds a simple dignity to the final lines.[24]

There is, however, another side to Cornford's verse. Committed so completely to communism as to be willing to die fighting for its advancement, he naturally confronted the problem of how to handle dogma in his work, how "to express in poetry the unity of thought and action, to translate necessity into terms of the poetic imagination," as Spender has put it.[25] That the pressure within Cornford to achieve a sort of orthodoxy resulted sometimes in the substitution of a strictly political muse for a poetic one is evident in the second half of "As Our Might Lessens." After stating that "No abstraction of the brain/ Will counteract the animal pain," Cornford propounds one of the party's nostrums as the answer to how man should confront pain and death : by actively participating in revolutionary struggles, which presupposes that such action will be completely fulfilling, man will face both unafraid. Activity alone will be the commencement of an entirely new existence :

> Action creates new ways of living,
> Shatters the old ideas of loving,
> Brings us in motion face to face with *fact*.

"Fact," of course, means reality itself. Only revolutionary action can destroy the old shadowy world of oppression and injustice and beget the new shining world of "fact." Action therefore becomes imperative. This political lesson is heavily underscored in the last three stanzas, and concludes with a promise that the future will belong to the "democratic forces" of the world:

> Though flesh is weak, though bone is brittle,
> Our sinews must be hard as metal,
> We must learn to mock at what makes readers wince,
> Our home, our job is everywhere,
> We have no time to stand and stare,
> Nor miss the fighter's nor the lover's chance.

> We cannot hide from life with thought,
> And freedom must be won, not bought.
> No talisman will keep us safe from harm.
> But moving in the masses' blood
> Vienna, Amsterdam, Madrid
> The ten-years-sleeping-image of the storm

> Shows us what we stand to gain
> If through this senseless-seeming pain,
> If through this hell we keep our nerve and pride.
> Where the nightmare faces grinned
> We, or our sons, shall wake to find
> A naked girl, the future at our side.

This peroration on the fruits of action, where pain is called simply "senseless-seeming," is not much more than a political lesson forced into verse.

In the conclusion of "Full Moon at Tierz," otherwise a

poem admirable for its restraint and convincing emotion, Cornford restated the Communist vision. But this time he relied on flat abstractions ("freedom" and "liberty,") and trite phraseology ("not in vain,") :

> Freedom is an easily spoken word
> But facts are stubborn things. Here, too, in Spain
> Our fight's not won till the workers of all the world
> Stand by our guard on Huesca's plain
> Swear that our dead fought not in vain,
> Raise the red flag triumphantly
> For Communism and for liberty.

The stanza, hollow and rhetorical, lacks the metaphorical force which elevates the similar conclusion of "As Our Might Lessens." Cornford relies too obviously on what might be termed "Party diction" to excite the proper enthusiasm among readers. But the final effect no doubt contradicts his intention, for we object, not so much to the insincerity of the passage, but to the unimaginative, banal treatment.

The form of his poetry is traditional. Except in "A Letter from Aragon," he used a four- or six-line stanza, with a regular rhyme scheme, interrupted occasionally by an off-rhyme. Few of the cant words, names of party heroes, and political slogans fit comfortably into the texture of the poems. Compare, for example, the deft use of a Marxist term in the metaphor of the past, in the first passage below, with the lugubrious use of names of party figures and events, in the second :

> The past, a glacier, gripped the mountain wall,
> And Time was inches, dark was all,
> But here it scales the end of the range,
> The dialectic's point of change,
> Crashes in light and minutes to its fall.

.   .   .   .

All round the barren hills of Aragón
Announce our testing has begun.
Here what the Seventh Congress said,
If true, if false, is live or dead,
Speaks in the Oviedo mauser's tone.

Three years ago Dimitrov fought alone
And we stood taller when he won.
But now the Leipzig dragon's teeth
Sprout strong and handsome against death
And here an army fights where there was one.

We studied well how to begin this fight,
Our Maurice Thorez held the light.
But now by Monte Aragón
We plunge into the dark alone,
Earth's newest planet wheeling through the night.

At best, his words and phrases are hard, clear, violent and strong, sometimes redolent of the muscle of Anglo-Saxon verse, such as in the description of the wounded militiaman :

Now out of danger, but still crying for water,
Strong against death, but unprepared for such pain.

His best metaphors, notably those of "Time," "History," and "Past," succeed because he rendered the special Marxist interpretation of those terms imaginatively. These lifeless, complex elements of a materialistic philosophy at times could become integral parts of a poetic fabric.

Donnelly's Spanish war verse, wrote Montagu Slater, shows the fusion of the poet's "emotional and intellectual life," the coming together of his "private and public living."[26] If Slater meant that Donnelly's verse shows the objectivity of a poet who has accepted the fact of the class struggle and who has consequently begun to participate actively in the revolutionary struggles of society and who has denied the existence of a sharp cleavage between the "public" and "private," or between life and art, then it would seem that Donnelly's objectivity is of a peculiar sort. For, although he did not predict certain defeat for the crusade in which he and his fellow volunteers were involved in Spain, he did show that that effort might be enormously impaired by the irresponsibility of some who were not actively engaged in it. For one in whom "private and public living" have merged, by which Slater meant that Donnelly had accepted the Communist hypothesis, Donnelly retained a secure hold on the value of private rebellion, and an almost omniscient view of the ways and ends of an ideological war. He began by distinguishing the real revolutionary from perhaps hundreds of others as the one who acts:

> Between rebellion as a private study and the public
> Defiance is simple action which will flicker
> Catlike, for spring.

Acting in accord with his ideals, he cannot rule out the possibility of dying for them, and should this occur his memory will become public property, available to anyone to use as he wishes:

> Your flag is public over granite. Gulls fly above it.
> Whatever the issue of the battle is, your memory
> Is public, for them to pull awry with crooked hands,
> Moist eyes. And villages' reputations will be built on
> Inaccurate accounts of your campaigns. You're name for
>   orators,
> Figure stone-struck beneath Dublin sky.
>
> Name, subject of all considered words, praise and blame
> Irrelevant, the public talk which sounds the same on
>   hollow

Tongue as true, you'll be with Parnell and with Pearse.
Name alderman will raise a cheer with, teacher make
    reference
Oblique in class, and boys and women spin gum of senti-
    ment
On qualities attributed in error.[27]

The application of all this to the Spanish situation is clear.
Like Parnell and Pearse, hero-martyrs of Irish freedom, the
Republican volunteer must anticipate that in the factious
atmosphere of public life his private deeds will be adapted to a
variety of situations, from inspiriting a politician's speech to
spicing a teacher's lecture. The ends, or issues, for which he
fought will become dissociated from him, distorted, or lost
completely. He will become, in a sense, a victim of a curious
kind of semantic switch : the perfectly natural act of renaming
any issue, ideal, or war so that its new name, or classification,
will produce certain desired results. Thus, if one wanted to
denigrate the Irish Volunteer movement, of which Pearse was
the symbol, one merely reclassified Pearse as a renegade. And
Donnelly was realistic enough to see that the same sort of
arbitrary reclassification could and probably would be used
to deride the dedication and idealism of the Loyalist volunteers,
who were all the easier to exploit because of the idealistic
nature of their cause. There was no defense against this kind
of abuse :

Man, dweller in mountain huts, possessor of colored mice,
Skillful in minor manual turns, patron of obscure sub-
    jects, of
Gaelic swordsmanship and medieval armory,
The technique of the public man, the masked servilities are
Not for you, Master of military trade, you give
Like Raleigh, Lawrence, Childers, your services but not
    yourself.

Donnelly intensified his detached, unheroic view of war by relying on judicious compression and some sharp, suggestive imagery in "The Tolerance of Crows" :

Death comes in quality from solved
Problems on maps, well-ordered dispositions,
Angles of elevation and direction;

Comes innocent from tools children might
Love, retaining under pillows,
Innocently impales on any flesh.

And with flesh falls apart the mind
That trails thought from the mind that cuts
Thought clearly for a waiting purpose.

Progress of poison in the nerves and
Discipline's collapse halted.
Body awaits the tolerance of crows.[25]

As in the other poem, Donnelly was again concerned with death and the mechanical and impersonal preparations which precede it. There is almost no feeling of sadness in this poem, nor is there bitterness. It is as though the poet were maintaining a kind of tolerance, almost a disinterestedness, toward the fact of death, which the simple structure complements.

The absence of party slogans, cant words and even the names of battles and regions where the war was fought makes Donnelly's poetry unique. Alongside some parts of Cornford's poems, Donnelly's verse seems calm and restrained, with no suggestion of hysteria or uncontrolled emotion. Inclined to be less personal than Cornford, less concerned with the effects of fear, loneliness and separation, he was capable of more objectivity than Cornford. He saw not just the possibility of sudden death, but the aftermath when ideals are cheaply and callously exploited, when revolutions go wrong. Donnelly's grasp of this theme alone suggests a breadth of imaginative experience quite beyond that of most poets of this war, particularly those who like himself were dedicated Communists.

Sacrifice without Heroism

The Spanish war poems of Ewart Milne, an Irishman who served with the British medical unit until the last months of the war, have imaginative and lyric qualities that are almost completely missing from the verses of the other volunteers. Milne goes well beyond trying to force political lessons into verse or recreating the surface drama of war. Not only has he assimilated the facts of war as well as the powerful human feelings and aspirations behind the sacrifice, but he has managed to render these human concerns honestly, without deliberate political twists. Milne's concern is with sacrifice, not with the heroism of war. He is interested in the long-range meaning of war, not the defeat of the Republic.

In "Thinking of Artolas," Milne speculates on the possible consequences of the struggle. Though the life forces of the Spanish people have burst forth in a movement that can alter the course of history, the cost has already been great and will continue to be. Milne's warning of the consequences of the expenditure is as solemn as Auden's : "You all know History is a cruel country / Where tiger terraces crouch drinking rivers waterless / And sheep immobilised by sombrero shepherds' piping." At this moment of History, however, the poet worries about his semidetachment. Although close to battle, he is not actually a participant, and he cannot escape from a sense of guilt, or the feeling that combatants discover more self-integration in the front lines than he :

All day I was a method of analysis . . . Did my heart,
   Thomas,

Or your depthless eyes tell me analysis was cowardly
While Los Madrileños were barricading their old Madrid
   out?

.   .   .   .   .

All day my heart with love was helpless, all day I knew
He had gone further than I towards finding a synthesis.

In the "cruel country" of History, where death is a permanent
resident, the living fight and die "because of Tone" or "human
love." The fortunate experience a synthesis of belief and
action:

Two, Gael and Jew side by side in a trench
Gripping antique guns to flick at the grasshoppers
That zoomed overhead and the moon was rocking.
Two who came from prisonment, Gael because of Tone,
Jew because of human love, the same for Jew as German—
Frail fragments both, chipped off and forgotten readily . . .
I set them together, Izzy Kupchick and Donnelly;

The sacrifice made, the brotherhood of mankind objectified
by Jew and Gael lying "side by side in a trench," what was it
worth? Did the death of Donnelly and Kupchick and nearly
four hundred volunteers at Jarama have a meaning? Milne
shuns heroism as well as flag-waving. He denies that there was
glory in the massacre; there was only cruelty. But History, he
recalls, is "a cruel country" for those who attempt to change
its contour:

And of that date with death among the junipers
I say only, they kept it: and record the exploded
Spreadeagled mass when the moon was later
Watching the wine that baked earth was drinking.[29]

Milne remained in Spain longer than most of the poet

volunteers. He saw the demise of the Republic, and felt the agony of lost liberal hopes and dreams. But his reaction to defeat was not despair. The ideals were not permanently lost. In lines redolent of Shelley's conclusion of "Ode to the West Wind," Milne assuages defeat with the prospect of resurgence :

> I am conscious of that quality inescapable
> In falling leaves of leaves in secret budding,
> Clad O in all winter's harness
> This glimpse comes brightening.[30]

Chapter 5 : Civil War Poets in England

MOST OF THE POEMS ABOUT THE SPANISH WAR WERE WRITTEN by Loyalist sympathizers who stayed in England and supported the Spanish Republic. Together they comprised a sort of rear-echelon commissariat, a vociferous cheering section, repeating and reinforcing in verse the slogans and opinions of the Popular Front. Temporarily, at least, they had succumbed to the seductive excitement of taking sides in the Spanish war, of becoming part of a cause for which men were dying.

But embroilment in a turbulent political world held forth certain hazards of which they could not have been fully aware. Since they had chosen to support one side, it meant that they had compromised their ability to think on all sides of an issue, that a mentality of war might come to dominate their minds entirely. That something like this happened, that the majority of these poets began thinking in opposites, in terms of black and white and good and evil, is clear from their verse. Having forfeited the freedom and expansiveness of mind essential to the poet, they almost had to depend for the substance of their verse upon the magisterial pronouncements of the Popular Front. Instead of rendering individually their own emotions and responses to the war in a personal idiom, they synthesized the decrees and slogans of politicians and propagandists.

The Burden of Guilt

But echoing pronouncements could fall short of providing a sense of wholehearted dedication to the Loyalist cause. These poets could not forget that volunteers like Cornford, Fox, and Donnelly had, after all, given their lives defending the Spanish Republic. And the volunteers still in Spain had every reason to believe that they might die too. Poets in England discovered that staying away from Spain could be almost as painful as being in the fight, but for different reasons. Whereas the volunteers experienced the ordeals of war, these poets were tortured by a conscience that said they should be doing the same. Thus, Jack Lindsay complained that "not being in the International Brigade" caused him to suffer "extremely from a bad conscience."[1] And C. Day Lewis admitted that not joining the International Brigade was a heavy weight on his conscience. "I believed I ought to volunteer for it, but I lacked the courage to do so."[2] As these statements suggest, even the pressing demands of the Popular Front, to which the majority of these poets responded, could fail to assuage the guilty conscience. We sense that relief from the burden of guilt, if it came at all, came infrequently.

Although nonparticipation in the Spanish war undoubtedly impressed many as evidence of complete sanity, to these poets it was demeaning if not shameful. Nevertheless their predicament was genuine, and it indicated that even the support given the Republic by its most enthusiastic supporters had limitations. The reality of their dilemma can best be seen in some verses that express guilt covertly or overtly. In several, such as "To a Free People" by John Gawsworth, we sense the urge to perform some expiable act. Gawsworth begins by sounding the slogan that "the free people" of Spain are defending "democracy" singlehandedly against the "totalitarian affront" while England stands by and refuses help. Nonintervention only exacerbates his guilt and causes his brain to smoulder resentfully. He generously extends his hand to his Spanish brothers, and then, rather embarrassed, relates that it grips only a pen :

> Here is my hand, brother
> Though it hold but a pen
> It would grip your grease of cartridge,
> The oil from the bolts of men
> Worthy of the name
> As the women of Spain.

The embarrassment, however, is unintentional. Gawsworth was certainly not trying to degrade himself and his pen as too inconsequential to be part of the war effort. He was striving for just the opposite meaning. Though he was not equating the pen with the gun, he implies that the pen can perform substantial service for the Republican cause. The poem, therefore, is an admission as well as an attempted expiation of guilt. But the confusing and synthetic images with which the poem ends ("The Cid has arisen / From out a Franco prison / And tilted at Death's windmill / Without a thought of gain,") suggest that Gawsworth's verse could never be of more than minimal service to the cause.[3]

While Gawsworth tried to wash his guilt feelings away with rhetoric, another poet, John Bronowski, nearly immolates himself on his own sense of guilt. Instead of offering his pen as an instrument of atonement, he extends his pity to the survivors of the Guadalajara battle, but not without realizing how inefficacious it is next to their sacrifices. The physical distance separating him from the combatants forces him to question his contribution :

> What is my pity worth? I fret
> no frozen body, but my mind;

and if I tremble, all my rage
weighs nothing in the bite of wind.

He asks for forgiveness and permission to phrase the soldiers' hopes:

Forgive me, men at posts, who stiffen
for furies such as Kings' or mine;
and suffer me no more than speak
the words your lips will never form,
the hope that hangs there like a breath
that fate shall break your frozen line,
break kings and break fanatic men;
that March shall break the world with storm.[4]

Guilt forms the core of both poems. Gawsworth enveloped his feelings in a cloak of verbiage; Bronowski used a personal idiom to inveigh against his inactivity. Gawsworth failed to transcend the mouthings of propagandists, under which the feeling of his poem is smothered. Only the self-conscious line, "Here is my hand brother, / Though it hold but a pen," suggests the emotion beneath the surface. Bronowski, on the other hand, exploited rather than repressed his sense of guilt and all but prostrated himself before the unreal image of hard-bitten soldiers who hold all civilians in contempt.

J. K. Raine (Mrs. Charles Madge), unlike either Gawsworth or Bronowski, discovered the roots of her guilt in a particular class. After finding it impossible to reconcile "The haven of a rentier indolence" with theories that she had "endured the worst," she began to connect her own incompleteness to a greater inadequacy that existed in the people around her. In a prefatory stanza to her poem, "Fata Morgana," she contrasts the impotence of this group with the sense of fulfillment felt by the soldiers in Spain:

> While those were on the march to their desires
> Through painful brilliance of Iberian day
> These arguing remained by their home fires
> Still living in the old, unhealthy way.

Parts I and II condemn the impediments that stand in the way of participating in the war : "books, idle books," "stupidity," "idleness," "the crowning joy of home," "incompetence"— these and other things may lay waste the will but they are not potent enough to prevent imagining "how it would feel to march / Guided by stars along the roads of Spain." Conscious that ends urged upon her by others, ends antithetical to those she really aspired to, have caused her to waste her energies in frivolous tasks, she longs to experience some kind of revolutionary change. Her longing, in fact, materializes in Part III. in a dream sequence in which she joins "unknown comrades" on a night march through embattled Spain. Casting off the guilty past presupposes physical sacrifice :

> I am no longer, alas, a charmed life,
> One whom the gods will favour, ill can spare,
> But target for the bullet and the knife
> Like any other soldier, wolf, or hare.

As restorative as the decision to sacrifice one's life is the self-liberation which occurs after having placed one's fate in the hands of others : "We swallowed back our pride, obeying orders / From leaders that in wiser days we chose." But since this is all part of a dream, a desire still ungranted, which those around her would ridicule if they knew of it, it does nothing to change the situation. She suggests the nullity of the experience in the final stanza :

> It is remarkable to dream so much
> And yet wake up to spend another day

With all the people I can only touch
With talks of long ago and far away.[5]

Troubled by the inertia that paralyzed the people around her, Miss Raine felt the reproach of her own conscience, and by revealing how she never attained her own ideals because she mistakenly sought those of the class she now repudiates, she endeavored to imbue the Spanish war with a selfless idealism which, being denied her, only underscores her own alienation.

Spain: Ideological Battleground

Guilt was just one theme that appeared in the verse written in England during the war. Another (and a far more popular one) depicted the struggle as an ideological contest between fascism and "democracy." By now it is hardly necessary to mention that this idea was being expounded regularly by every left-wing periodical and by dozens of speakers at Popular Front demonstrations and rallies. The poets who elaborated upon this theme were presumably at least as interested in re-affirming a political viewpoint as they were in recording their own responses, if not more so.

If, because of the familiarity of the topic, this verse was supposed to arouse man's "latent idealism"—as C. Day Lewis put it—its manner was somewhat unappealing. First, it strikes one as being on the defensive. It often possesses a strident, sermonizing quality, as though these poets hoped to drown out the opposition by hard words and philippics. A kind of cock-sure self-righteousness that permeated so much of it is apparent in Rex Warner's polemic:

It is we who feel future flowing in our veins,
    the past and the pressing present:

What was stifled stirs : what was hoped is in our hands :
What betrayed in the dark is now the desperate visible foe.

.   .   .   .   .

It is the aim that is right and the end is freedom.
    In Spain the veil is torn.
In Spain is Europe. England also is in Spain.
There the sea recedes and there the mirror is no longer
    blurred.[6]

Warner exploits the meaning implicit in the line, "In Spain
the veil is torn," the veil being outworn beliefs, traditions, and
customs which volunteers from all over the world will help the
Spanish people destroy but which still blind some to the true
nature of the struggle.

Convinced of the moral and political rightness of the Loyalist cause, Warner and others never even deigned to investigate
the arguments of the Insurgents. Whatever reasons the Rebels
had for revolting were not worth consideration. Their black-
and-white view was symtomatic not only of a certain illogi-
cality, but also of an apparent reluctance to cope with a world
composed of shades of gray. Whether for political or psychological reasons, or both, they simply refused to differentiate
between cause and effect, between the relative merits and
weaknesses of both sides.

Conceived in the impassioned atmosphere of rallies and
demonstrations, their verse conveyed almost no sense of the
reality of war. Everything the organized Left did tended to
minimize it, from the surcharged speeches of Popular Front
orators to the one-sided pseudo-documentary articles in leftist
publications. Generating enthusiasm for the cause was the *sine
qua non*. Consequently, the war functioned very often as an
enormous backdrop which was just real enough to give meaning to the demonstrations and to the verse. So long as it
retained at least a nominal reality, it lent this verse an un-

earned longevity and postponed serious consideration of its poetic worth.

The difficulties involved in attempting to harmonize the vision of poetic experience with the dogma of Spain's ideological significance can clearly be seen in three poems by H. B. Mallalieu. The first, "Welcome in August," published in *Left Review*, October, 1936, contrasts some idle British vacationers, sporting their "neutral conscience," with the knowledgeable comrades who have aligned themselves with the force that will eventually win victory in Spain. Although the determinative nature of the struggle is not mentioned specifically, it is certainly implicit in the final stanza, where Mallalieu issues a call to arms:

> The solid line which money's weight may bend
> However bruised with shell or beaten cruelly
> Needs the surety of a united hand—
> Comrades, this is more than sympathy.[7]

Later, in the sonnet, "Spain 1938," Mallalieu turned from chiding British neutralists to exposing "pity and love" as qualities incapable of assuring the peace and sanity of Europe. They have neither saved "ten thousand who are dead," nor "brought relief to peasants" who now wait to be bombed out of existence, nor have they "stifled horror nor killed hate." Does Mallalieu have an enfeebled view of the salutary powers of love and pity? It is hardly likely. Is he then building a case for something that necessitates reducing pity and love to flabby, ineffectual emotions? This seems more likely. His remedy for Europe's ills comes in the clumsily organized sestet, in which tears and "the suffering mind" are also demeaned:

> Tears are no use, the suffering mind is mad.
> Let sanity have strength and men unite

> Who in their individual lives are glad
> That what remains of peace may yet prove strong.
> We have the will, then let us show the might,
> Who have forborne and pitied far too long.[8]

Through the muddle of these lines comes the revolutionary message, a little weighted down, but still recognizable : the sword must supersede the once acceptable, but now ineffectual, virtues of love and pity if the world is to be turned into a place worth inhabiting.

Mallalieu's third poem, "The Future Is Near Us," develops the belief that Spain is the focal point of the world. But unlike the others it benefits greatly from a directness and lucidity of statement and a richness of imagery. The blissfully ignorant Englishmen, who in "Welcome in August" still sheltered a "neutral conscience," have now "caught the signal of the sentinel dead." "The signal was Spain," and now they know they cannot afford to ignore events in that land. "Distance is death now and the carrier seas / Hurl on these cliffs their message of despair." Spain's struggle has "imposed new frontiers" and thrown light on long-neglected problems ("Light revealed in woodland unexpected dearth"). Up to this point the imagery conveys the multiple implications of the war and impregnates the poem with a good deal of imaginative excitement. We sense the triumph of vision over exhortation.

But the last triumph is reserved for the demands of the Popular Front. Our antagonism stiffens as the poet warns us that "the black / Night of hatred has set boundaries to delight" and that "Love is too large for the short day before us." Words like guns must "discharge their shells into the doubtful ear," for "Ours is not the unquestioning strength of stones, / But the future is near us and our line is clear." The intrusion of these covert political messages interrupt the communicative process. They are alien to the preceding parts of the poem, and they make it more difficult to respond to the poem as a whole.[9]

One additional example should suffice to make the point clear. In "This New Offensive, Ebro, 1938," Margot Heinemann used a topical development—the final Loyalist offensive of the war which, when it failed, sealed the fate of the Republic—to coax British sympathizers into making greater contributions to the Republican cause. More realistic than most of her cohorts, she scolds those who dream of victory but do nothing to bring it about :

> Let Fools and children dream that victory
> Drifts lightly on the waves of chance,
> And all that riveted and smooth-tooled army
> Should melt before this proud advance.
>
> Not this war's weathercock, brave when things go well,
> Afraid to think of a retreat,
> By turns all singing and all sorrowful :
> We've not to watch, but win this fight.
>
> Offensives must be paid for like defeats,
> And cost as dear before they end.
> Already the first counter-raids
> Take no positions but they kill our friends.
>
> A miracle is not what we can hope for
> To end this war we vainly hate.
> We shan't just read it in the evening paper
> And have a drink to celebrate.
>
> For two long years now when you sighed for peace
> To slip from heaven as an angel drops,
> You were confronted with your own sad face,
> And once again time holds the mirror up.

The meaning of the war thus far, she contends, is not that the antifascist forces have incurred defeat but that they have fought to gain a "narrow ridge of time," enough for all to discover that "this new offensive is your life and mine" and that "one nation cannot save the world for ever."[10] While we admire the acumen in spotting the unexpressed desire for an adventitious victory, we chafe at the polemic that Spain fights to save the world. Not only is it a standard propaganda nostrum, but nowhere in the poem does Miss Heinemann prepare us for the final exhortation. It is simply an urgent reminder attached to a desperate summons. What power the poem has comes from the use of words that have a kind of aseptic quality that contributes to an over-all concreteness and directness. But the language fails to provide meaningful overtones. We assume that a clear statement of the urgency of the "New Offensive" strongly conditioned the writing of this poem.

Moral Regeneration

Not only could the war be depicted as embodying opposing ideologies, with the balance of goodness on the side of "democracy," but it could also be presented as a contest between opposing views of morality. And the same oversimplification that applied to ideologies recurs in the presentation of what were considered opposite moral views. The opposition is strongly put in Stanley Richardson's poem, "The Calpe Hunt," where the "Old World," symbolized by "traitor generals" on horseback rattling their skeletons across the fields, ride out for the last time to hunt down their prey.[11] But this "Old World" is self-destructive. It "blasphemes the glory of the rising moon" and thus reveals its depravity by setting itself against "life" and "truth" which have allied to expel the "world's decay."

Though it is difficult to find a definable content in Richardson's abstractions ("Life" and "truth" are so flaccid in this context that, without the help of some informing detail, I am hard pressed to assign a satisfactory meaning to them.), I assume he is predicting that a morally corrupt, enervated "Old World" of privilege will at last be destroyed by the stronger forces of life itself (i.e., those embodied in the Republican cause).

The belief that an old world was near death and a new about to be born prompted Richard Church to herald the emergence of a new morality. His poem, "The Madrid Defenders," begins where Richardson's ended and predicts the disappearance of a personal, selfish, restrictive, "individual love." Out of the cohesion of the masses of Spaniards in places like Madrid will come the new morality, a love for mankind:

> Our love is another,
> Much greater than one
> For husband, for mother,
> For wife or for son.
> No longer human,
> Compelled by our need,
> Neither child, man nor woman;
> An act, not a Creed;
> The People, the One![12]

The feeling that the Spanish masses were advancing toward greater moral freedom, that out of their struggle would emerge a fuller and freer life, kindled the hopes of most of these poets. But none was as inclined to celebrate the "new life" as vigorously as Jack Lindsay. Already aligned with the communist movement, Lindsay associated the Spanish war with his own new allegiance. "It represented the new life with the immediate threat and attack it aroused from all the forces of evil, of power and property." Even his "aspirations were indistinguishable from what [he] felt of the Spanish people." His chief aspiration, as he put it, was "to express the full meaning of proletarian unity." Yet, in a sense, the fullest expression of unity—to join the International Brigade—he could not achieve. Instead he joined the Communist Party ("To join the Communist Party was for me tantamount to going into the International Brigade"). What remained? Only to celebrate, loudly and exuberantly, the concern he felt for the "People's struggle," and to create the vision of the new life awaiting him and the Spanish people.[13]

A glimpse of that new life appears in "Looking at a Map of Spain on the Devon Coast," the first of several poems Lindsay wrote on the Spanish theme:

> The girl with the cap of liberty at the loom
> weaves the fate of Spain,
> the web of brotherhood on the warp of courage.
> The factory-windows crimson with the sunset
> flash signals to the fields of toil;
> the slow echelon of sickles
> advance upon the wheat. Now in the battle
> the Spanish workers ride
> the horses of the year, wild mountain-horses,
> tamed to draw the ploughs of man.
> Hear the confederate engines throb
> the belts whirr and the hammers of power leap thudding,
> to bring about at last the generous hour
> When man and nature mate in plenty's bed.[14]

The poem is all vision. It idealizes the war by substituting a vision of a marvelous future for the unpleasant realities of the present. It even fails to make clear (as Auden did) that the promise of tomorrow is contingent on the action of today, and that a proletarian paradise can be realized only through the discipline of shared suffering. To write of "the web of brother-hood," when one of the Republic's most serious problems was maintaining unity among the disparate elements that supported it, is dubious poetizing.

Lindsay's fervor for the cause manifested itself no more exuberantly—and one might add, hardly more tediously—than in "On Guard for Spain!", a 350-line tirade lambasting the "fascist vultures" and exalting the "Spanish people." Subtitled "A Poem for Mass Recitation," it was frequently delivered at Loyalist rallies, apparently with great success, judging by how frequently it appeared on Popular Front programs. Ostensibly, the object of the poem was to restore "the traditional link between poetry and the people,"[15] and as Lindsay himself wrote, to create "the most direct contact with the new audience." He contended that mass recitation occupied "the position of norm" in the recreation of poetry for the people; it could become "the form of contact from which endless new developments" might stem; it could become, insofar as the poet found "a conscious relation to the revolutionary proletarian forces," a form of poetry that was at once a "revolutionary weapon."[16] And like his hard-working colleagues in the Poetry Group of the Left Book Club, who turned out similar declamations and trained eager members to recite them, Lindsay was probably at least as much interested in writing verse that would sell the Loyalist cause to the people as he was in forming a new contact with them.

In his reply to Nancy Cunard's questionnaire, Lindsay wrote that "to be above the battle, when such a cause is concerned, is to be sub-human." While he was certainly moved by the battle, there is some question about whether he ever really descended from a position "above the battle." When he presumes to speak "for the Spanish people to the workers of the world," when he assumes the role of a militiaman, and when he becomes the arbiter of right and wrong, we might ask whether he descended very far. There is too much questionable generalization and moral reprobation in "On Guard," and not enough careful representation of the particularities of the war. It is absurd to write that the "workers, going to battle,/ Went as to a fiesta." And it is just as bad to say that the fascists "gouged and scourged and maimed and lamed and murdered,/blew up with grenades the wounded in hospital wards." These horrifying images and others, such as "fascist vultures gathering/to pick the bones of Spanish cities," do not strengthen the Loyalist cause, they have the reverse effect. Instead of shocking us into anger, they deaden our nerves, which grow weary when such horrors are retailed. And even the moral supplication with which the poem ends depends partly on calling the enemy "wolves of death":

> Workers of the world, unite for us
> that bear the burden of all.
> You shall not hear us complain
> That the wolves of death are ravening in our streets,
> if you but understand, if your bodies flow
> into this steel of resistance, this welded mass,
> making you one with us, and making us
> unconquerable.[17]

If "On Guard" had any value at all, it was the somewhat negative value of supporting the work of propagandists. If it enjoyed a certain popular acclaim, it was because those who heard it were already excited about Spain. Its only striking feature was a fresh, vigorous style, redolent of the style of the eighteenth-century periodical broadsheets, which, if recited by the trained person, might make even the substance of the poem palatable.

The Satirist's Victims

A few poets attempted to satirize particular grievances that had long piqued the Left. Though the subjects of their satire were usually legitimate—that is, they deserved to be exposed—that fact alone could not guarantee the success of the satire. For in far too many instances the poets vitiated the satire by relying upon invective and sarcasm to deliver a crushing blow. What might have been, say, an amusing and effective unmasking of the nonintervention policy often lapsed into a piece of sarcasm and anger. Apparently, the urge to destroy the opposition, instead of revealing just enough of its weakness to provide a tantalizing satiric effect, proved irresistible, and insofar as these poets succumbed to their angry desires they failed to write satire which might have had more than transient interest and value.

A poem that illustrates the point is Edgell Rickword's "To the Wife of Any Non-Intervention Statesman," which attacked the policy of nonintervention. Certainly the duplicity in the Nonintervention Committee was sufficient to make this a suitable, if not an excellent, subject for satire, and therefore one can hardly deny Rickword's sound choice of topic. But the way in which he handled this subject is another matter. At the beginning of the poem, he imagines himself stealing into the boudoir of the wife of a nonintervention statesman; he at once assures her that he is there for her good. "No ballyhoo, what I've to say/May stand you in good stead one day." After reminding the lady that "mutual trust" is the secret of a successful marriage, he demands to know what her reaction would be should her husband confide that he was one of the instigators of nonintervention. The reply (Rickword's—the wife is not permitted to speak) begins in a controlled and witty fashion:

> Traitor and fool's a combination
> To lower wifely estimation,

> Although there's not an Act in force
> Making it grounds for a divorce :

But then it suddenly degenerates into rancor :

> But canon law forbids at least
> Co-habitation with a beast.

As Rickword lists additional injustices which nonintervention ("the Gentlemen's Agreement") has perpetrated upon the Republic—he claims that brave Basques die because Britain's fleet respects Franco's blockade, that Germany and Italy have gained time to prepare for future wars and have also exploited Spanish natural resources, and that hundreds of Spanish are killed daily in bombing raids over unprotected cities—his ire builds up until it erupts in a torrent of abuse :

> Would not a thinking wife condemn
> The sneaking hand that held the pen
> And with a flourish signed the deed
> Whence all these hearts and bodies bleed?
> Would not those fingers freeze the breast
>   Where the young life should feed and rest?
>
> Would not his breath reek of the tomb
> And would cold horror seal her womb?
> Could a true woman bear his brat?
> The millions wouldn't
>   Thanks, my hat.[18]

In this, the concluding passage, Rickword's rage triumphs. But most of his spleen is lavished on the "beastly" nonintervention statesman, who is nothing more than an ogre Rickword created to destroy. In other words, although Baldwin's policy was grist for the satirist's mill, Rickword was not satisfied until he had fabricated a revolting monster called a nonintervention statesman, whom he equated with beasts and with whom, if she had any conscience at all, his wife would refuse to live. What he tried but failed to do was condemn the statesman as morally impoverished. He failed because the statesman is false, an obvious "hate symbol" intended to intensify the indignation of the Left. Finally, however, the only vivid impression is the author's own fury.

One reason why the British Government refused to relax its nonintervention stand, according to the Left, was because it aided the Nationalists, whose victory was viewed as an essential part of protecting British investments in Spain. Brian Howard, in "For Those with Investments in Spain," treated this theme with almost smothering irony, much too heavyhanded to be effective. Sardonically, he requests that those with interests in Spain be patient and understanding:

> I ask your patience, half of them cannot read,
> Your forbearance if, for a while, they cannot pay,
> Forgive them, it is disgusting to watch them bleed,
> I beg you to excuse, they have not time to pray.[19]

But a more successful handling of this theme, because more controlled and less noticeably angry, is Sagittarius' "They Got What They Wanted." The poem was addressed to the Friends of Nationalist Spain who, in the author's opinion, now that the war was over (the poem appeared in the *New Statesman and Nation*, May 13, 1939), would discover they had supported the wrong side. A kind of taunting levity and subtle but piercing irony distinguish the verses, and there is enough accuracy in what she said to give point to the satire:

> Though Nazi Party enterprise
> Will British interests displace,

> Though legionaries mobilise
> In bristling camp and beetling base,
> Though Franco dam the stream of trade
> His friends still give their glad accord—
> Armed intervention must be paid
> But friendship is its own reward.

The poet's jab at the avowed and hidden motives behind the Nationalist revolt suggests a nice irony of cross purposes:

> The extirpation of the Red
> The victor of all blame acquits
> Who saved the day for Christ instead
> With Heinkels, Fiats and Messerschmidts.

Finally, she ironically notes the disappearance of liberty in Franco's Spain and the desultory way the Nationalists have gone about recognizing foreign interests:

> Where liberty and faith return
> Mere business claims may be ignored
> So British friends of Franco learn
> That friendship is its own reward.

Hardly memorable satire, "They Got What They Wanted" nevertheless wittily dissects the incredulity of the Franco partisans while avoiding the invective and sarcasm which vitiated the poems of Rickword and Howard. Her weapon— and it served her well—is a bantering irony which skillfully plays on the notion of "friendship is its own reward."[20]

One other topic treated satirically was the role of the Roman Catholic Church in the Spanish war, primarily because the Church seemed to be in the anomalous position of condoning the rebel attack on the Republic. That the role of

the Church, for a multitude of reasons, was deliberately mis-
stated or distorted is true. Despite the mass of conflicting
evidence, however, there is good reason for believing that the
Church had at least taken a tacit stand against the Republic,
particularly if, by Church, we mean the Spanish Church,
which had and continues to have an autonomy all its own.
And the confusion over its role was compounded by the
presence of ardent Catholics, like the Basques, fighting on the
side of the Republic. The important point, however, is that
outside Spain, especially in England and the United States, it
was taken for granted that the Church was in league with the
Nationalists. Given a situation, therefore, in which the exact
position of an institution was far from being clear in the
country where it existed, but which everywhere else seemed
entirely clear, we should be surprised if left-wing poets had
not seized the opportunity to castigate the Church for its
duplicity.

The opportunity was not lost to Stanley Richardson, who,
in his sonnet, "To a Certain Priest," could hardly contain his
indignation in describing a priest accused of "propagating lies"
to praise "Franco's Fascist Hell" while ignoring Guernica and
"bloody Badajoz." By focusing on the sins of the Church,
Richardson intended to condemn the Right. But his attempt
at whitewashing the Left, by magnanimously asking God to
show charity on the wayward priest, while intended to be
sarcastic, seems hollow charitableness:

> God, in that day when every proof is read,
> Show all thy charity to this poor priest
> Who basely wore the livery of thy Son;
> Thy mercy on the traitor's tonsured head,
> Who heaped this cruel message on thy least,
> And served the rich, and knew it, and sinned on.[21]

The anomaly received more imaginative expression in Elizabeth Cluer's "Analogy in Madrid," where, except for some rather forced *double-entendre,* the imagery conveys the startling impropriety of Christianity joined to a military attack :

> Christ brings a sword, the Archbishop said.
> The wide jaws of the newly dead
> And their appearance of surprise
> Testify this. From innocent skies
> Out of wind's mouth or sun's breath
> Came the most high, the triple death
> And with its omnipresent purr
> Drew out the thirsty listener.

Yet with Franco heralded as a Christian crusader, the analogy seems to have some validity :

> Thirsty still, under jungle law
> The deer lies under the striped death's paw;
> And who can be sure of the ways of the Lord?
> Both Christ and Franco carry a sword.[22]

Of a less serious character, though related to the religious question, was the satirical verse about the Irish Christian Front and its militant leader Eoin O'Duffy. The Front was formed by priests and laymen who believed that the whole weight of Irish public opinion ought to support Franco, whom they regarded as the Church's defender. Though it attracted few supporters, it was influential enough to persuade the Church hierarchy to decree a special collection to restore burned churches in Spain as part of a campaign to "knit all Catholic opinion together in proper relation to the Spanish struggle."[23] In the shelter of the Front, General Eoin O'Duffy, a former commissioner of the Irish Civil Guards, found a small, enthusiastic band of men willing to form a brigade to fight for the Church in Spain.[24] That they were sincere about the Spanish undertaking, particuarly concerning the religious mission with which they felt they had been entrusted, and that they were politically more naïve than their counterparts on the Left, are matters which are entirely sound in spite of what their disparagers have contended.[25]

What seems distressingly clear now, however, is that Franco capitalized on their religious fervor. Bound by the fact of their inexperience and small number (there were only seven hundred) to be of minimal military value to the Insurgents, they could nevertheless serve an important propagandistic purpose. The presence in Spain of a group of Irish volunteers, willing to die for the Church, was a situation too good to remain silent about. Even the agreement O'Duffy made with Franco, to stay for a period of six months (from November 1936 to May 1937), and the fact that all but nine volunteers returned to Ireland on schedule, in May, suggest that the entire expedition was being used for propaganda.[26]

Of the almost comic war experiences of O'Duffy's brigade, which to his credit he recounted in his book *Crusade in Spain,* the Left poets made surprisingly little use. But about his anti-Republican background, his quasi-fascist beliefs, and the fact that he supported Franco, several poets wrote scurrilous verses, of whom the most prominent and by far the most entertaining was the Irish poet Somhairle Macalastair. Two of his ballads make oblique references to the Irish Civil War ("Lombard-Murphy's crew," "Ballyseedy") and Irish politicians, past and present (Connolly, Liam Mellows, Paddy Selton), but his principal target is O'Duffy, whom he depicts with mock seriousness in "Off to Salamanca":

> My name is Owen O'Duffy,
>> And I'm rather vain and huffy,

The side of every Bolshie I'm a thorn in.
　　But before the break of day,
I'll be marching right away,
　　For I'm off to Salamanca in the morning.

Chorus
With the gold supplied by Vickers,
I can buy Blue Shirt and knickers,
Let the Barcelona Bolshies take a warning,
For I lately took the notion,
To cross the briny ocean
And I start for Salamanca in the morning.[27]

The bantering tone of "Off to Salamanca" changes to derision and scorn in "Ballyseedy Befriends Badajoz," where the worst sort of wickedness is laid at O'Duffy's feet:

O'Duffy's dupes are killing as their Fascist masters bid.
　.　　.　　.　　.　　.
God, they claim, is Fascist—The Voice that Pilate feared
Is pitting streams of hellish hate from a Moorish soldier's
　　　　beard!
They use the Cross of Calvary to veil their foul designs.

Even the possibility that O'Duffy plans to weld a fighting force in Spain, to use later in Ireland, is explored:

They hope to lure out Irish youth to learn their murder
　　　　trade
And bring them back to Ireland as a Fascist Shock Brigade.

But should O'Duffy and his followers attempt to make use of such a brigade in Ireland,

When they get kicked out of Spain,
　　And they travel home again,

Let them hearken in good time to this, our warning.
If they try their Fascist game
They'll be sorry that they came
Back from Salamanca in the morning.[28]

Macalastair's ballads, with their jingling rhymes and
monotonous cadences, typify a form of verse eminently suited
to fulfill the demands of propaganda. The observation can be
substantiated by the considerable number of political ballads,
many of them written by combatants, which circulated continuously among the soldiers in Spain. Simple and direct, they
appealed while more sophisticated forms of verse failed. The
easy, roughshod rhythms and the structural simplicity reached
the generally nonliterary soldier. And the demands on the
poet, as the two ballads by Macalastair indicate, were not
great. For the most part his task was to avoid subtlety and
write simple abuse of the enemy.[29]

Heroes : Dead and Alive

As the war continued into the second and third year, certain
individuals or groups were gradually fashioned into heroes of
the Left. Above all, however, the "Spanish people," an omni-
bus term that had obvious propagandistic value, remained
the one symbol—however indefinite its connotations—most
often used by pro-Loyalist poets. In their early accounts of the
war, Langdon-Davies, Pitcairn, and Sommerfield had idealized
the masses who rose up against the rebels in the first days of
the struggle, assigning to them virtues like courage, nobility,
and determination. The individual Spaniard who perhaps did
not quite possess all these virtues was unimportant. What
mattered was the collective whole, the masses of Spain considered as a single body. These people, depersonalized and

anonymous, symbolized a nation's heroic struggle.[30] Of course
nothing was said about Spaniards who fought against the
Republic. Presumably they were no longer considered
Spaniards.

Occasionally, from out of this mass emerged a group which
for a brief moment occupied the world spotlight, such as the
Basques and the Madrileños, whom Church and others
rhapsodized. But it was inevitable that besides the "People,"
the struggle would create some additional popular heroes. One
was Dolores Ibarruri, or "La Pasionaria" (the Passion Flower),
as she was commonly called at her own suggestion. The
daughter of an Asturian miner, she had become known as a
fiery speaker and revolutionary before 1936. But it was during
the early months of the war that her impassioned speeches
were heard all over Spain. In the language of most who heard
her, she could not be equaled for the inspiriting effect she
produced on audiences.[31] Coming from that region of Spain
where revolution was always threatening to break out and
from a background at once poor but proud—attributes she
seldom failed to mention in her speeches—she made a deep
impression on several British and American writers, including
Charlotte Haldane and the American poet Edwin Rolfe.[32]
Miss Haldane's treatment of "La Pasionaria," in her poem
reverently entitled "Pasionaria," exemplifies the crudest sort of
propagandizing. She begins by likening her to a "great figure-
head" on the prow of a ship, which somehow is supposed to
embody Spain itself. The rest of the poem is simply a catalog
of the great lady's virtues, and the eulogizing has the
simplicity of a primer:

> You are good, You have stood
> Always in the vanguard, leading,
> Hands held out to uphold

Children and women above this sea
Of hatred and of blood.
You are wise. In your eyes
That smiled at me so lovingly
I saw and understood
Also the buried tears,
Crystallized toil and struggle,
Years of hardship, privation, sorrow.

Finally the panegyric ends with a tawdry reference to the war :

In you I salute, Comrades Dolores,
Spain, forging a new world for us too ![33]

This kind of hero-worship, naïve and crude in both sentiment and manner, suggests a sense of imbalance in the author, a loss of perspective. Miss Haldane forewent the necessary job of experiencing the impact of "Pasionaria" upon her, or upon Spain, imaginatively, and instead simply recounted, in the manner of a pamphleteer, the qualities she felt should exist in "Pasionaria" and in the Spanish Republic. But unsurprisingly her effort reads like a tract, not a poem.

Miss Haldane's poem illustrates the worst result of too fervent a desire to create a hero for the Republic. Other poets, however, succeeded in giving the Republic considerable cultural prestige by connecting their poems with prominent Spanish artists. Ruthven Todd, perhaps aware of the *Left Review*'s campaign to identify fascism with the destruction of Spanish culture, called his poem depicting the physical destruction of Spain, which he envisioned happening in a painting by Joan Miró, "Poem for Joan Miró," thereby implying that the war Franco started destroyed art.[34] And Albert Brown, in "From a Painting by Picasso," not only publicized the position taken by Spain's outstanding artist, but predicted that a Republican defeat would destroy Spanish culture as well.[35]

By far, however, Garcia Lorca generated more interest among this group of poets than any other Spaniard. Despite Lorca's political indifference, the Left went right ahead and canonized him as a political and artistic martyr. Why Nationalists shot him outside Granada in 1936 remains uncertain even today. Nationalist defenders like Roy Campbell blame it on "a private grudge."[36] But Loyalist Arturo Barea says that the proletarian quality of his work was sufficient to identify him with the masses, and that the "emotional forces he released became part of the shapeless revolutionary movements of Spain whether he intended or not. Thus it was . . . inevitable that he was killed by obscure fascist brutality and that his work became a banner to the Spanish masses."[37] The opportunity to locate in Lorca's assassination all the callous destructiveness of fascism was not lost on the Left; he made an especially useful symbol.

The section John Lehmann and Stephen Spender entitled "Lorca" in their anthology of Spanish poems (*Poems for Spain*) contains three poems about the Spanish poet, two by English poets and one by Leopoldo Urrutia. While each poet celebrates the achievements of the dead poet, only Urrutia commemorates the humanity of Lorca, who could not believe that his life was in danger and whom death "took by surprise."[38] The British poets Geoffrey Parsons and John Bronowski are more interested in the political significance of Lorca's death. For instance, Parsons recounts Lorca's final hours; each act of the poet is used to enhance the Loyalists and denigrate the Insurgents. Even the mysterious circumstances of his death fail to deter Parsons from fixing the responsibility for it, as well as the motivation:

The Fascists have only one answer for a poet

.   .   .   .   .

And for Lorca the civil guard had a special hatred
A personal spite : there were certain deeds in the past
Had been pilloried, had been whistled through Spain in a
        ballad.
So they smelt him out and marched through the town, to
        the trees,
He walking straight as a tree, and knowing to what end :

The heart of the poem pictures Lorca—entirely helpless but
without fear—facing a firing squad :

And he stopped and turned and faced them standing still;
He stared at their aiming eyes, his imminent murder;
He was one with the people of Spain and he stood as they
        stood.[39]

Here is Parsons' message : Lorca's heroism before his executioners is symbolic of the heroic struggle of the "people of
Spain." And "So Lorca merges with Spain," his songs destined
to be sung by "His friends, the people, the peasants," who
thereby put the lie to the "foul-mouthed general in Seville,"
Queipo de Llano, who announced his death. Claiming Lorca
for his side—unnecessary since he had already shown his
attachment to the masses—forces Parsons to ignore the pitiful
loss which his death meant to humanity.

    Although Bronowski's poem, "The Death of Garcia Lorca,"
contains some similar political haymaking, it also conveys a
different interest. Whereas Parsons emphasizes politics,
Bronowski concentrates partly on the incalculable loss to the
world of the poet's unwritten work. The slow cadence of the
opening imparts a feeling of awe and sadness :

> Step after step into the darkened landscape
> we mourners walk with you : until the guns speak.
> Speak to the muffled dead for the loss
> of the gipsy's glory and the matador's.

His lonely death becomes still more moving by suggesting that
some of those the poet had befriended have turned against the
people with whom he was most at home—the gipsies, tramps,
bullfighters, and the peasants—and who are now facing a
similar fate :

> You joked with the dead : did you not hear
> their voices lower year by year?
> their dumb trumpets? and the word Doom
> when the gun's echo answered the drum?
> You walked with ghosts, and their time is done.

But Bronowski cannot refrain entirely from reading into
Lorca's fate a political message. It is less excited and arbitrary
than Parsons' and only faintly suggests that Lorca had political
leanings, but with them Bronowski harmonizes his own
sympathies :

> Ours is the cause
> of the grinding mill and the crowded house
> and the men who walk between mill and home.
> Our future is not easy come.
> Step by step into the darkened country
> we walk with you there; but the light gentry
> walks no more, nor the gipsy kings.
> And out of that dark the poet sings.[40]

Before long the Left had its own Lorcas; Ralph Fox, John
Cornford, Charles Donnelly, Christopher Caudwell, and
Julian Bell were all killed in the early months of the struggle.
And in addition to the writers, several promising young

scholars lost their lives fighting for the Republic, among them Lorimer Birch, David Guest, Lewis Clive, and Leslie Maugham. When the British volunteers finally returned home, in the closing months of 1938, they left behind in Spain close to five hundred of their comrades.[41] Poetic tributes to the dead volunteers were plentiful, and in most of them the deceased achieved an easy immortality as martyrs to truth ("Remember the youth that died for truth/on the battered fronts of Spain"),[42] to freedom ("So they fought and died for their grave, proud duty. . . . And will be remembered in the songs of a new freedom")[43] and to emancipation ("And I longed to release her people/Out of their pit of pain. . . . And my bones now lie in Spain").[44] Jack Lindsay composed a 136-line "Requiem Mass" for the "Englishmen fallen in the International Brigade," in which he painstakingly illustrated the heterogeneousness of the British volunteers. Lindsay's roll call was packed with "types of English dead": heading the list were writers Fox and Cornford, followed by an assortment of comrade-workers, including two seamen and a London businessman.[45] What most poets tried to say was that the dead volunteers had not died for a defeated cause, but rather for a cause that could not be defeated. This was the point of the preamble to a short account of the XV Brigade that formed part of the Memorial Souvenir, which brigade members distributed to the crowd that attended the memorial meeting on January 8, 1939. The brigade dead were immortalized as participants in the "long struggle for freedom, carried forward from Wat Tyler through men like Byron and movements like the Chartists, through Keir Hardie to the present day." They went to war "to safeguard peace and the arts of peace . . . to help the defenceless Spanish people fight the invading armies . . . to save their loved ones, and us, from the horrors of fascism."[46] In short, the struggle that claimed them was the

eternal struggle for freedom which, of course, no one assumed
had ended with the Republican defeat.

Certainly for the majority of poets associated with the
Popular Front the indestructibility of the cause helped make
the defeat in Spain bearable. It was also responsible for tempering their grief over the loss of friends and kin. For example,
it was clear that T. E. Nicholas could bear the loss of a son of
Wales as long as he respected the cause for which the dead
man had sacrificed himself. Couched in the most banal
abstractions, the cause seems to predominate over the fact of
death :

> Far from the hills he loved, he faced the night,
>   Bearing, for freedom's sake, an alien yoke;
> He fell exalting brotherhood and right,
>   His bleeding visage scorched by fire and smoke;
> E'en as the sweetest note is born of pain,
>   So shall the song of songs be born in Spain.[47]

By celebrating the "song of songs" and "brotherhood and
right," Nicholas makes the fact of death seem less important
than the slogans the volunteer died defending, and which like
all slogans came closer to being bright euphemisms than
realizable tenets of a definite program.

As expected, Hugh MacDiarmid's reaction to death was
violent. In the midst of the war he vilified the fascists who
were killing his comrades :

> FASCISTS ! you have killed my comrades
>   And their wives and children !
>   You have killed them !
> It were better that you all should rot in your vices,
>   In the bottomless filth of damnation,
>   And that they should live ![48]

MacDiarmid tried solving the annoying problem of explaining the presence of fascists inside Spain by identifying them as Christians ("cannibals, blood-suckers, carrion beasts that feed on the dead"), and executioners who, like Napoleon's soldiers pictured by Goya in *The Executions after the Dos de Mayo,* vented their rage by firing upon captured civilians. The "twisted zeal of the Inquisition," the "hag-ridden mythology of the peninsula," the "pretty, distracting duchesses," all cited as the corrupt motivating forces behind the fascist blood siege, also served as counterattacks against the proclamations made by Roy Campbell, Lady Margaret Sackville, Shane Leslie and other contributors to the pro-Franco magazine *Spain,* that the conflict was a holy crusade, in fact, God's war.

Two years later, the war ended, MacDiarmid attached a "Postscript" to his indictment of fascists, which is as calm as the other is impassioned, and reveals how deep his involvement in the struggle had become. Defeat has deadened anger, hope has replaced zeal. The Spanish landscape, now full of tragic portent, is the setting for an agony which can only be expressed in tears, tears, however, which clear the eyes and bring the future into focus:

> Spain! The International Brigade. At the
>   moment it seems
> As though the pressure of a loving hand had gone,
> The touch under which my close-pressed fingers
>   seemed to thrill
> And the skin to divide up into little zones
> Of heat and cold whose position continually changed
> So that the whole of my hand, held in that clasp,
> Was in a state of internal movement.
>
> My hands that were full of love
> Are empty again . . . for a while
> For a little while![49]

As in the Nicholas' poem, the defeat is once again seen simply as a hiatus in the unbroken struggle.

While still in a reflective mood, MacDiarmid turned to eulogizing the entire Republican army, a "citizen army" greater than any in history, a "symbol of human freedom" based on neither lies nor legends, but truth. Casting himself in the role of priest (but "outside all systems of theology") with powers oddly similar to those Roy Campbell claimed he possessed, MacDiarmid announced that within the Republicans

> . . . unconscious processes may be intelligent and aspiring,
> Generating images and intuitions of moral import,
> Solutions of conflict, desirable avenues of advance,[50]

and that "every man and woman of you on the Republican side" could be "platonic forms or archetypes," images illuminating, guiding and giving significance to "trivial occurrences." Behind everything is an idea of the soul, its "creative evolution" and search for fulfillment, not with deity, but "with the boundless potentialities of other creative individuals." As such, the total effort is a "revealing mirror," a timeless lesson, powerful enough to "instigate a resurrection from the dead" and to grant immortality to the people of the Republic. The lesson can be read in the examples of Chartes and Versailles, the latter, standing empty and silent, a symbol of "kingship in our civilization" and an unreal, sterile life; the former, the embodiment of the "living force and beauty in the minds and souls of many men," an example of the "free and many-sided spirit of humanity." When the struggle is renewed in Spain, nothing will have changed. Once more the people will oppose despotism ("vain titles and vicious wealth of a worthless few"); the "People of Spain on the one side" and "wealth, superstition, and traitor soldiery on the other"; one already dead, the other alive and determined to grow.

Chapter 6 : Anarchism and Humanism

IN 1936 NEITHER HERBERT READ NOR GEORGE BARKER belonged to a political organization, and for the duration of the Spanish war they remained politically unaffiliated. Yet as a few poems written between 1936 and 1939 show, they were strongly moved by events in Spain. But what sets Read and Barker apart from the majority of the left-wing poets who were attracted to the war, besides not sharing their political views, is a well-defined "humanistic" attitude toward the struggle. Both were evidently more appalled by the inhumanity of the conflict than by the attack against "democracy" which their left-wing colleagues were denouncing so vociferously. Their compassionate, humane feelings had been stirred; their political beliefs, for what they amounted to, had been moved only slightly. They also differed from the others in their highly imaginative treatment of the struggle in their verse. And their small body of war poems—each wrote but two or three—further suggests that their first consideration was their art and not the insatiable demand of the Popular Front for verse that would extol the Loyalist cause.

The Anarchists Lose Again

Asked in October, 1934, if he stood "with any political or political-economic party or creed," Herbert Read replied with a flat "No."[1] If he had been asked the same question three years later, in the middle of the Spanish war, when he was enthusiastically supporting the Catalonian anarchists, his answer probably would have been the same. For anarchism, he believed, was by its very nature the antithesis of a static system of political ideas. While fascism and Marxism imposed severe restrictions upon man by drastically limiting his freedom and equality, anarchism sought instead to reaffirm a kind of "natural freedom," opposed to all systems of government, in which man might re-experience the goodness of nature and the value of organic growth. At the center of anarchism lay the concept of religious as well as political brotherhood. Unlike either fascism or Marxism, which to their disadvantage failed to recognize the social necessity of religion, anarchism embodied a mystical ethos of its own based on the relationship of brotherhood and the freedom, emotion and intellect implicit in that relationship. In political terms, brotherhood meant "the free association of producers working for the common good" and "according to their abilities and receiving according to their needs."[2] Therefore, since Read believed that anarchism stood in the largest sense for freedom as opposed to regimentation, for the highest kind of individuality instead of passive cooperation, for "direct communion with universal truth" as opposed to the inherited dogma of fascism or Marxism, he could readily deny, in 1937–38, that in espousing anarchism he was backing a political party. Anarchism was apolitical, because it exalted a life of organic change and freedom. It sought to extend the principle of equity until it superseded statutory law. At the time, Read would have agreed that he stood for the rebirth of "the system of nature, of man living in accordance with the universal truth of reality," and not for a man-made form of government.[3]

Apparently, his espousal of anarchism resulted partly from a disappointment with communism as the foremost socialist force:

From 1917 onwards and for as long as I could preserve the illusion, communism as established in Russia seemed to promise the social liberty of my ideals. So long as Lenin and Stalin promised a definitive "Withering away of the State" I was prepared to stifle my doubts and prolong my faith. But when five, ten, fifteen, and then twenty years passed, with the liberty of the individual receding at every stage, a break became inevitable. It was only delayed so long because no other country in the world offered a fairer prospect of social justice.[4]

However, it was not only in matters involving social liberty that Read found communism deficient. He claimed its bureaucratic atmosphere had stifled the artistic impulse. The persecution of Mayakovsky, and later of Bukharin, Pasternak, and Shostakovich for introducing into their art a "formalism" that allegedly detracted from the party's standard of "objective realism," offered disquieting proof that the revolution had not succeeded in liberating the artist. In fact, it seemed probable that he had been made almost entirely ineffective by a system interested primarily in capitalizing on his art for its own purposes and that the values he respected and for which he lived had been shut out. So relentless an exploitation of the rights of the artist contradicted Read's belief that the poet had to be a catalytic agent whose responsibility for insuring progress depended partly on the freedom to break form and distort pattern deliberately. He wrote to this point:

In order to create it is necessary to destroy; and the agent of destruction in society is the poet. I believe that the poet is necessarily an anarchist, and that he must oppose all organized conceptions of the State, not only those which we inherit from the past, but equally those which are imposed on people in the name of the future. In this sense I make no distinction between fascism and marxism.

The work of art, by processes which we have so far failed to understand, is a product of the relationship which exists between an individual and a society, and no great art is possible unless you have as corresponding and contemporary activities the spontaneous freedom of the individual and the passive coherence of a society. To escape from society (if that were possible) is to escape from the only soil fertile enough to nourish art.[5]

Thus, in Read's concept of anarchism the poet was the chief anarchist. And he could become one and remain one only if he were allowed to develop freely, according to his own laws and unaffected by inhibiting political directives. The same standard applied to a work of art, which in order to be a work of art must emerge out of the artist's unique position in society, and which, accordingly, must evolve a form which will meet its own demands and correspond to its own laws. As the basis of his poetics, anarchism seemed to be as satisfying as it was for his vision of a co-operative commonwealth.

Having rejected Russia as the vanguard of social progress, Read transferred his hopes for constructive socialism to Spain, and particularly to the Catalonian anarchists, whose spontaneous counteraction against the Insurgents had been widely credited with saving the Republic in the first weeks of the war. Even the gradual banking of the fires of anarchism, which had been practically accomplished by May, 1937, did not change his belief that the triumph of anarchism was imminent. In 1938, when it was clear to most that the Republic could not win, Read could still write hopefully that

At the time I write the outcome of the struggle is still uncertain, but it is impossible to believe that the conscience of a modern people, once roused to a sense of its human rights, will ever again submit to a medieval tyranny. It is impossible to believe that with the examples of Russia and Germany before them, they will pass from a medieval to a *modern tyranny*. Let us rather believe that there are possibilities in the present situation which justify a renewal of our faith in human humility and individual grace. The will to power, which has for so long warped the social structure of Europe, and which has even possessed the minds of socialists, is renounced by a party that can claim to represent the vital forces of a nation. For that reason I do not see why intellectuals like myself, who are not politicians pledged to an immediate policy, would not openly declare ourselves for the only political doctrine which is consistent with our love of justice and our need for freedom.[6]

As this passage reveals, Read considered the struggle a war of "will" and "justice," in which anarchism was at last manifesting itself, warring on tyranny and suppression, and working to create the Golden Age. More practically, anarchism had combined with syndicalism and established collectives which had not only proved the efficiency of the system but had provided "a standard of living far higher than that realized under any previous form of social organization."[7] At a time of rebirth and renewal even the efforts of Russia to foist upon the Spanish a program inimical to their wishes would fail. "The demand for provincial autonomy, for syndicalist autonomy, for the abolition of the bureaucracy and the standing army," Read contended, "springs from the deepest instincts of the Spanish people."[8]

Despite the enthusiasm he felt for the Spanish anarchists, he managed in a dedicatory poem, "A Song for the Spanish Anarchists," to preserve remarkable restraint. The spare, lucid diction and the sharp, carefully hewn imagery give the poem a hard outline. Economical almost to the point of being austere, it is the epitomy of controlled emotion. He even seems less concerned about the contemporary struggle of anarchism than in its basic, almost primitive, dignity and rightness.

The golden lemon is not made
   but grows on a green tree :
A strong man and his crystal eyes
   is a man born free.

The oxen pass under the yoke
   and the blind are led at will :
But a man born free has a path of his own
   and a house on the hill.

And men are men who till the land
   and women are women who weave :
Fifty men own the lemon grove
   and no man is a slave.[9]

He appeals to man's desire to be free so that he might realize
himself as an individual and work in harmony with his fellows
amidst the goodness and bounty of nature. The poem's implicit
revolutionary message, intentionally understated and played
down by the quiet tone, carries more conviction and far
greater impact than the collection of slogans and shibboleths
found in so many of the Spanish war poems. Read sublimated
his enthusiasm and rendered the essence of the anarchist
struggle in a few spare, yet meditative, images which appeal
to man's love of justice and need for freedom.

   In view of the fact that Read had experienced the trench
warfare of World War I and had contributed to the antiwar
literature of the twenties and thirties, his position as a supporter of the Spanish war, in spite of its special classification
as a "just" war, might strike one as somewhat anomalous.
However, two other poems, "The Heart Conscripted" and
"Bombing Casualties," suggest that his belief in the justice of
the war was at times tenuous, and while they are not defeatist
poems they do show that Read was aware of the penalty war
exacts from everyone, including the poet. The most remark-

able characteristic of "Bombing Casualties" is the acuity of observation :

> Dolls' faces are rosier but these were children
> their eyes not glass but gleaming gristle
> dark lenses in whose quicksilvery glances
> the sunlight quivered. These blenched lips
> were warm once and bright with blood
> but blood
> held in a moist bleb of flesh
> not spilt and spattered in tousled hair.
>
> In these shadowy tresses
> red petals did not always
> thus clot and blacken to a scar.
>
> These are dead faces.
> Wasps' nests are not more wanly waxen.
> Wood embers not so greyly ashen.
>
> They are laid out in ranks
> like paper lanterns that have fallen
> after a night of riot
> extinct in the dry morning air.[10]

Again, as in "A Song for the Spanish Anarchists," Read retained a tight control over his material. Without resorting to denunciations of aerial bombing, he conveys in a few concrete words and images the physical horror as well as the inhumanity of the act. His concentration on the condition of the victims may at first suggest that his interest is only clinical, and the absence of any overt condemnation of the act may tend to reinforce this impression. But the condemnation is implicit in Read's emotional involvement in the situation of the poem. The selection of the most gruesome phase of a bombing raid as the subject of the poem, while intended to shock, actually exemplifies the poet's revulsion. And by using child victims, rather than a more heterogeneous group, he intensifies this feeling. The graphic description of the dead children, particularly their distorted faces, although controlled and quiet, suggests the terror and nausea which the poet himself felt.

But in "The Heart Conscripted," the most personal of his Spanish war poems, Read made no attempt to suppress the personal loss which the war brought him. The elegiac mood, the meditative ruminations on the past, the note of despair, all create an impression of irremediable despondency.

> The shock of silver tassels
> the sledded breath . . .
> I who have fought my battles
> keep these in a sheath.
>
> The ulcer of poetic pride
> from which the Lake Poet perished,
> the owl's indifferent hood—
> these have vanished.
>
> I only hear the sobbing fall
> of various water-clocks
> and the swift inveterate wail
> of the destructive axe.
>
> Lorca was killed, singing,
> and Fox who was my friend.
> The rhythm returns : the song
> which has no end.[11]

The sense of loss which pervades this poem might almost stand as the poet's final comment on the Spanish war. As the defeat of the Republic drew closer and as the spirit of Spanish anarchism gradually died, he could no longer sustain an

interest in the war. After the capitulation of the government
forces in March, 1939, he looked upon the whole affair "with
a certain indifference." As his reply to the *Left Review*
questionnaire two years previously had suggested, his interest
was fixed primarily on the emergence of Spanish anarchism.
"In Spain, and almost only in Spain," he wrote, "there still
lives a spirit to resist the bureaucratic tyranny of the state and
the intellectual intolerance of all doctrinaires. For that reason
all poets must follow the course of this struggle with open and
passionate partisanship." [12] But when anarchism was put down,
Read's "open and passionate partisanship" soon faded. The
war inspired no additional poems. His disappointment, if not
actual disillusionment, was reflected in *The Philosophy of
Anarchism,* written in 1940, in which the baleful instruments
of the Comintern are castigated as inimical to the emergence
of a classless society :

The point I wish to make is that there is all the difference in
the world between a movement that aims at an exchange of
political institutions, which is the bourgeois socialist (Fabian)
notion of a revolution; and a movement that aims at getting rid
of these political institutions altogether. An insurrection, therefore, is directed against the State as such, and this aim will
determine our tactics. It would obviously be a mistake to create
the kind of machinery which, at the successful end of a revolution,
would merely be taken over by the leaders of the revolution, who
then assume the functions of a government. That is out of the
frying pan into the fire. It is for this reason that the defeat of the
Spanish Government, regrettable in that it leaves the power of
the state in still more ruthless hands, is to be looked upon with
a certain indifference; for in the process of defending its existence
the Spanish Government had created, in the form of a standing
army and a secret police, all the instruments of oppression, and
there was little prospect that these instruments would have been
discarded by the particular group of men who would have been
in control if the war had ended in a Government victory. [13]

"Women Weeping in Irun's Ruins"

Like Herbert Read, George Barker refrained from participating in activities organized on behalf of the Spanish Republicans. Nor did he lend his name to a particular political group or creed. As far back as 1934, he had declared that he was unaffiliated with any party,[14] and even in 1937 his specific political preferences were still indefinite, although as the following statement suggests he had clearly moved leftward with many of his contemporaries. His reply in *Authors Take Sides* was perhaps deliberately evasive: "I am for the people of Republican Spain, for the people of China, for the people of England, for the people of Germany, etc. I am against Fascism, Franco, Mussolini, Japanese Generals, Hitler, Walter Chrysler, the Archbishop of Canterbury, etc."[15]

Evidently, Barker hoped, as did Spender, to avoid making firm political commitments as long as possible. And unlike Spender, he preserved a political anonymity throughout the Spanish Civil War. Nevertheless the war exerted considerable influence upon him and his work. But whereas with the majority of left-wing poets the influence of the war was primarily political, with Barker it was humanitarian. That is, instead of being interested principally in social reforms, or the kind of government the Republicans were fighting for, Barker was concerned with the immediate effect of war on the Spanish people, with the pain and misery they were enduring.

The degree to which the Spanish struggle affected him is evident in the final section of the long personal poem, *Calamiterror*. It begins as a lament for the poet's dead child and ends, after he has passed through an agonizing period of introspection when he envisioned himself in a world made almost uninhabitable by ugliness and guilt, with the realization that it is because of self-interest that this sort of nightmare of existence can become a reality. Then, into the poet's imagined chaos, breaks the sound of "Women weeping in Irun's ruins," or, in other words, the cry of suffering humanity. Hearing their cries, the poet realizes he must share their agony, which is symbolic of the agony of an entire people. Once he has made this decision, he finds that he has exchanged a life of self-indulgence, bound to lead only to an artistic impasse, for one based on fellow-feeling:

> He loved himself so much that the act of love
> Made with himself, gave him, as hybrid, death.
> But phoenix, beetle, snake, from his blood,
> I rose and felt the throes of Spain.

> Continually the women weeping in Irun's ruins
> Call in distress with voices like swans;
> I hear that cry which breaks the womb or room
> Wherever I stand, and forces me to go.
> The swan my world with a myriad at her breast,
> The foaming human struggle, I hear their cry;
> The feminine weeping and masculine agony
> Meet at the throat and make the swan's song.[16]

Suffering Spain has shown the poet the way out of his nightmare. Assuming social responsibility has given him a less personal but more objective and adequate view of the world. Behind him he leaves his "predecessor," a "serpent continually swallowing itself." Ahead lies Spain, "labouring to let out liberty, with the rat and rot at her heart."

Calamiterror is not a poem expressly about Spain. It is a rambling, often indistinct, intensely personal vision of a world made loathsome by the absence of love and responsibility. Intruding into this vision come the "women weeping in Irun's ruins" who, although symbolic of Spain, have not been introduced to preach a sermon or force a political lesson. Their purpose in the poem is symbolic in another sense; they suggest that the poet has solved his problem himself and that the answer lies partly in assuming greater social responsibility. Barker has not projected the problem outward into the external world of politics, rather, in solving the problem privately, he has used a symbol from that "outside world," which he has personalized and rendered imaginatively.

Both of Barker's Spanish war poems are elegies on the defeat of the Republic. A sonnet, "O Hero Akimbo on the Mountains of To-morrow," written first, appeared in *Poems for Spain* and is the prototype for the more ambitious "Elegy on Spain," which appeared anonymously in August, 1939. The former poem, while refreshingly free of political jargon, depends too much upon a medley of strained and scarcely homogeneous images for its effect. Those in the octave seem particularly forced:

> Star crossed on its own limbs I saw
> Spain like a rose spreadeagled to a knife :
> The mountain muscles and the Gibraltar jaw,
> The French forehead and the fist of grief
> Seized by a sadist for a Caesar's leaf
> Big on the head : browbeaten I saw
> The face of Spain struck to a badge of war
> For a king's coat, but to a heart's grief.

The sestet develops the theme of a resurrected Spain, which MacDiarmid, Wintringham, and Campbell, among others, foresaw in their verse. Barker's hopeful vision, however, suffers from a lack of imaginative unity, especially where he envisions the resurrected hero "gallivanting on the hills again." And it is disappointing to read that nothing more formidable than the poet's hope for a reborn Spain lies behind his confident vision :

A hero akimbo on the mountains of to-morrow,
Star crossed spreadeagled and browbeaten Spain—
I see your starved shape grow more strong from pain,
Leap finer and freer from the grave of sorrow,
I see you go gallivanting on the hills again—
O hero akimbo on the mountains of to-morrow.[17]

No doubt the strict confines of the sonnet form proved too limited for the fuller development which this theme needed. Such compression is technically pretentious and hardly conductive to ready comprehension. In "Elegy on Spain," however, Barker reworked the subject, not only including much informative detail but also achieving considerable imaginative intensity, which gives it a poetic value far above any political importance it may have had. In a dedicatory poem "to the photograph of a child killed in an air-raid on Barcelona," Barker, like Read, exhibits a concern for the fate of the child victims of war; it also comments on the poet's expanding social consciousness. For such is his concern for humanity that he makes himself responsible for vindicating the death of the child : "I hold/ The crime of the bloody time in my hand . . . And if I feel your gaze upon me ever,/ I'll wear the robe of blood that love illumines."[18]

The theme of "Elegy on Spain" is announced in the first part, which is dominated by the figure of a fallen hero, a "red rag . . . laid across his eyes," lying "by the Madrid rock," and baptizing the sand with his blood. Cut down "by the fist of the beast" and indirectly by the inactivity of sympathetic supporters, he lies prostrate but not defeated. The theme of the poem is that Freedom has been nourished by the struggle in Spain, and that in spite of what seem to be tragic reverses, it has actually imbued those who witnessed the struggle with the courage and endurance to continue the fight for liberty.

Besides the fallen hero, Barker makes effective use of a stricken
bull and the capital of Madrid as symbols of Spain's temporary
condition, and throughout the three parts of the elegy skillfully
interlaces the various elements of his theme—loss, hope, resurrection—in images far less strained than those of *Calamiterror:*

> The flower Freedom needs blood at the roots,
> Its shoots spring from your wounds, and the bomb
> Booming among the ruins of your houses, arouses
> Generation and generation from the grave
> To slave at your side for future liberation.
>
> .   .   .   .   .
>
> Drop, drop that heavy head, my less and more than dead,
> Bled dry a moment, tomorrow will raise that hand
> From the sad sand, less than death a defeat.
> Beaten by friend, not enemy, betrayed, not beaten,
> Laid let that head be, low, my bull, stunned,
> Gunned from the royal box by a trigger pull.
> Bigger no courage is than the blood it can spill.
>
> Not in a wreath I write the death in a ring,
> But sing a breath taken by heroes, a respite :
> No fight is over when Satan still straddles a man;
> Then the real battle begins which only ends
> When friends shake hands over the break of evil.

The theme reaches its climax in the final stanza, where the
sense of eventual triumph is clearly expressed :

> So close a moment that long open eye,
> Fly the flag low, and fold over those hands
> Cramped to a gun : gather the child's remains
> Straining the wall and cluttering the drains;
> Troop down the red to the black and the brown;
> Go homeward with tears to water the ground.

All this builds a bigger plinth for glory,
Story on story, on which triumph shall be found.

What started in *Calamiterror* as an expression of guilt over excessive self-interest has here reached its climax. The antithesis of his former egotistical self, the poet now broods hopefully over the tragedy of Spain and the possibility of a resurrected Spain and a new era of Freedom.

Chapter 7 : Roy Campbell: The Voice of the Insurgents

Prelude to Battle: "Light on a Dark Horse"

THE ATMOSPHERE OF SOCIAL PROTEST IN WHICH MOST LEFT-wing poets lived and which they helped to perpetuate was almost entirely foreign to Roy Campbell, at least until the months just before the outbreak of the Spanish Civil War. His South African background had scarcely made him conscious of the problems of a heavily urbanized society. Nor did being in England awaken any strong interest in postwar economic problems or in the importance of the Russian revolution. A sturdy belief in the supremacy of a practical knowledge gained from action rather than reading—a belief which was probably strengthened when Campbell was forced to leave Oxford for failing the entrance examinations—had already, in fact, formed the keystone of his pragmatic philosophy. It asserted itself most noticeably at this time in his expressions of dislike for Aldous Huxley, with whom he shared a London flat following the sojourn at Oxford. To Campbell, who had learned to respect the challenges of life in the raw, Huxley's pedantry and inexperience with the practical side of life were anathema. "I felt ill at ease with this pedant who leeringly gloated over his knowledge of how crayfish copulated (through their third pair of legs) but could never have caught or cooked one; let alone

177

broken in a horse, thrown and branded a steer, flensed a whale, or slaughtered, cut, cured, and cooked anything at all."[1]

This disparagement of Huxley is symptomatic of the contempt which Campbell eventually expressed for nearly all left-wing writers. He considered them too cerebral, too mincing and prissy, too fearful of the cruder elements of life, and, worst of all, too far removed from life itself. Lacking practical knowledge and experience, they substituted cleverness, sophistication, and bookish knowledge, which violated one of Campbell's basic convictions: "I have always known that the non-bookish existence underlies and precedes the bookish one, which should ornament and implement the latter."[2]

In the twenties Campbell took no interest in politics, social causes, proletarian reforms, and stayed clear of leftist groups, although he did not refuse a job as book reviewer for the left-wing *Daily Herald* and later for the *New Statesman and Nation* on the ground that reviewing involved no politics. What political philosophy he had at the time he has summed up himself in two sentences: "The only possible idea of government is charity and generosity on the part of the strong and the rich—as opposed to envy or greed on the part of the weak and the poor. A full well-fed shark (and all politicians are sharks) is unlikely to bite off so many heads as a hungry one."[3]

Between 1928 and the outbreak of war in 1936, Campbell provided for his growing family by raising olives in Martigues, bullfighting in Provence, fishing off southern France, and steer-throwing and horse-breaking in Toledo. The intensity and excitement and demands of this life did little to quicken an interest in politics, although his animosity against the Blooms-bury literati as well as their politics grew stronger, especially after he learned a few of them had banned his poem *The Georgiad*. But the political detachment ended around 1935. As the signs of unrest began increasing in Spain, Campbell, then living in Toledo, was forced to recognize, if not to sympathize with, the power of an ever more daring and hostile Left. To the frequent outbursts of lawlessness, he reacted vehemently, accusing the Spanish Communists of deliberately creating disorder preparatory to launching an attack on the state. Their goal, he believed, was a Communist-dominated Spain. Sometime before the war which he considered inevitable came, he had declared that for him there could be no compromise. It would clearly be a determinative battle "between the East and the West, between Credulity and Faith, between responsible innovation (which catches all 'intellectuals' once they have been hereditarily derailed) and tradition, between the emotions (disguised as Reason) and the intelligence," and in such a struggle he would unequivocally stand with the "West," "Faith," "Tradition," and "Intelligence."⁴ Even as the power and rebelliousness of the Spanish Left increased, following the February elections, Campbell made little effort to hide his opposition to the actions of the new government, which he condemned as deliberate maneuvers to deliver Spain into Communist hands. Warned that he was exposing himself to possible harm if he persisted in denouncing the state publicly, he nevertheless continued and, in addition, openly proclaimed his allegiance to the Church, which had already become a target of leftist incendiaries.

The two events that eventually persuaded him to "step into the front ranks of the Regular Army of Christ," as he described joining the Church as well as the Nationalist force, occurred in 1936. The first concerned the February elections, by which a Republican government had once again got control of the country. According to Campbell, he had been forced to vote "Red" in that election, and when the Republicans took office on what he claimed was a minority vote, he lost all faith in the fairness of Spanish elections and was certain that the people had been hoodwinked into accepting a government opposed to their will. The second was a personal attack on his life.

Shortly before the war began, Campbell was arrested and beaten by two assault guards a few miles from Toledo and forced to march into the city at pistol point. He only just escaped more severe punishment because he was a foreigner. This frankly unwarranted and brutal attack, and the more or less systematic terrorism carried on by the fanatical elements of the Left, convinced Campbell that the Right, who in his opinion still had a majority, "had turned both cheeks so many times that it began to look cowardly rather than Christian." His final act of defiance occurred on the eve of the war, in June, 1936. Already a nominal but not a confirmed Roman Catholic, Campbell, along with his wife, accepted the offer of two Carmelite monks, whom the poet was later to celebrate lengthily in several of his Spanish war poems, to be confirmed, just in case their well-known anti-Republican views should incite their enemies to retaliatory action. The ceremony— indeed an act of some daring even for a foreigner—was the overture to a new life:

At 3 A.M. while it was still pitch dark, we picked up the two Fathers at the Carmelites' in their "full-regimentals" as Carmelites, and walked through the dark, empty streets to the Cardinal's palace. We were thrilled and exhilarated, like children robbing an orchard, for we were committing an entirely innocent but extremely dangerous crime in the eyes of our new masters. On that day, before dawn, began an entirely new chapter in our lives, which had hitherto been somewhat drab and dull compared with the new splendours of experience for which we were lucky enough to be preserved.[5]

"Men" versus "Wowsers"

Without meaning to be deliberately incautious or to pun at an inappropriate time, I would suggest that the Spanish war was a godsend for Roy Campbell. At least if the number of poems Campbell wrote on the struggle is important, there is reason to believe that as an event capable of initiating considerable poetic fermentation that war held unusual powers. In all, Campbell wrote eleven poems based on the war, and while the number may seem small, it must be said that they form the most elongated compendium of the Spanish Civil War by a single author. In the *Collected Poems, Flowering Rifle,* the longest, fills nearly 125 pages; "A Letter from the San Mateo Front," which formed Part I in the original version of *Flowering Rifle,* covers sixteen pages, and several others, such as "The Carmelites of Toledo," "The Hoopee," and "Talking Bronco," run anywhere from five to ten pages. What provoked this really sizable production was more than just the excitement of witnessing a war and the natural desire to write about it, although these clearly influenced Campbell. What really lay behind it, I believe, was the poet's firm belief that the Nationalist cause embodied most of the values and ideas with which he as a man and poet profoundly agreed or at least respected; and that, on the other hand, the Loyalist cause of "freedom and democracy" was nothing but camouflage to conceal the ambitions of a ruthless group of Communists to seize control of Spain. He believed, furthermore, that Republican leaders had licensed disorders of the worst sort, and to their party had attracted nearly every enemy he had ever made, right down to particular left-wing poets.

To discover his beliefs, indeed to find his friends and enemies so felicitously arranged into opposing camps—and in such extraordinary abundance—was indeed a happy occurrence. For here on a single battlefield, so to speak, tearing at each other's throats, were the very creeds as well as people on whom the poet had long spent his wrath or approbation. To divide the combatants into groups representing right and wrong was therefore probably an easier task for Campbell than it had been for the Left. Only the terminology differed. Where the

Left used the terms "fascists" and "democrats" to designate the combatants, Campbell chose more personal descriptions like "Wowsers" and "Reds" for the Loyalists, and the simple but ennobling epithet "Men" for the Nationalists. As the terms themselves suggest, Campbell was as inclined to forejudge the combatants as the most prejudiced left-wing poets. He began *Flowering Rifle*, for example, by making his biases clear :

> A hundred years of strife with warring vans
> Had winnowed Spain in two distinctive clans
> Upon the left, inflammable, the chaff,
> Corn to the right, the vulnerable half,
> And thus in Spanish history began
> The war between the Wowser and the Man—[6]

In a note he added to *Flowering Rifle* in 1938, Campbell admitted that "like all English writers on Spain I am biassed," but then added that he was biased, "unlike any of the others, by a thorough first-hand experience of life under both regimes as one of the working population."[7] While it is probably true that Campbell was more familiar with the workaday world of Spain than any other English-speaking writer who became involved in the war, with the possible exceptions of Ralph Bates and Peter Chalmers-Mitchell, there was one additional consideration, not primarily social, which played an extremely important part in forming his bias and which probably motivated more of his Spanish poetry than any other single factor. And that was religion. As a new convert who had described his conversion as "stepping into the front ranks of the Regular Army of Christ," Campbell was especially sensitive to attacks on the institution for which he obviously held an intensely emotional respect. His relationship with the Carmelite fathers of Toledo, who had heard his confession and had received him into the Church, was of the most personal and moving sort.

That it was their courage as much as their holiness which impressed him is suggested in his description of the part they played in defending the Alcázar :

> His radiant face when last I saw
> Eusebio bade me task delight :
> His flesh was flame, his blood its light
> That sought the fire as fire the straw,
> And of his agony so cruel
> As ruthlessly devoured the spite
> As eager flame devours the fuel.
>
> Small wonder then as trash to earthly
> The gunbutts drove me from the pin
> They smashed to let such Princes in
> When, too presumptuous, as unworthy,
> My carcass for a crown to barter,
> The blows acceding to the Martyr
> Rebuffed me for a Harlequin.

And it was with this sort of determination and courage, Campbell felt, that the Church warred on the "godless horde" of Republicans. It was, in fact, the heroic defense of the Alcázar that Campbell fashioned into a symbol of the "phoenix-birth" which Spain was about to witness :

> A phoenix from its ash to father,
> A greater, in its turn, to shire—
> It was to be to the Alcázar
> What the Alcázar is to Spain,
> And Spain is to the world entire;
> Unanimous in blood and fire
> A single purpose lit the twain.[8]

He conceived of the Church as a church-militant, forced to fight for its own survival and determined to resurrect a new

Spain out of the ashes of war. It was in the vanguard of a great crusade to expel the heretics whose "dogmatized Utopias" threatened to destroy the religious as well as social and political traditions of the country. It alone gave purpose and symbolic value to the cause:

> The Army of the People of the World,
> The hoarse blaspheming of the godless hordes
> Against the Cross and Crescent of the Lord
> The Cross, our Hammer, and the Quarter Moon
> Our Sickle, and Hosanna for our tune![9]

Campbell often stated that when Spain would again be ruled by the Right it would experience an unprecedented economic revival. Under the Nationalists, he foresaw a much improved standard of living for everyone, an abundance of food, more work and even greater international prominence. In fact, he declared that the economic transformation had already begun wherever Franco's soldiers had won victories; wherever, that is, the influence of the Church had been restored, for he believed that a fruitful economy simply could not exist under the Left. The wealth of Spain, in other words, remained out of their reach; it flowed only where "Christ is King," but

> Where the Red Curse is, there will Hunger be!
> .   .   .   .   .
> They (the liberated) gasp to see our half-ton bullocks bleed
> Whom wealth of mighty nations failed to feed,
> To see the flocks of fat merinos spring
> From some poor provinces where Christ is King,
> Where loaves are multiplied from scanty grain
> And fishes seem deserters from the main.

Not only would the starved survivors of "Red" rule be taught the science of husbandry, but having seen the prosperity of their former enemies, they would themselves set about laboring to improve their conditions :

> Now through the Nation as our legions spread
> The richer by the Poorer half is fed :
> Beside the lewd inscription, where they sprawl,
> From loafing idly charcoaled on the wall
> Hammer and Sickle to their labour fall,
> Storks to the steeples, rollers to the wires
> Return, and swallows to the broken spires—
> And men to the religion of their sires ![10]

Such was the restorative power of the Church that it would effect not only a religious but an economic recovery. The whole Nationalist effort Campbell viewed as an "extraordinary awakening of a national consciousness in a ruined and pros-trate country."[11] It represented the needs and desires of the majority of the Spanish people, including most of the workers; only the "literate lounging class . . . that first conceived this Rabies of the brain,"[12] or communism, tried to obstruct this demonstration of the people's will. But the help this class received from alien "Reds" or "Wowsers" amounted to almost nothing. When they did not run away from battle, they either surrendered or defected; their very presence in Spain, Camp-bell contended, augured the defeat of the Republic :

> Vultures and crows so rally to the field
> And where they "group" you know the doom is sealed
> Before it hits our nostrils ripe and hot
> They've long ago divined the inward rot
> And as by sympathy I sense the rose
> Of Victory before its buds unclose,
> So they (before it trumpets to the nose)

Anticipate the maggot on its way,
With it co-operate in swift decay,
And so with one more carcass strew the way.[13]

The Hoopoe's Prophecies

Whether Campbell's conversion in any way strengthened his belief in his prophetic powers is questionable. But that he took more than a delight in offering proof of such powers is obvious. The role he assumed was similar to that of the Hoopoe, whom Campbell celebrated in the poem of the same name as the "Sergeant of the Birds . . . who knows that deeds say more than words."[14] Besides preferring action, Campbell and the Hoopoe have something else in common; they are both harbingers of war, and hence both had been banned or ignored.[15] Campbell evidently felt that the time had come to demonstrate the accuracy of his prophecies, "to scoop the news / That is not printed in reviews / The kind they stoned the prophets for."[16] To begin, he claimed that the bulk of his Spanish war poems "were printed in England two or three years before the war, and that the last one to appear, early in 1935 . . . clearly symbolized the Spanish war in a nutshell, together with the Red Débâcle."[17] But though foreseeing such a war and especially its outcome was indeed a perspicacious achievement, it can hardly be regarded as prophecy, especially given the peculiar knowledge of the country which Campbell possessed. And if he had claimed no more than this, we should scarcely give his prognostication a second thought. But, in fact, Campbell did claim more than this, a great deal more; however, it appears that all his predictions benefit greatly from having been made, or, at least, revealed, as predictions of long standing, after the completion of the events which they forecast. For example, the one occurrence in *Flowering Rifle*, "A Letter from the San Mateo Front," and "Talking Bronco" which Campbell claimed he foresaw, and which actually did happen in 1938, was the capture of three hundred British volunteers at San Mateo. As proof of his prescience, he cited the dedicatory poem to *Mithraic Emblems* (1935), where a surrender is described, which he claimed was based on a vision he had had of the actual capture. It "couldn't have been bettered had I written it retrospectively,"[18] he wrote afterward.

Now it is, of course, perfectly possible that Campbell did envision the capture of the British volunteers and that the surrender described in the dedicatory poem to *Mithraic Emblems* is the same surrender that occurred later at San Mateo. But there are no specific details in the latter poem to satisfy the dubious mind that the foreordained capture *is* the one that actually took place. Indeed, the capture is described in the most general terms:

> But when the bullets whistle
> Up goes the white flag, and down comes the Thistle. . . .
> .   .   .   .   .
> These are the guys that have no time to wait
> Though wisdom has a trick of coming late,
> A butterfly that stops at every flower
> And with a golden leisure hoards the hour,
> With these have squandered in their breathless haste
> And through their open bilges run to waste.
> So how to round them up? and where impound
> This legion of the lost that can't be found?
> No need to hurry; with an easy mind
> We catch them—where they left themselves behind![19]

While this passage unquestionably depicts a surrender, there remains the important question of who surrendered and where and when. Since the rest of the poem provides no additional information, it behooves us to accept the poet's explanation that he was, indeed, forecasting the surrender of the British volunteers. But while Campbell's story must be respected, is it not possible that he saw an opportunity, following the capture of the volunteers at San Mateo, to use the dedicatory poem as proof of his prescience? Campbell's prognostications, his pronouncements, and his theories had, he believed, been deliberately ill-received and even ignored in England, particularly by critics of the Left. Is it possible, then, that still angry over what he considered unfair treatment, he sought to vindicate his powers and, since the unfortunate prisoners in both vision and reality were members of the Left, to ridicule those who had abused him and his writing so badly?

Campbell himself, I believe, adds weight to this conjecture by referring to the incident repeatedly throughout *Flowering Rifle* and the two shorter poems, always in a snickering and vindictive manner. But even more revealing than the frequent repetition of the event is his explanation of why it occurred. The volunteers were captured, he argued, not because of an accident or military blundering. They were captured because Campbell himself had willed that they would be taken prisoner. He evidently believed that his prophetic words had somehow directed the volunteers to their ignominious fate:

> But let these prisoners speak for my precision
> And answer for my range and drive of vision,
> Who promised this before the war began,
> And drilled them with my pen before my gun
> To dance in dudgeon what I wrote in fun:
> And come like "Calais Burghers," as I planned,
> "With their pink halters tamely brought to hand"
> In every detail fleshed, as fancied them,
> When first the sword was fathered by the Pen:
> Surrendering without a single blow
> For nothing, save that I foretold it so—
> To make this great round-up at San Mateo

A film of my original rodeo—
To see them act down to its quaintest antic
The verse they dared to dream of a "Romantic"
When (ere they dreamed of it) I had portrayed
The British International Brigade,
And twice predicted clearly in advance
Lest any fool should foist it on to chance
If only one I'd whirled the whistling line
To get them hog-tied with iambic twine,
Preventing all suggestions of coincidence
When the live words should burgeon into incidents,
As in a tame hypnotic trance they follow
My verse, the flaming lariat of Apollo.[21]

This magical power over man and events was not Campbell's alone. Claiming nature as a colleague, he maintained that nature also contrived to frustrate the labor of the Republicans by refusing to allow grass and corn to grow in their territory. All of its elements, he asserted, "will shun the Communist's convulsive hold";[22] but wherever that hold is loosened nature will respond with flowery beauty :

But where his lore [Communist's] we trample and oppose
Reviving Nature thanks us with the rose
And the live earth recovers from his blows—

Matter in Campbell's animistic universe does its part, too, to defeat the enemy, by showing a sort of natural hostility toward those whose insensitiveness to order would force it into incongruous forms :

In its behaviour, Matter proved no dolt,
And that it has opinion of its own—
. . . . . .
Whether it's guns to fire, or bricks to pile,
Matter is always sensitive to style

(Which is the breathing rhythm of the soul)
And shows itself Devout from pole to pole :

.   .   .   .   .

But when democracy begins to soar
To whom the jail, the brothel, and the store,
Stand for the Church, and tries for like proportions
Matter complies with sorrowful distortions.
And rather as a slave than an ally
"Co-operates" to raise them to the sky,

Even the sun is made a fascist co-partner, and on one occasion literally bakes Russian tank crews into surrendering :

And what the sun began, the iron heated,
The Fahrenheit and Centigrade completed,
To save us any need of work more fiery,
As they came nosing to our mazed inquiry,
For the good sun, our ally and physician,
Had kept those dread-vans in the best condition,

As though it were not enough to have the natural universe take sides, Campbell declares that even the Loyalist's war machinery rebelled : "For even their machinery rebelled / And as by miracles, our armouries swelled : / Till we could almost pray for what we wanted / And take the answer to the prayer for granted." [23]

This all-out effort to consecrate the Nationalists by claiming that nature, matter, and even God actively interposed on their behalf to defeat the Republicans sounds suspiciously like the efforts of a man who is determined to win support for his side, even if it means endowing fatuity with a kind of breathtaking sanctification. *Flowering Rifle* really develops no argument that might conceivably persuade anybody that the Nationalists had the better cause. For Campbell cannot imagine that any logical argument about economics, for example, could possibly outweigh the fact and for him it was indeed a fact—that the

Nationalists had been blessed with holy sanction. To dispute about politics, land reform, social rights, or about the respective merits of the belligerents was all immaterial and superfluous : the Nationalists were "holy crusaders," the Loyalists were "godless marauders," and this distinction, in Campbell's opinion, not only obviated any need for disputation but made all the difference between right and wrong. And it was this distinction that was responsible for turning *Flowering Rifle* into a polemic, and Roy Campbell into a sort of sham *vates*. The latter role rather naturally led to the polemic. It is not so much Campbell's claiming to have forensic powers that we find objectionable, although his boasting gives off a hollow sound, it is rather the tediousness of the ex-cathedra tone in which these prognostications are uttered that annoys us. And the tedium is intensified by the regularity with which these prophecies are recited or defended. Campbell's determination to impress us with "the constant certitude of his pen" has led to a monotonous tirade in his own defense, which all but overshadows his primary purpose, which, I gather, was to herald the supremacy of the Nationalist cause. Repetition is one of the propagandist's most effective tools, but it is fatal to poetry, especially when it is used as a means of self-glorification, having little to do with the principal subject of the poem.

When we couple Campbell's efforts to build his reputation as a seer with his paean in defense of Franco and the Nationalist cause, we have joined, as it were, Campbell the *vates* to Campbell the propagandist, and the two are complementary. In fact, it seems certain that Campbell saw little, if any, distinction between them, although it is also clear that the latter role was one he would deny having played. The certainty of his prophecies, together with his knowledge of Spain and Franco, made deliberate distortion for any propagandistic purposes, in his opinion, impossible :

The Pen a sword, prophetic in advance,
Deriding probability or chance,
That with unerring skill and biting scorn
Can sack a dud republic ere it's born![24]

But that he made the most preposterous claims for Franco's campaign, in addition to proclaiming it a holy crusade, is undeniably the case, whether or not he would consider such absurdities propaganda. The extravagance of his allegations defeats their purpose. It seems incredible that Campbell actually thought anyone would believe such patent falsehoods about the belligerents as these : that the Republicans, besides acquiring foreign aid before Franco, received alien soldiers who outnumbered foreign enlistees on Franco's side four to one; that whatever aid Franco received—less than the Loyalists—"was proffered, not entreated"; that the Moors, first approached by Azaña, preferred to serve as mercenaries with Franco; that the Nationalists, naturally peace-loving, were forced to fight in order to preserve Spain from the Red menace, often using only arms they captured from the Reds themselves; that Mussolini's invasion of Ethiopia was simply a matter of settling a score with an old enemy;[25] that the Left, naturally siding with "filth and famine," was completely devoid of any morality,[26] but that the "clean hands" of the Nationalists would clean up the "filth and dirt" of these would-be reformers; that the Left was guilty of the most callous sort of aerial bombing; that the destruction of Guernica was the work of Loyalists who tried to blame the Nationalists for the tragedy; that in contrast to the heroic defense of the outnumbered Nationalists[27] the Reds were not only uncommonly cowardly (one wonders what is the point in opposing a cowardly foe) but afraid to save their wounded lest they spread demoralization behind the lines;[28] and finally, that Franco clearly bespoke his greatness by bidding "the epic years begin,"[29] while the Red leaders revealed their cowardliness by escaping Spain weeks before the war ended.[30]

It is not so much the absence of political neutrality with which we argue; that aspect of his poetry, although unacceptable to the impartial reader, quickly recedes into the background. More objectionable is the personal and spiteful tone which animates so much of his satire of "Reds" and Republicans. The contemptuousness with which he castigates them is scathing; the words are hot from a mind boiling with hatred. And it is this spirit of hatred which in the end predominates and which starts the seeds of disbelief growing in our minds. For our reacton is likely to be negative. We resent Campbell's attempt to bludgeon us into accepting his own hatred, and we reject as too uncontrolled to be valid what he has written.

As objectionable as the scurrility is the almost total lack of form in *Flowering Rifle*. It has already been pointed out that the poem suffers from extreme repetitiousness, even in one or two instances repeating the same lines without representing some artistic design.[31] It appears that Campbell simply piled one contention on top of another indiscriminately, without any careful consideration of how the finished product would look. For instance, an argument favoring the Nationalists suddenly ends, a passage of autobiographical boasting begins, which, in turn, stops, and a piece of satire on British intellectuals commences—all perhaps within the confines of a page or two, and done without the aid of transitions.

The Shame of "Joint MacSpaunday"

Campbell's most effective satire is leveled at the British intelligentsia. As was noted in the discussion of the San Mateo affair, the poet's hostility toward this group, particularly the left-wing poets and critics whom he contended had deliberately neglected his poetry, was prodigious. And, unfortunately, the result too often is that the satire is marred by a kind of vicious savagery which throws more light on Campbell's angry mind than on the faults of those he was satirizing. Relying on invective, sarcasm, and cynicism, he seemed more intent on crippling —permanently if possible—than correcting his victims. However, despite the questionable motivation, he often succeeded in inflaming the susceptibilities of left-wing poets. For example, he ridiculed the sort of sham communism of the Bloomsbury intellectuals, who remained "bourgeois" in spite of ostentatious efforts to prove the contrary :

> As doomed anachronisms, Sire and Son,
> Capitalist and communist make one,
> The scrawny offspring and the bloated sire
> Sentenced by nature to the same hot fire;
> So in red Bloomsbury the two are tied
> Like gangsters to be taken for a ride—
> Smug rebels to Society, the tame
> Charaders in a dreary parlour game,
> Where breaking crockery gives a lawless thrill
> And Buffaloes each smug suburban Bill,
> Where the Left Fist will pelt you from the fence,
> But when you lift a hand in self-defence,
> Although it scorns the bourgeois law and state,
> Off to the lawyers takes the broken pate,
> And at the first sign of a lifted quirt
> Will cling his Mother Grundy by the skirt.
> From every communist you can unsheath
> The snug fat "bourgeois" creeping underneath,
> And every Babbit is a foxes' hole
> From which a scrawny "comrade" snarls for dole !

And he was equally effective when criticizing their inactivity and ignorance of Spain. While he worked and fought in Spain, they imbibed what they could from books and then foolishly claimed to know all about the "Spanish worker" :

> Since my existence has been lived and fought
> As theirs at Oxford ready-made was bought
> And in my teens I'd shed like threadbare trousers
> Every experience possible to Wowsers;
>
> .   .   .   .   .
>
> Grown wiser in the company of mules
> Than they with learned pedantries of fools,
> And, since I was not sent with foreign cash,
> Like some, to spread the bolshevistic rash,
> Able both to explain the "Spanish Worker"
> From the inside, as to expound the Shirker,
> The Communist, whose bungling Left we fight
> With this Right hand—in every sense the Right!

As long as Campbell concentrated on exposing these and other weaknesses of the literary Left Wing, he was entirely successful. Even his contention that the Left had created a monstrous myth about "democratic" Spain being attacked by international fascism in order to bamboozle young Englishmen into volunteering to fight for the Republic has bite and perhaps some truth. Deliberate romanticizing of a political sort of the Spanish war was commonplace. There was point in Campbell's exposure of this tendency, although the assertion that his own poetry was the quintessence of realism can certainly be questioned :

> Some fools may find Romantics in my Obra—
> But where's a Realism that is sob'rer
> When heroes Rooperted in Spauden's line

> As dying stoics, nonchalant and fine,
> Like numbed, frostbitten bullfrogs to a Cobra,
> Galvanically volted through the spine,
> Confront the cold Reality of mine?[32]

But when in "Talking Bronco," which seems to be an appendage to *Flowering Rifle* and a receptacle for leftover spleen, he accused the left-wing poets, whom he fused into "Joint MacSpaunday," of deliberately exploiting the Spanish war for financial gain, we are inclined to think that vengeance has gained the upper hand. Furthermore, to say that they were well-paid propagandists who collaborated with the workers' parties "while it paid" is to misrepresent completely their part in the Spanish war. Nothing could be further from the truth than the contention that self-interest motivated their actions, or that their verse was cheap recruiting propaganda to inspire volunteers to go to Spain. Among other things, it is certainly a question of deciding whether the left-wing poets inspired the volunteers, or whether the volunteers inspired the poets, and most signs point to the latter as being closer to what actually happened. The charges of exploitation are intended to destroy not to illumine, but they do neither because they contain no truth :

> While joint MacSpaunday shuns the very strife
> He barked for loudest, when mere words were rife,
> When to proclaim his proletarian loyalites
> Paid well, was safe, raked in the heavy royalties,
> And made the mealy mouth and Bulging Purse
> The hallmark of Contemporary verse.
> A more ferocious, bloodthirsty poltroon
> Has never howled for blood beneath the moon
> Than joint MacSpaunday, when his leash of heads
> To murder, rape, and arson roared the Reds,
> For then he "stamped with emphasis" or tone
> For "Energy and Energy alone."[33]

Finally, as though to impress once more that the Left carried within it the seeds of corruption, a kind of "inward rot" that contaminated everything it touched, Campbell declared that the publication of *Poems for Spain* (1939) signaled the collapse of the Spanish Republic :[34]

> You will not find such virtues in a Tyke
> That follows beaten armies in the rear
> Alternately beset with greed and fear
> And brings bad luck to every cause he scabies
> Far worse than if he's bitten it with rabies.
> No sooner his anthology came out
> Than at the sign Spain had no further doubt :[35]

Correspondent or Combatant?

It should be clear that Campbell went to considerable trouble to create the impression that the substance of his verse was authentic, that it was the work of one who, having lived in Spain, had considerably chosen to defend the side that was fighting to preserve Spain's best traditions. *Flowering Rifle* bears the description, "A Poem from the 'Battlefield of Spain,'" and like "A Letter from the San Mateo Front" and "Talking Bronco," it contains myriad details about the war and the author which can only be obscure to most readers. Indeed, Campbell assumed that his audience knew far more about the Spanish Civil War and his personal feud with the British Left than they could possibly have known. But whether one could identify each battle, each allusion to the banned *Georgiad,* or each political reference may not have concerned Campbell very much; at least the scarcity of explanatory notes in *Flowering Rifle* would indicate that this was his feeling. But what this mass of detail does do, however, is give *Flower-*

ing Rifle a verisimilitude. It appears to be a trustworthy
document where all the facts have been meticulously recorded.
And this illusion of conscientious reliability Campbell cared
very much about. Above all, he cherished the role of
"Hoopoe," the "Talking Bronco," which made him perspicacious and the only one knowledgeable enough to write about
Spain truthfully:

> The sword a pen to chronicle its deed
> And write in scarlet for the world to read:
> And both the lightning's thunder-scribbled ray
> To singe the daft illusions of the day.[36]

He likewise plied his audience with the hard fact that, while
most left-wing poets shunned the war they "barked for
loudest," he had not, but instead had taken up arms to defend
the rights of the natural leaders of Spain. Repeatedly, he
endeavored to give the impression that he fought in the front
ranks of Franco's army, and in one footnote to *Flowering Rifle*
he actually stated as much.[37] His battle scenes, especially those
describing the siege of the Alcázar, are brilliant pageantry that
provide some additional insight into his attitude toward war.
He found much to celebrate in what often seems to be a
glorious contest, perhaps not much different, at least in the
danger and excitement involved, from bronco-busting or bullfighting. Indeed, he felt an overwhelming ecstasy marching
into battle:

> How thrilling sweet, as in the dawn of Time,
> Under our horses smokes the pounding thyme
> As we go forward; streaming into battle
> Down on the road the crowded lorries rattle
> Wherein the gay blue-shirted boys are singing,
> As to a football match the rowdies bringing—

But of this match the wide earth is the ball
And by its end shall Europe stand or fall.[38]

There is, however, some evidence to show that Campbell was not the front-line combat soldier that he claimed to be. Robert Graves, for example, wrote that Roy Campbell "was evacuated from Spain early in August, 1936 . . . and returned there only as a well-protected war correspondent" and that Campbell himself later said "that the authorities discouraged him from volunteering 'since they had enough rifles but not enough pens.'"[39] It appears, however, that Campbell tried to maintain the fiction, at least for the duration of the war, perhaps in the interest of adding weight to his proclamations.[40]

Whatever the truth is, there is no suggestion in *Flowering Rifle* that war had had a sobering effect upon him. He is like a great titan standing in the middle of a battlefield, defying his enemies to strike, certain that his own superior weapons can crush them out of existence. The conflict almost seems to be a personal one between Roy Campbell and the British Left, and insofar as he allowed his hatred for this group to seize him, he was unable, as one critic has said, "to differentiate between himself as an outraged human being and himself as a poet."[41] Campbell, at least in *Flowering Rifle,* "A Letter from the San Mateo Front" and "Talking Bronco," cannot resist attacking the Left whenever he felt inclined to do so, and it is because of this lack of control that these works are marred by a seemingly endless and decidedly wearying satire.

The Peace of "La Mancha"

When Campbell was less activated by scorn, less intent on sanctifying the Nationalists or proving his prophetic abilities, he was capable of writing about the war with considerable tolerance for both sides and with a feeling for suffering that we would not have thought possible. When he forgot for the moment the hateful Left, the valiant Nationalists and all the causes, good and bad, he liberated himself, as it were, from those unpleasant duties which he felt were his to perform. He could see the war from a greater distance, realize its larger significance, observe the wounds it had left on all alike. And it is in this less angry verse, too, that his rhapsodic powers, which were only occasionally demonstrated in the tirades, are most fully revealed. The opening lines of "La Mancha in Wartime," for example, beautifully conjure up a broken landscape in which the poet sees both despair and hope :

> A land of crosses, in the law's despite,
> Where every chance designs a crucifix.
> For the cicadas, in their choir of sticks
> And for the wider, in the kestrel's flight.
> The kestrel, and the stationary mill
> That sail-less hangs upon the tide of war,
> Had not this one significance before
> With which their merest shadow signs the hill.
> Where men have waifed the land with fire and steel
> Of all it spreads its arms to represent,
> Amidst their huge abortion of intent,
> That symbol is the only thing that's real.[42]

And the calm, almost wistful mood of these lines appears again at the end of "Dawn on the Sierra of Gredos," where the poet, imagining himself in the company of life, makes one last survey of the destruction of war and then turns homeward to begin the task of rebuilding :

> We gazed into that light primordial
> That filled with love the whole vast region

Whereunto death had passed from here :
So comradely, so frank, so cordial—
Like re-enlisting in the Legion
It made the thought of death appear.

Freed from the locustries of Marx,
The plain sent up a myriad larks.
And Life and I, with time to spare,
Rode homeward down the slope abreast,
And hung our rifles up to rest.
And yoked the oxen to the share.[43]

In moments of such placidity, Campbell gained in tolerance and saw that wherever and whenever enemies fought there would be not only suffering and death but endless charges and countercharges—the whole degrading sequence of recriminations—and that finally even the illusions themselves would begin to fade; and quite characteristically all that remains whole amidst the rubble, he wrote, was the Church :

We all become the thing we fight
Till differing solely in the palms
And fists that semaphore (to Right
or Left) their imbecile salaams.
Each of the other, fifty times,
Will plagiarise the stock-in-trade
Of purges, massacres, and crimes,
Before their hatred is allayed.
For I have lived, of three crusades,
The heroism and the pathos,
Seen how the daft illusion fades,
And learned of victory the bathos.
But when the lava has been poured
Through huge ravines of change and less,
Of all most hatred or adored.
One thing remains intact, the Cross![44]

Chapter 8 : Oxford Poets and the Spanish War

The Movement Begins

W. H. AUDEN, STEPHEN SPENDER, C. DAY LEWIS, JOHN Lehmann, Rex Warner, and a few others first gained wide prominence in two anthologies, *New Signatures* (1932) and *New Country* (1933), which linked their names for at least the remainder of the decade. Originally, their work had much in common, particularly in its underlying political attitude and in the use of imagery drawn from contemporary life. But it also reflected certain marked differences which seemed less important than the similarities and which, even today, tend to be slighted or overlooked. Foremost among the critics responsible for defining what came to be called the Movement in the literature of the thirties was Michael Roberts, the editor of *New Signatures* and *New Country*. In introductions to the two anthologies Roberts set out to interpret as well as defend the poets he had brought together. He began by noting that although none had been old enough to fight in the First World War, they had nevertheless been deeply affected by the social upheaval that followed it. He argued that there was no alternative for them but to reject the standards of the society in which they had been born. Not only had they "found themselves in a world which possessed no traditions by which they could regulate their lives," but they discovered that the older generation was totally incapable of feeling or understanding their "moral scruples." They were compelled, therefore, "to attack consciously problems which, in a stable society, would be solved by the social convention. They became self-conscious, self-analytical, dubious of the wisdom of their own decisions."[1]

The break with tradition, however, led to a way out of the individualistic predicament. Conscious of the barbarity and inhumanity of war as well as the social and economic problems it had created, and, more importantly, of the blighted condition of their society exacerbated by a broken, blundering, inhuman economic system, they experienced what Roberts implies was a kind of moral conversion. They felt guilty about enjoying class privileges which only the exploitation of the masses made possible, and they repudiated a system that condoned such slave-market practices. They realized, as Roberts put it, that they were "no more important than a flower in a field." The revelation was nothing less than the expression of "the essence of the communist attitude"; it led to the rejection of selfhood and to a desire for greater communication with the masses. It was a sort of impersonality which "comes not from extreme detachment but from solidarity with others. It is nearer to the Greek conception of good citizenship than to the stoical austerity of recent verse."[2]

Proof of their desire for "solidarity with others" appeared in their writing, where they endeavored to show that their interests were "bound up with those of the working class." In poetry free from "complexity and introspection, the doubt and cynicism" of the past, they articulated the revolutionary message. The break with tradition, the frightful consequences of the economic crisis, and the perils of incipient fascism combined to enhance the appeal of social communism as the best possible means for rectifying the injustices of the past and meeting those of the future. It was this common morality, or ideology, which bound them together. Far from being intractable and dogmatic, demanding servitude instead of generating enthusiasm, it was an "extension of personality and consciousness," concluded Roberts, "which comes sometimes to a group of men when they are working together for some common purpose."[3]

Though Spender, Auden, and C. Day Lewis emerged as spokesmen for the Movement, there was considerable disagreement on whether they represented the interaction of politics and art. Especially unfriendly were Julian Bell, John Cornford, and Christopher Caudwell, who accused them of holding on to their middle-class privileges while writing verse that was at least revolutionary in spirit. Bell dubbed them "Hot Marxists," full of enthusiasm, violence, emotionalism and unreasonableness, whose communism consisted of a mystical search "for salvation and a savior." He condemned as misleading their optimism about the chances of winning a class war and recommended that, instead of so much effusion and enthusiasm, they "get down to the business of providing leadership."[4] Cornford and Caudwell both claimed that they had not chosen between the bourgeoise and the proletariat. Rejecting the politics of their class was only the first step toward participating in the revolutionary struggles of the masses. That they had gone no further was obvious in their poetry, which was still written for a middle-class audience. They were playing at revolution, asserted Cornford, and their poetry was "a kind of utopian wish-fulfillment." It was the poetry of revolution "as a literary fashion, not as an historic necessity."[5] And it was a fashion, a pseudo-revolutionary literature, because Auden, Spender, and Day Lewis had failed to choose between revolution and reaction. Since they had not joined the revolutionary struggle by joining the proletariat, the old separation between life and art remained real to them and made impossible the true revolutionary writer's "objective" view which denied that such a separation existed. In the final analysis, they denied the class struggle by refusing to take part in it. Caudwell flatly stated that their reluctance to disclaim outmoded standards of art was disastrous:

They often glorify the revolution as a kind of giant explosion which will blow up everything they feel to be hampering them. But they have no constructive theory—I mean as artists: they may as economists accept the economic categories of socialism, but as artists they cannot see the new forms and contents of an art which will replace bourgeois art.

They know something is to come after this giant firework display of the Revolution, but they do not feel with the clarity of an artist the specific beauty of this new concrete living, for they are by definition cut off from the organization which is to realize it; and which therefore alone holds in its bosom the nascent outlines of the future.

They announce themselves as prepared to merge with the proletariat, to accept its theory and its organization, in every field of concrete living except that of art. Now this reservation— unimportant to an ordinary man—is absolutely disastrous for an artist, precisely because his most important function is to be an artist. It leads to a gradual separation between his living and his art . . . this separation cannot take place without a mutual distortion. His proletarian living bursts into his art in the form of crude and grotesque scraps of Marxist phraseology and the mechanical application of the living proletarian theory. . . .[6]

In a sense, the Spanish war became the crucible which tested the charges Cornford, Bell and Caudwell made against the "Hot Marxists." How would those poets who had been widely acclaimed the leading literary Marxists of their time react to the responsibilities demanded by the Spanish crisis? Would the struggle provide an emotional center for their beliefs that would be so moving and so impervious to any arguments based on a need for artistic isolation that they would naturally gravitate to a position of greater harmony with the proletariat? Would the formation of a Popular Front in England, dedicated to actively supporting the Spanish Republic, convince them that would-be leaders could not remain passive, that as intellectuals it was their duty to provide leadership? Would considerations for the welfare of English society convince them that their art should henceforth be a revolutionary weapon rather than a receptacle for private matters?

Auden's "Spain": End of an Era

On W. H. Auden, to whom one naturally turns first for some sign of how the Oxford poets reacted to the struggle, the Spanish war seems to have had a cathartic effect. Precisely what Auden did or saw during a brief visit to Spain, from January to March, 1937, still remains a mystery, which Stephen Spender, with whom Auden spent some time after his return to England, makes no effort to solve. Having gone to Spain to offer his services as "a stretcher bearer in an ambulance unit," wrote Spender, Auden "returned home after a very short visit of which he never spoke." A short time later, however, and, according to Spender, "as a result of this visit," he wrote and published "Spain," the proceeds of which he donated to the British Medical Unit.[7]

Despite whatever merits "Spain" has as a poetic statement of the Republican case—and Spender and John Lehmann both considered it the finest that had appeared up to that time—it marks the beginning as well as the end of Auden's involvement in the Spanish war. Afterward he neither wrote nor spoke publicly about Spain. "Spain" is also the last poem in which Marxism plays a conspicuous part, and, ironically, it is Auden's most ambitious Marxist poem, being a kind of projection of what a successful socialist revolution might accomplish. But in addition it contains an implicit condemnation of Marxism. When Auden wrote of "the conscious acceptance of guilt in the necessary murder," he was mindful of something besides being in the unhappy position of having to kill your enemy before he killed you. He was cognizant, as well, of the consequences of the Marxist hypothesis which condoned the most reprehensible conduct so long as it advanced the socialist cause. Whether for some reason Auden had never before considered the theoretical or practical applications of the hypothesis cannot be conclusively determined. But that it began to bother him following his return from Spain seems certain. To Spender, "he stated emphatically that political exigence was never a justification of lies."[8]

If "Spain," besides being a defense of the Spanish Republic, works out to its logical conclusion the Marxist hypothesis, which Auden's statement to Spender virtually rejects, is it not possible to consider the poem Auden's renunciation of Marxism? If this contention be permitted, it can only be assumed that his visit to Spain played a prominent part in this rejection. Certainly it is likely that during a war the unsavoriness of a politics of expediency might well be dramatized in some unforgettable manner, as Spender, for example, discovered frequently in Spain. Auden, too, may very well have had his eyes opened for him. What he saw or heard may have precipitated his repudiation of Marxism and eventually of politics altogether.[9]

The severely impersonal quality of "Spain" might almost be taken as presaging Auden's withdrawal from politics. The detachment he maintained throughout the poem amounts nearly to anonymity. We search for signs of his emotional involvement in the struggle, but the search is futile. Auden the politically committed man eludes us. We can only assume he is on the side of truth, but nothing in the poem will substantiate our assumption. This aloofness is no doubt intentional. By remaining detached from the actualities of the struggle, emotional as well as physical, Auden perhaps felt he would be in a better position than many of his contemporaries to envisage the possible historical significance of the Spanish war. Part of the poem is a theoretical analysis of the issues at stake in Spain, and, as such, it is a sort of blueprint of history, past, present and future, with Spain the key to the direction history will follow. Since from his position above the battle Auden surveys rather than participates in the struggle, the poem is not only theoretical and impersonal. It is also almost completely lacking in excitement of a personal kind. In some respects it sounds more like a well-deliberated history lesson in verse than a poem about a revolutionary struggle by a poet who had professed Republican sympathies. In rigidly excluding the personal element—providing, of course, that Auden was still pulling for the Republic when he wrote "Spain"—he may have deprived the poem of the vital force needed to bring to life the rather massive rhetorical analysis. Insofar as the poem is an attempt to work out the Marxist tenet of political exigency and to comment on the pivotal position of Spain in the historical dialectic, it is an interesting exercise in ratiocination. But it fails to convince us that Auden, beyond offering the Republic the nominal support expected of him, could have personally been very much concerned over the fate of Spain. His speculations are dry of emotion; they offer only minimal insight into his feelings.

This is not to say, of course, that "Spain" is entirely academic and uninteresting. On the contrary, Auden's imagery, suggesting the diversity and at the same time the essence of past or present cultures, evokes considerable imaginative excitement. He begins with yesterday :

Yesterday all the past. The language of size
Spreading to China along the trade-routes; the diffusion
    Of the counting-frame and the cromlech;
Yesterday the shadow-reckoning in the sunny climates.

Yesterday the Sabbath of Witches. But today the struggle.[10]

As man triumphed over ignorance and superstition—or merely
substituted new superstitions for old ones—he learned to use
mechanized power, made discoveries about his origin, and
gradually grew less dependent upon antiquity's inviolate
example :

Yesterday the installation of dynamos and turbines;
The construction of railways in the colonial desert;
    Yesterday the classic lecture,
And the origin of Mankind. But today the struggle.

Yesterday the belief in the absolute value of Greek;
The fall of the curtain upon the death of a hero;
    Yesterday the prayer to the sunset,
And the origin of Mankind. But today the struggle.

Auden introduces the idea of struggle ("But today the
struggle") to prepare for the final stanzas in which the actual
demands of the struggle are set down. Beforehand, however,
he divulges the sad truth that humanity will try, if possible, to
avoid becoming involved in another's struggle. Timorousness
often triumphs when men face decisions that require action.
The poet, the scientist, the poor, and the nations each protest
that changing the course of things is not their duty; it is the
concern of the Creator, the Prime Mover, whom they entreat
to intervene :

And the nations combine each cry, invoking the life
That shapes the individual belly and orders

The private nocturnal terror :
"Did you not found once the city state of the sponge,
Raise the vast military empires of the shark
And the tiger, establish the robin's plucky canton?
    Intervene. O descend as a dove or
A furious papa or a mild engineer : but descend."

But their entreaties fail. Their responsibility to Spain cannot be evaded. Life, in the guise of Spain, challenges all who would mold their destiny. Whatever they decide on Spain will shape their future :

And the life, if it answers at all, replies from the heart
And the eyes and the lungs, from the shops and squares of
    the city :
    "O no, I am not the Mover,
Not today, not to you. To you I'm the
"Yes-man, the bar-companion, the easily-duped;
I am whatever you do; I am your vow to be
    Good, your humorous story;
I am your business voice; I am your marriage.

"What's your proposal? To build the Just City? I will.
I agree. Or is it the suicide pact, the romantic
    Death? Very well, I accept, for
I am your choice, your decision : yes, I am Spain."

If they choose to fight, what will they be fighting for? The next section describes the fruits of victory, the rich Tomorrow that is contingent upon victory Today. Auden's Tomorrow, however, seems scarcely more than a return to normal :

Tomorrow, perhaps, the future : the research on fatigue
And the movements of packers; the gradual exploring of
    all the
        Octaves of radiation;

Tomorrow the enlarging of consciousness by diet and
    breathing.

Tomorrow the rediscovery of romantic love;
The photographing of ravens; all the fun under
    Liberty's masterful shadow;
Tomorrow the hour of the pageant-master and the
    musician.

Tomorrow, for the young, the poets exploding like bombs,
The walks by the lake, the winter of perfect communion;
    Tomorrow the bicycle races
Through the suburbs on summer evenings : but today the
    struggle.

When Auden revised "Spain," he deleted a stanza in this
section of the poem which provided a tantalizing picture of the
type of government he foresaw after the victory. On the political content of this stanza, one is tempted to hypothesize that
Auden had been thinking along the lines of some form of
popular democratic government which, as he became less
political, he found somewhat embarrassing and subsequently
omitted :

The beautiful roar of the chorus under the dome;
Tomorrow the exchanging of tips on the breeding
    of terriers,
    The eager election of chairmen
By the sudden forest of hands. But today the struggle.

Finally, Auden repeats the refrain, "But today the struggle,"
and announces what Today's struggle involves. If this poem
sheds any light on Auden's flirtation with Spain and his rejection of Marxism, the last three stanzas provide the most fertile
material for speculation. The first explores the communist
thesis that the ends justify the means, as well as the less serious

but nonetheless exhausting responsibilities of writing the deliberately propagandistic pamphlet and attending the "boring" political meeting, of which, it is worth noting, Auden did neither :

> Today the deliberate increase in the chances of death;
> The conscious acceptance of guilt in the necessary murder;
>   Today the expending of powers
> On the flat ephemeral pamphlet and the boring meeting.

In the revised version of "Spain," Auden describes the increasing "chances of death" as "inevitable," rather than "deliberate." The latter adjective, it seems to me, comes nearer to describing the communist insistence on making the "necessary sacrifice" than the former. "Deliberate" suggests the dedication and willingness with which Cornford, Donnelly, and Bell made their sacrifices to the cause. On the other hand, "inevitable" merely describes the situation in any war; one places oneself, or is placed, in a position where the chances of death multiply. If these connotations exist, then Auden has substituted a rather bland word for one which once had fairly meaningful political overtones. And the substitution suggests the direction of Auden's thought after "Spain." A second alteration in the next line, where in place of "the necessary murder," Auden substituted "the fact of murder," supplies material for further speculation. Certainly "the fact of murder" is applicable to any war, but "necessary murder" carries suggestions of Marxist revolution and deliberate slaughter to secure certain ends. And it was this hypothesis, we recall, that Spender said Auden had found untenable and had rejected.[11]

The next stanza recounts relatively ordinary hardships, but the last is a challenge and a warning and a rejection of the Marxist theory of historic necessity :

The stars are dead; the animals will not look :
We are left alone with our day, and the time is short and
    History to the defeated
May say Alas but cannot help or pardon.

While Auden obviously recognizes the urgency of the Spanish struggle, he also admits that, should the battle be lost in Spain, the struggle will thereby terminate. "History to the defeated/ May say Alas but cannot help or pardon." The true Marxist, as we have seen, would never agree that defeat in Spain meant the end of the struggle. Only a temporary subduing of the forces of socialism and the unfortunate suppression of the Spanish people would be accomplished.[12] Auden, however, in a sense, betrays the Marxist doctrine, for he states, or at least implies, that history cannot be altered. This conclusion, while not exactly defeatist, is certainly far from optimistic, not to mention orthodox.

The composition of the poem is indeed exceptional, and marks a considerable advance from the rather shapeless verse which Auden had written just previously. The logical development of the thought, advancing from Yesterday to Today to Tomorrow, gives it a firm structure and a concentration and a fullness of interpretation to each part. The revised form is even more compact since Auden deleted two stanzas from the middle section, which may have been too long in the original. If my contention is right, however, that Auden's alterations were influenced by his withdrawal from politics, then the canceled stanzas provide some noteworthy evidence. For more than any other stanzas in the poem, they convey the political idealism of the volunteers, the personal identification they felt with the Spanish people, and their hopes for the final triumph of the "people's army" :

> Our thoughts have bodies; the menacing shapes of our
>   fever
> Are precise and alive. For the fears which made us respond
> To the medicine ad and the brochure of winter cruises
>   Have become invading battalions;
> And our faces, the institute face, the chain-store, the ruin
>
> Are projecting their greed as the firing squad and the
>   bomb,
> Madrid is the heart. Our moments of tenderness blossom
>   As the ambulance and the sandbag :
> Our hours of friendship into a people's army.

In 1935, Auden wrote that "poetry is not concerned with telling people what to do, but with extending our knowledge of good and evil, perhaps making the necessity of action more urgent and its nature more clear, but only leading us to make a rational and moral choice."[13] As this statement suggests, Auden, like his colleagues, distrusted the means and ends of propaganda. If he intended to say that poetry may inform but not try to coerce, "Spain" exemplifies his point. Although Auden had theoretically made a choice, he certainly refrained from foisting his decision upon others. Not only is the tone of the poem impersonal, but the language contains none of the slogans or cant words so frequently used to exhort sympathy for the Republic. As an interpretation of the historic position of the Spanish struggle, the poem can be taken as an argument in favor of the Loyalist cause. But "Spain" is not an over-simplification or a romantic idealization of the war. On the contrary, the less pleasant demands of the struggle are clearly stated in the last three stanzas. The poem, then, outlines a course one might follow in regard to the Spanish war. Its value to Auden, however, was that it showed him how impossible such a course was. The close-up view of the inventions of propagandists, the visit to Spain, which he probably realized had been a mistake, and, perhaps, even a premonition that the Republic had already lost the war, all influenced the writing of "Spain," which as a watershed in Auden's development is of inestimable importance.

The Quest of Comrade Spender

Just how far Spender was from identifying himself fully with the Movement, it became possible to reckon in 1935, in the long poem *Vienna,* in which the poet denounced the suppression of the Austrian workers' movement. The poem revealed more than an expression of disgust. It was also the first of several attempts Spender made to relate a "public passion," or experience, to his "private life." In other words, in *Vienna* Spender tried to solve the problem of how to reconcile a public point of view with a private vision. Was it possible to adapt one's own experience so that it would complement or unite with the "impersonal public point of view"? He concluded that the poet's private vision, since it was truthful to his experience, had to prevail over what might be a formidable but nonetheless impersonal expression of the public mind. He later justified this position :

I think I was probably right to enter deliberately into a confused situation, and reject the great simplifications of a deeply felt but impersonal public point of view. The truth of my own existence was that, in spite of everything, I did not plunge myself wholly in public affairs. Therefore a poetry which rejected private experience would have been untrue to me. Moreover, I dimly saw that the conflict between personal life and public causes must be carried forward into public life itself : it was my duty to express the complexity of an ambivalent situation.[14]

Vienna confirmed what several observers, notably John

Lehmann, had discerned in Spender's essay in *New Country,* "Poetry and Revolution" : that as far as literature was concerned Spender was outside the Movement. His belief that personal experience and private emotion were the basis of poetry made it impossible for him to write from the point of view of the wider, less personal emotions of a vast public. Yet all his sympathies were directed toward Marxist means to improve the condition of the masses. Much later, when Spender called his generation a "Divided Generation," he may have been mindful of his own ambivalence. For as a poet he insisted on remaining a kind of anarchist. But as a man, as a public figure, he called himself a Communist. These opposites he never reconciled (indeed, they are irreconcilable), and the "divided mind" remained until he had abjured communist views.

His position as a sort of devil's advocate became more pronounced in the *Destructive Element* (1936), where he implied that the Russian government occasionally suppressed or opposed freedom and truth, and again in his guarded and not always lucid commitment to communism, *Forward from Liberalism* (1937). In the latter book, the ambivalence of his position again became evident. On the one hand, he encouraged the union of the artist and the worker so as to bridge the gulf between their different conditions and backgrounds. Moreover, he suggested that "art must spring, not from the sensibility of a few segregated individuals, but from roots which reach toward the lives of the whole people." He also insisted, however, on the poet's right to present his personal truths and warned that he would betray both himself and society if he forsook those truths to write verse to incite social action. Furthermore, he maintained that the artist had a right to criticize the party and that it was "fatal to sacrifice truth to the functions of discipline and dogma. Unless there is criticism the political movement is liable to fixation." As though to illustrate his point, he condemned the Moscow trials on the ground that the accused had never actually been found guilty of the crimes with which they had been charged.[15]

What *Forward from Liberalism* made clear was that Spender had not advanced very far beyond liberalism and that the freedom he demanded for the artist was not the Marxist concept of social freedom, which only those who immersed themselves in the proletarian struggle could enjoy, but a sort of bourgeois freedom which included preserving certain class privileges and, at least, the concept of artistic individuality. Above all, Spender wanted to maintain what he termed "disinterestedness," that is, some separation between political commitment and artistic creation. While the "Why I'm a Communist" statement in *Forward from Liberalism* had sincerity, it underscored Spender's hesitation to put himself in the position of being under the party's control. His communism was more theoretical than integral; his commitment was based on reason and emotion; however, it did not go the final step and include joining the Party and participating in the revolutionary struggle. Nevertheless, he agreed to support procedures that promised to effect an improved social and economic condition, but not if this required, as Communists insisted it did, becoming a member of the proletariat and writing revolutionary verse for that class. In that case, Spender, perforce, felt he had to refuse in order to continue to function as a poet. He did not join the British Communist Party until after the Spanish war had begun, and only then with very precise reservations.

Spender's membership in the party lasted for a brief and uncomfortable period. Called by Communist Party secretary, Harry Pollitt, to the party's King Street offices one day in the winter of 1936, he was asked if he believed in the cause of the

Spanish Republic. Since he did, Pollitt suggested that he ought to support the Republic by joining the party, since it was the only group in England supporting the Loyalists. Spender accepted the proposition on condition that he be permitted to state his reasons for joining in an article to appear in the *Daily Worker*. He rejected, however, Pollitt's suggestion to go to Spain as a member of the International Brigade, maintaining that he was unqualified for soldiering, but that he would go in any "useful capacity." Much later, in *The God That Failed*, Spender said that it was Pollitt's appeal that pushed him "over into the Communist Party."[16]

While Pollitt's gambit succeeded in bringing Spender into the party, the transition from nonparty to party member scarcely altered his outlook. In one sense, joining the party was simply another way of showing that he supported the Republic. And when his statements appeared in the *Daily Worker*, the party rank and file erupted, questioning the wisdom of turning over a whole page in the midst of a war for an apology by one who was so obviously a "poor risk" to begin with. Not surprisingly, being a Communist gave him no "blessed sense of being right about everything" which most Communists, in his opinion, seemed to feel,[17] and his relations with party members only confirmed his suspicion that they were at the mercy of dogma. It was clear, even before he had made the first of three trips to Spain, that it had been a mistake to join an organization in which he could only be a misfit. Pollitt's gambit could only have unfortunate repercussions, both for the party and the poet.

Spender's first visit to Spain grew out of an assignment from the *Daily Worker* to investigate the fate of the crew of a Russian ship which Italians had sunk in the Mediterranean. This, his first experience working politically with others, amounted to little more than quizzing supposedly informed officials in North Africa and Spain. The investigation finally fizzled out when someone inquiring at the Italian consulate learned that the crew had been interned at Cadiz. The trip did, however, provide some concrete experiences that matured his Republican sympathies. At a pro-Loyalist rally in Tangier, while watching "the poor, the sick, the maimed and the blind —their upturned faces illumined by a smile of hope"—straining to hear the words of the speakers, he was overwhelmed by a sense of "devoutness, a sense of hope."[18] And the sight of busy, noisy revolutionary Barcelona, the streets swarming with people examining the city as though it had just come into their possession (and in some ways it had), convinced him that the war "was between a small, ferocious, reactionary, clinging class, and an awakening, ignorant, combative proletariat, who looked to the Spanish Republic as the realization of their aspirations." Conversely, however, Spender's relations with Communists deteriorated. In one incident, an officious British Communist refused to recognize his passport and did so only after Spender had produced a copy of the *Daily Worker* in which his picture appeared next to an article he had written. "When he had discovered the article in his file of *Daily Workers*," Spender wrote with obvious asperity, "even he could not pretend I was someone else. But I was left wondering what happened to people who had no better evidence than passports with which to prove their identity."[19]

More disagreement with the Communists resulted from his second visit to Spain, the primary purpose of which was to take a position as head of English broadcasting for the radio station of the Socialist Party in Valencia. When the position failed to materialize, he decided to remain in Spain. The experiences during the next few weeks not only provided most of the material for his Spanish war poetry, but also seriously undermined his Communist ties. At brigade headquarters in

Albacete, he learned that Communists controlled most of the units in the brigades. Their method of recruiting members under the guise that they represented the Popular Front of the Republic offended his sense of honesty, and he was shocked to learn that the deception had precipitated at least one tragedy, that of a young British schoolboy who had run away to join the brigade because "he identified the Spanish Republic with the cause of Liberalism." When he discovered that the Communists, with whom he disagreed, were in charge, he told Spender that "the rest of my life is to walk every morning up here [a ridge] until one day I am killed."[20] Six weeks later he was killed, and Spender wrote an article for the *New Statesman and Nation* in which he assailed party functionaries for enlisting men in the brigades without telling them they were Communist-controlled.

Besides sharing George Orwell's suspicions of Communist involvement in the attack on the POUM, Spender coldly assayed the party's practice of attributing countless atrocities to the Francoists, while absolving the Loyalists from similar crimes. It was nonsense to maintain that only one side committed atrocities. In the long run such distortions might irreparably damage the Republican cause, which, since it was already just, would only suffer from falsehoods. He objected to propaganda which painted "friends entirely white and enemies black . . . [and] human events as abstractions." Perhaps Communist "double-thinkers" could say that all elements in the Republican army stood for "freedom, democracy and the Popular Front." But when they found a recalcitrant group, such as the POUM, they speedily labeled it "fascist" and struck it down.[21]

The practice of expedient reclassification of men and events to fit the designs of the party taught Spender two lessons. First, he found that people "have an extremely intermittent grasp on reality"; that is, they see as "real" only those things in which they are interested. Other things, equally "real," they conjure up as abstractions. Thus, enemies become "tiresome, unreasonable, unnecessary theses," but comrades are "real human beings with flesh and blood and sympathies." The second lesson was that he found himself guilty of this sort of thinking. He noted that when he saw photographs of children murdered by fascists, he saw "corpses," but when he heard Franco's supporters describing Republican crimes, he saw "only words." Realizing the probable consequences of thinking this way, he decided that one had to care about all humanity, regardless of classifications. "Unless I cared about every murdered child impartially," he maintained, "I did not really care about children being murdered at all."[22]

During the second visit, Spender spent considerable time seeking the release of his friend Jimmy Younger, who had deserted from the British Battalion and was confined in a brigade prison. Younger, whose war adventures appear in *World Within World* as notes kept by Younger, had been Spender's companion and secretary since 1932. The two men had traveled widely, and their relationship, though often quarrelsome and empty, had developed into one of mutual dependency. But, in 1936, when Spender married a young Spanish scholar he met at an Aid to Spain meeting, Younger, out of pique, joined the Communist Party and went off to fight in Spain with the International Brigade. For both acts Spender assumed responsibility : "Without my influence he would never have joined the Brigade. . . . I had put myself in a position where I could not prevent him from making what I was sure was a mistaken decision."[23]

Younger's letters from Spain confirmed Spender's worst fears about life in the brigades. Besides being at odds with the party, Younger soon learned he was not a soldier, and after the slaughterous battle of Jarama, he no longer felt any "anti-

Fascist anger, but only overwhelming pity." His main objective was to leave Spain before he was killed. Asking that Younger be released from prison (he had deserted a second time during the battle of Guadalajara, saying that he had stomach ulcers) seemed to Spender a reasonable request. But to go further and insist on repatriation to England might be wrong, because others would wish to do the same and thus the discipline of the brigades might be weakened. Being linked with Younger evidently led to some discomfiture, for it was evident to all who knew about their relationship that he was not on the "side of the heroes." However, the argument that hoarding the weak was scarcely justifiable when the brave had spent themselves so well did not prevent him from petitioning for Younger's release. "I could not give up a life which might be saved, and which was of no value in this war."[24] Eventually, and probably partly because of Spender's efforts, Younger and several other intractable comrades were released and returned to England.

Spender's third and final visit to Spain during the war occurred in July, 1937, when he joined a small band of British party writers at an International Congress in Madrid and Valencia. For ten days, intellectuals and writers from several European countries and Russia discussed their attitude toward the Spanish war. However, a more intense discussion soon arose over André Gide's book, *Retour de l'U. R. S. S.*, in which the noted author had made some uncomplimentary remarks about his recent Soviet tour. Because he had written that in Russia he felt "an atmosphere of suspicion and fear which he found distasteful," the Soviets had begun denouncing their one-time comrade as a "Fascist monster" and "a self-confessed decadent bourgeois." This was the kind of volte-face with which Spender was already familiar. The Gide affair split the Congress wide open and threatened to overshadow its principal purpose, namely, to show the world that intellectuals supported the Spanish Republic. Spender's "strongest experience" of the meeting was a "deep dissatisfaction."[25]

Spender had joined the party partly because of a sense of "social and personal guilt" that prompted him to do more than just sympathize with the Republic. And Pollitt's rather surprisingly accommodating offer made the move into the party easy. But, in addition, Spender must have realized that being a party member would facilitate getting Younger out of prison and out of Spain. In the end, however, the generally unhappy relations with Communists turned him against the party but not against the Republican cause, which he continued to call one of "social justice and freedom." What Spender really represented was liberalism. He was convinced it was the source of the real energy behind the Popular Front. When he called the Spanish war a "poet's war," he meant that it was one "in which the individual with his passions and his comparative independence of mechanical methods still counted." But Communists threatened to arrest the expansion of liberal ideals. Basing every action on exigency, they "always had reasons for silencing those who saw more than one point of view." Moreover, he disagreed with the party on the need to criticize its activities, which really amounted to insisting on the freedom to say and write what he wished. The result was that he severed whatever tenuous ties bound him to the Party. As he put it, he reacted against attempting "to achieve communist self-righteousness" by turning away from public activity to "problems of self."[26] It was in this mood that he wrote his Spanish war poems.

Only occasionally in his poems does Spender allude to the themes of freedom and liberty, or to the democratic nature of the war, or to the humanitarian feelings it evoked, all of which he had espoused at Loyalist rallies and praised in numerous articles. And references to politics and ideologies are completely absent. It is, indeed, surprising and a little perplexing to find Spender's Spanish war poetry devoid of the humane and political ideals of the period, especially since he himself had defended these ideals. Surely there were occasions when he found himself in total agreement with the will of the "public mind." Why, then, did he not express some of this sympathy which millions in England, including himself, felt for the struggle of the Spanish people? Why did he maintain a rigid political neutrality when he had joined the Communist Party partly because it supported the Spanish Republic? Why did Spender adopt such a cautious attitude toward an event which, while admittedly often rendered theoretically and in oversimplifications, he had actually experienced himself?

There are at least three possible answers. First, he may have been so distressed by Communist practices in Spain that he was determined not to write anything which the party could possibly use for propaganda. Second, when he wrote his Spanish poems he had dissociated himself from the party, but he was probably much too close to politics and the war to express the political despair he had experienced. Under the circumstances, he might have thought it well to omit references to political experience until the outlines of what had occurred became sharper. The third reason he suggested himself in an article published in the autumn of 1937, following the third trip to Spain and written about the time he was writing his war poems. Here he spoke of being annoyed by the "uncritical and heroic attitude towards the war" which so many poets assumed in their verse. He defined his own attitude : "I myself, because I am not a writer of heroics, have felt rather isolated from the cause and the people I greatly care for, because I do not share this uncritical attitude."[27] The statement suggests that whatever ardor Spender felt for the Republic had noticeably cooled by the end of 1937. Furthermore, it implies that, emotionally, the Spanish themes were no longer so compelling, and that he was forced, so to speak, back upon himself for material, with the result that the war was surbordinated to his personal problems. Simply stated, the larger ideas which the war had set in motion had ceased to inspire him; the only alternative, therefore, was to approach the subject from a personal angle, which, along with other matters, could ignore the reasons why men were fighting in Spain.

Probably because he had been such a strong public supporter of the Spanish Republic, Spender included an apologia in *The Still Centre* (1939) to explain his "unheroic attitude." The explanation is redolent of an argument he had advanced in an essay in *New Country* several years before—that the poet should be concerned only with the particulars of his felt experience and not with the larger, impersonal reality outside himself :

As I have decidedly supported one side—the Republican—in that conflict, perhaps I should explain why I do not strike a more heroic note. My reason is that a poet can only write about what is true to his own experience, not about what he would like to be true to his experience.

Poetry does not state truth, it states the conditions within which something felt is true. Even while he is writing about the little portion of reality which is part of his experience, the poet may be conscious of a different reality outside.[28]

The statement reveals how distrustful Spender had become of verse containing "propagandist heroics," and how determined he was not to write anything that could possibly be construed as either heroic or propagandistic. His intention was to limit his work to the "smaller unheroic truths" of his own experience, which could in no way weaken the Republican cause. He defined his position in the poem, "Port Bou," in which he pictures himself standing alone "at the exact centre" of a bridge, some distance from and yet within earshot of the firing practice going on nearby. The location almost perfectly represents his disengagement :

> And I am left alone on the bridge at the exact centre
>> Where the cleaving river trickles like saliva.
> At the exact centre, solitary as a target.[29]

Spender's Spanish war poems fall into two groups : those that depict the impact of war upon his sensibility and are defeatist; and those that render wartime events objectively, with a few oblique references to the struggle's tragic implications. The first group of poems is indebted for more than their mood and tone to Wilfred Owen. The construction, which in each poem amounts to focusing on one aspect of war and then building around it, was a technique Spender had observed in the verse of the World War I poet.[30] His intention was to create a composite picture of war.

The first group indicates that Spender was as troubled and conscience-stricken about war as Owen. Antiromantic, full of pity for the victims of war, and obsessed with the incalculable losses felt by all humanity, these poems not only embody Owen's ideas, but benefit from a similar solemnity of tone and ironic mood. Like Owen, Spender conceives of war itself as the great destroyer, a kind of impersonal entity indiscriminately brutalizing and maiming humanity. Behind it may lie the interests of the wealthy ("The guns spell money's ultimate reason"), or the desire of a few for power. But whatever it is, it makes a mockery of the individual life. The theme is developed in "Ultima Ratio Regum," in which the death of a soldier, "too young and too silly" to have been important before the war, is ironically compared with the enormous "expenditure" required to destroy him:

> Consider his life which was valueless
> In terms of employment, hotel ledgers, news files.
> Consider. One bullet in ten thousand kills a man.
> Ask. Was so much expenditure justified
> On the death of one so young, and so silly
> Lying under the olive trees, O world, O death?[31]

The anonymous boy lying dead "under the olive trees" was, perhaps, ultimately the victim of an economic system. There was another, however, who suffered the same fate because he had been tricked into fighting by the propagandist's "false promises." This was the coward, more complex and closer to Spender's experience than the hero. In the final moments of life, he seizes "the naked revelatory truth" about himself and dies knowing the agony of his inadequacies. The psychology of "The Coward" might stem from Spender's knowledge of Younger's dilemma, or from a personal experience he had at the front near Madrid when he was invited to fire "a few shots into the Moorish lines. I did this," he wrote later, "positively praying that I might not by any chance hit an Arab." And when he was asked if he wanted to remain at the front, he quickly fabricated a reason to depart. "The fact is that I was frightened and wanted to get away as soon as possible."[32] It is unsurprising, then, to find Spender defending the coward. The villains are the propagandists, not the dead man who experienced "rings of terror" more dreadful than any hero has ever known. For him there can only be everlasting pity:

> I gather all my life and pour
>   Out its love and comfort here.

> To populate his loneliness
>   And to bring his ghost release
> My love and pity shall not cease
>   For a lifetime at least.[33]

This concern for the weak and unheroic extends, in "The Two Armies,"⟨ to all the men who became involved in a struggle they would gladly abandon if they could. The idea— that the exigencies of war act as a sort of neutral agent, or common enemy, and create a bond between combatants of both sides—suggests how really traditional Spender's attitude toward war is:

> Deep in the winter plain, two armies
> Dig their machinery, to destroy each other.
> Men freeze and hunger. No one is given leave
> On either side, except the dead, and wounded.
>
>   .   .   .   .   .
>
> All have become so nervous and so cold
> That each man hates the cause and distant words
> Which brought him here, more terribly than bullets.
>
> From their numb harvest all would flee, except
> For discipline drilled once in an iron school
> Which holds them at the point of the revolver.[34]

The defeatist sentiments here are probably thinly veiled references to what Spender considered the Communist strangle hold on the Republican army, although they are applicable to any war. But Spender had objected to the ruthless methods Communists used to maintain superiority and to force men to stay in the line, among which firing on a "comrade" was not unknown.[35] United by common suffering, these men "cease to hate," and like "tormented animals" practice a "dumb patience" while waiting for the fighting to end. This is the sadness which men at war share:

Finally, they cease to hate : for although hate
Bursts from the air and whips the earth like hail
Or pours it up in fountains to marvel at,
And although hundreds fall, who can connect
The inexhaustible anger of the guns
With the dumb patience of these tormented animals?

Clean silence drops at night when a little walk
Divides the sleeping armies, each
Huddled in linen woven by remote hands.
When the machines are stilled, a common suffering
Whitens the air with breath and makes both one
As though these enemies slept in each other's arms.[36]

The idea of common suffering is personalized in "Thoughts
During an Air Raid." Instead of the sacrifice of the coward or
the dispirited volunteer, the poet contemplates his chances of
dying. The whole effort, Spender contends, "is to put myself/
Outside the ordinary range/ Of what are called statistics" and
to maintain an "impersonal" attitude which can ignore the
hundred killed "in the outer suburbs." Above all, everyone
"should remain separate . . . and no one suffer/ For his
neighbor." That among people subjected to war the thought
of personal survival may predominate over any humane concern for others is entirely possible, and perhaps normal. But
Spender's repulsion forces him to draw too weighty and ironic
a moral : for the unfeeling "horror is postponed . . . until it
settles on him/ And drags him to that incommunicable grief;
Which is all mystery or nothing."[37] The same theme recurs in
"War Photograph." Visualizing this corpse "a photograph
taken by fate," he imagines it withstanding the passage of
time, by maintaining its "wooden continual present," so that
the moment of death will live on forever. While the "years
and fields forget," the "whitened bones" will remember; they

will become part of the human condition and lasting reminders of a terrible sacrifice.[38]

Much less subjective, the second group of poems attempts to express the feelings of a people struggling for their existence. Though hardly heroic, these poems nevertheless hint at the generous emotion and courage and devotion of the Spanish people. In "At Castellon," for example, where a few realistic images successfully evoke the tense atmosphere of a city about to be bombed, Spender's depiction of the "workingman" is warmly sympathetic. Ordered to drive a comrade (presumably the poet) away from the city to a safe place, he lifts the ravaged lines of his face into a smile, "the eyes gleam/ And then relapse into their dream./ Head bent, he shuffles forward/ And in without a word." The man embodies the will of a people "who dared to move/ From the furrow, their life's groove."[39] Examples of partisanship seldom occur in Spender's verse. But what he celebrates here is not a political ideal. Rather, he projects an almost timid admiration for a people who dared to disturb "life's groove." Their idealism and devotion can be short-lived, however, as "Fall of a City" illustrates. The poem presents a pathetic trial of defeat which yokes a whole population to the alien ideology of the victors:

> All the names of heroes in the hall
> Where the feet thundered and the bronze throats roared.
> FOX and LORCA claimed as victory on the walls,
> Are now angrily deleted
> Or to dust surrender their dust,
> From golden praise excluded.
>
> All the badges and salutes
> Torn from lapels and from hands
> Are thrown away with human sacks they wore
> Or in the deepest bed of mind

They are washed over with a smile
Which launches the victors when they win.

All the lessons learned, unlearnt;
The young, who learned to read, now blind
Their eyes with an archaic film;
The peasant relapses to a stumbling tune
Following the donkey's bray;
These only remember to forget.

As in all wars the defeated must at least pretend to embrace
the ideology of the victors, for the success or failure of their
hypocrisy may mean the difference between living and dying;
and if Spender had described the volte-face as facile hypocrisy,
"Fall of a City" would come close to being defeatist. But the
final stanza spares it that appellation. The spark of a once vital
idealism will pass to a new generation; the deception is mere
expediency; beneath the guise a vivid memory exists:

But somewhere some word passes
On the high door of a skull, and in some corner
Of an irrefrangible eye
Some old man's memory jumps to a child
—Spark from the days of energy.
And the child hoards it like a bitter toy.[40]

The rather sharp disparity between Spender's public
statements about Spain and his Spanish war verse, or between
Spender the politician and Spender the poet, was nowhere
more clearly illustrated than in the introduction he wrote to
Poems for Spain, the anthology of Spanish war poetry he
compiled with John Lehmann. Here he defended the role
poets had played in the war, because "the struggle of the
Republic . . . seemed a struggle for the conditions without
which the writing and reading of poetry are almost impossible

in modern society." The poets of the English liberal tradition, he went on, responded to the threat of fascism in Spain with the same hope and energy that their predecessors had once shown in the face of the Napoleonic invasion of Spain. And in such a crisis there was apt to be "a revival of the fundamental ideas" of liberty and freedom. Moreover, he declared there could be "an identity of the ideas of public policy and poetry," and, in this sense, poetry would become really political, for it was "always concerned with the fundamental ideas, either because they are being realized in action, or satirically, to show that they are totally removed from public policy." He concluded, therefore, that the action of the Republic was "the subject of poetry because the Spanish Republican leaders act with an awareness of men's psychological needs, and understanding of the fundamental nature of political ideas, which is a subject worthy of poetry."[41] However worthy they were of poetic treatment, these fundamental ideas were not themes that appealed to Spender. For reasons already stated, he preferred to treat this most political of wars in a personal, nonpolitical, and traditional manner. Instead of fundamental ideas about freedom and liberty, his poems expound upon death, suffering, fear, and concern over the fate of the innocent and cowardly. They are the antithesis of poetry which fuses "public policy and poetry."

C. Day Lewis at Queen's Hall

Of the leading poets of this group, C. Day Lewis was unquestionably the most fully committed Marxist. From 1933 to 1938, he was a member of the Communist Party, which made extremely heavy demands upon both his time and talents. Besides turning out pamphlets and articles for *Left*

Review, he took on several public duties not closely connected in all cases with his writing. He became chairman of the British section of the Communist-controlled International Association of Writers for the Defense of Culture, a regular speaker at Popular Front meetings; and during the Spanish Civil War, along with Harry Pollitt, the Duchess of Atholl, Ellen Wilkinson, he was a familiar figure at rallies for the Spanish Republic. Speaking publicly, a task he always considered burdensome and distasteful, finally was the duty that convinced him he was not suited to be an amateur politician. At Queen's Hall, one night in 1938, while addressing a packed audience at an antifascist meeting, he sensed that what he was saying, although true and for a good cause, had for him a certain unreality. After he had finished, a small voice inside his head whispered, "It won't do. It just won't do."⁴² Either he felt that he was the wrong person to plead such a cause, or he had simply undergone a rather sudden loss of revolutionary zeal. In either case, the Queen's Hall meeting ended his political career. He withdrew from public life to devote himself once again to his writing, which both Edwin Muir and T. E. Lawrence had warned him was steadily worsening.

In his recent biography, *The Buried Day* (1960), Lewis took to task some of the shibboleths of the thirties, that "tricky, darkening decade," when "it seemed possible to hope, to choose, to act, as individuals but for a common end." He pointed out that his generation "had not vision equal to desire," that their hopes for humanity contained a fanciful element which contradicted the reality of the situation. They "lived too much in the future, and in abstractions." Romantic by instinct but classical by intention, they failed to reconcile in their verse the values they revolted from with the values they imagined would exist in a future society. Their poetic response to the world "was rendered ambiguous by this contradition." Apart from this general inadequacy, however, Lewis defended the sense of commitment which he and his colleagues experienced at the time. "I cannot regret that desire to be committed, that positive sense of engagement which our upbringing and the weather of the times combined to produce."[43]

Perhaps one reason why Lewis can write so positively about a period which some of his contemporaries have taken pains to explain away, or have simply refused to discuss, was because his attachment to Marxism was intellectually and emotionally more complete and satisfying than that of some of his friends, notably Spender and Auden. Perhaps because he was more familiar with the Marxist classics than either of the others, he could unreservedly accept the thesis that in order to improve society, capitalism, which was responsible for maintaining class distinctions and the system of profit, would have to be destroyed. And to do this he was prepared to act. But while he agreed with the Marxian premise and saw that communism was as much an economic idea as a moral concept, it was to the latter that he was more attracted. His essay, "Letter to a Young Revolutionary," published in *New Country,* made this point clear. Its serious tone and sense of urgency suggest how much Marxism had moved him.

To the Young Revolutionary, he affirmed the need to be converted to a faith in revolution, and he warned that to make a personal religion out of communism, "a danger to which . . . poets might be particularly susceptible," was to weaken its power to effect change through unity. Therefore, "If you must join yourself to this body, then let it be without reservations, a submission of your self entire."[44] As these bits of advice show, Lewis conceived of communism as a moral code, a religion, whose difficult and relentless demands might tax the individual as severely as those of Christianity. Joining the party was an

act of conversion, requiring the submissive but zealous
devotion to the party's objectives. For Lewis personally, becoming a Communist probably helped fill the void created by his
rejection of Christianity, which, as he suggested in his novel,
The Starting Point,[45] came as a reaction to an ultraconservative
religious background. Marxism offered the "authority" and
"logic" to fill the void, and as a faith it "would make sense of
our troubled times and make real demands on me."[46]

Moreover, it was exhilarating to be part—even an anonymous part—of a revolutionary movement which claimed to
discover reality by acting upon it, rather than by simply
thinking about it. "It appealed . . . to that part of me," he
wrote, "which from time to time revolted against the intolerable burden of selfhood and desired the anonymity of a unit
in a crowd." There was, perhaps, an inevitable romantic
element attached to leaving one's class and siding with the
workers; it gave one a feeling of being in the company of
society's new heroes. And it was their heroic struggle, roman-
tically symbolized by a worker "mounted upon his magnificent tractor," chugging "steadily towards the dawn and the
new world," which joined with Lewis' "natural partisanship
of the underdog to create a picture, romantic and apocalyptic,
of the British worker at last coming into his own." No less
oversimplified was his concept of the class enemies, the
financiers, industrialists, high-ranking Cabinet ministers, and,
of course, the complacent, selfish bourgeoisie. The former, he
reduced to "a sort of composite caricature, simplified and
melodramatic," and the System they represented "personified
itself in a figure of cunning, hypocrisy and spiritual inertia,"
around which were ranged the church, the press, and the law.
The middle classes, upholders of the System, became "figures
of fun, philistines, self deceivers, playing golf and bridge
while their world crumbled beneath them." We can surmise

that Lewis' conversion was less a matter of accepting Marxism
intellectually (that element, of course, affected his decision,
although he has admitted to being skeptical "about a good
deal in Communist theory" at the time) than it was an act of
conscience, a decision based on the belief that communism
offered the greatest hope of putting the world to rights.[47]

Although being a party member simplified some aspects of
his life, it complicated others. Tolerated by his friends and
teaching colleagues, who were perhaps influenced more by the
sincerity with which he held his views than by a generous
wish just to be tolerant, he nevertheless felt uncomfortable in
the anomalous position of occupying two worlds at the same
time. It was too much like sitting on the fence. "It certainly
must have encouraged my own chronic malady, the divided
mind. I never ceased to be aware of the forces in myself
which kept pulling me towards the past, the status quo, the
traditions and assumptions in which I had been brought up."
But as party activities multiplied following the outbreak of
war in Spain, the position of occupying two worlds apparently
bothered him less. Moreover, there was the pull of Spain
itself. Should he volunteer to fight with the International
Brigade? "I believed I ought to volunteer for it, but I lacked
the courage to do so." Eventually, a greater division of mind
preoccupied him. This was the problem of how to reconcile
his social conscience and his conscience as an artist; that is,
how to function as a poet and a politician simultaneously, or
if holding two positions meant doing neither well, which to
surrender. Political duties absorbed much of the time he
normally spent on his art, and he came to resent whatever
disturbed his concentration. "If my poetry had gained by the
enlargement of my interest, it was now losing because of the
many distractions this border life had brought with it." The
decline that Muir and Lawrence had observed confirmed what

he had himself suspected. If he had to choose, the choice should certainly fall on the side of poetry, for there was little hope of becoming more than an amateur political worker, but there was a good chance of developing into a better poet. "My poetic habit," he noted, "seemed hopelessly at odds with a genuine public-spiritedness."[48] The decision to break with public life and eventually with the party came, almost apocalyptically, at the Queen's Hall meeting.

Several factors account for Lewis' decision. One has already been discussed. The demands of the political life cut too heavily into the time needed to develop his art. But, in addition, despite his commitment to Marxism, Lewis—like Auden and Spender—never made what Lindsay, Swingler, and other thoroughgoing Communists called the "necessary leap" from the middle class to the proletariat. Always at least a spiritual member of his class, he refused to turn his poetry into an instrument for advancing the socialist cause. In *A Hope for Poetry* he had maintained that there need not be any separation between the feelings of the artist and the public man, but that the artist must always express first what he felt as a man. It was no good trying to advance Marxist interests by writing "people's poetry" about the dirty fascists and the reactionary conservatives when such sentiments were the mere pap of propagandists. The only political poems he considered of any value, "The Conflict" and "In Me Two Worlds," showed, he says, "the turmoil of the 'Divided Mind'," the tug of war between his heritage and progressive ideals. "The others, with their shrill, schoolboyish derisiveness," demonstrated "the unnatural effort I had to make in order to avoid seeing both sides."[49] The break with the party came when he realized that politics and poetry did not always mix, and that the time devoted to the former, in his case, had had a deleterious effect upon the latter.

Finally, Lewis realized that Marxism was incompatible with his heritage of "romantic humanism." He imagined with what amazement and, no doubt, contempt Communists would receive the news that he had refused to indoctrinate his students with left-wing ideas, and that he had joined the party only after he was earning enough to satisfy himself that he was joining from a "disinterested motive, not as one of the lean and hungry who would personally profit by revolution." In the end, he rejected communism for the same reason Auden and Spender had; he could not subscribe to a doctrine that pursued its ends regardless of the "corrupting and dehumanizing effect of the means employed,"[50] one that so consciously adhered to a policy of opportunism and forced its followers to support its deceptions.

Since Lewis belonged to the Communist Party and supported its role in the Spanish war, it is hardly surprising to find a more positive and heroic note in his Spanish war poems than in those by Spender and Auden. How wholeheartedly he backed the Republic his reply to Miss Cunard's questionnaire made clear: "I look upon it [Spanish war] quite simply as a battle between light and darkness. . . . Both as a writer and as a member of the Communist Party [note that Lewis implies there is a separation between the two roles] I am bound to help in the fight against Fascism, which means certain destruction or living death for humanity." There are no detailed arguments here about opposing the "materialism of the Catholic Church in Spain" and the need to defend the "principle of democracy," with which Spender dressed his answer to the questionnaire, nor is he concerned about what implications a fascist victory in Spain would have for the creative artist, which Auden seemed to be most worried about. Lewis reduces the conflict to a battle "between light and darkness," a point of view certainly common among extreme left-wing writers. It was just such a simplified version of the war, we recall, that both Auden and Spender rejected, either because it allowed for the propagation of lies or because the facts of the conflict simply would not substantiate it. It was, however, the official view of the Communist Party, as the speeches of Pollitt abundantly illustrated, and as a party member Lewis was naturally committed to this view, even if he believed the issues were more complicated. But for purposes of propaganda the "black-and-white" view of the struggle was practically essential. It could be argued that subtle arguments and contradictory details had to be ignored in the interests of making the greatest appeal to the widest audience. The oversimplification was deliberate and done in the belief that to interject complexity into the conflict would only bemuse rather than inflame public opinion.

But besides being the basis for propaganda, the "black-and-white" view provided a ready-made version of the struggle. It permitted a writer to line up on the side he supported and write about the monsters fighting on the other side, a simple exercise in vendetta. As we have seen, Roy Campbell and most of the left-wing poets adopted this attitude to the detriment of their poetry. And Lewis' reply in *Authors Take Sides* indicated that he, too, might write verse in which the struggle of opposites would predominate. However, whether he was a more serious and, indeed, a more experienced poet than so many who seized upon Spain as a subject of poetry, or whether he consciously maintained the separation between what he felt as a man as opposed to what he was supposed to feel as a poet, his Spanish poems show surprisingly few signs of conforming to the party's "black-and-white" view. While his poems are partisan, and in the case of *The Nabara* openly heroic, they contain a subtlety of emotion and action which is not found in mere polemical work. Lewis' diction and imagery are not deliberate or unconscious echoes of the slogans and clichés of the party. And the quiet and yet urgent tone of these poems differs vastly from the noisy hysteria so often found in the verse of his contemporaries. Lewis relied on his own resources for these poems, although the communist vision must have provided the impetus. But the direction they took and the sentiments they contain were not dictated by party interests alone. In each of them the greatest single idea is the need to defend liberty and freedom, and this idea was hardly the exclusive property of the Communist Party. In brief, Lewis may very well have seen the conflict in "black-and-white" terms, as he wrote, but he did not depend exclusively on the particular vision of the party for either the attitude or the content of his poetry. Both were influenced as much by his "romantic humanism" as by the communist vision.

Two of Lewis' poems depict particular phases of the Spanish war, and one, "Bombers," uses a general condition to issue a warning. As an example of the climate of the late 1930's, "Bombers" has a prophetic quality that must have been oppressively moving at the time. The bombing raids, carried out with such destructive efficiency upon unprotected Spanish towns and cities, stirred Lewis as deeply as they did Read, Barker, Spender, and several others. Pictures of the mutilated bomb victims, circulated by partisans on both sides, inspired several poets to protest against man's most inhuman method of destruction. "Bombers" is also a protest. But, in addition, it is an appeal to man's reason, not just to his pity or his desire for revenge. In a well-sustained sequence of images, in which the approaching planes seem like death-carrying angels, Lewis makes convincingly terrifying the experience of being subjected to a bombing raid. The steady build-up from the first inkling of sound to the thundering roar of low-flying planes and exploding bombs is accomplished by paralleling the increasing volume to the growth of a seed. And as the sound grows louder and then materializes as a bombing plane, we realize that this is a life cycle in reverse. A bomb, "conceived in fear," becomes the "iron embryo" which, upon being delivered, brings death instead of life. The juxtaposition of seed and bomb, bees and vermin, and "flares" and "screeching fire," and the inversion of the natural cycle of growth and birth into a death-dealing experience, provide a fine irony :

> Through the vague morning, the heart preoccupied,
> A deep in air buried grain of sound
> Starts and grows, as yet unwarning—
> The tremor of baited deepsea line.
>
> Swells the seed, and now tight sound-buds
> Vibrate, upholding their paean flowers
> To the sun. There are bees in sky-bells droning,
> Flares of crimson at the heart unfold.
>
> Children look up, and the elms spring-garlanded
> Tossing their heads and marked for the axe.
> Gallant or woebegone, alike unlucky—
> Earth shakes beneath us : we imagine loss.
>
> Black as vermin, crawling in echelon
> Beneath the cloud-floor, the bombers come :
> The heavy angels, carrying harm in
> Their wombs that ache to be rid of death.
>
> This is the seed that grows for ruin,
> The iron embryo conceived in fear.
> Soon or late its need must be answered
> In fear delivered and screeching fire.

The final stanza poses a question, and although the imagery is still effective, the stanza becomes rhetorical. The question of whether to choose life or death seems flat; it might have been shouted from a political platform :

Choose between your child and this fatal embryo.
Shall your guilt bear arms, and the children you want
Be condemned to die by the powers you paid for
And haunt the houses you never built?[51]

In the largest context, the poems that depict particular
phases of the war celebrate the defense of freedom. However,
to make this theme concrete, Lewis uses two groups of people:
volunteers who fought in Spain because they felt they could
prevent a second world war, and a group of Basque seamen
who sacrificed themselves for their belief in freedom. Lewis'
estimate of the value of the volunteer's role in Spain may
have been partly formed by his own lack of courage in taking
up arms for the Republic, or by his lack of knowledge of the
realities of life in the International Brigades. Unlike Spender,
whose antiwar attitude was intensified by his visits to Spain,
Lewis remained in England and, if "The Volunteer" reflects
his attitude, saw the volunteers as men who had dedicated
themselves to the cause of freedom. The poem begins by
defending their decision to fight:

> Tell them in England, if they ask
> What brought us to these wars,
> To this plateau beneath the night's
> Grave manifold of stars—
>
> It was not fraud or foolishness,
> Glory, revenge, or pay;
> We came because our open eyes
> Could see no other way.
>
> There was no other way to keep
> Man's flickering truth alight:
> These stars will witness that our course
> Burned briefer, not less bright.

However, their idealistic dedication to preserve "man's flick-
ering truth" has meanings which transcend the immediate
crisis. Defending freedom abroad is tantamount to defending
it at home. The English volunteer foresees that victory in
Madrid will one day mean victory in England too:

> Beyond the wasted olive-groves,
> The furtherest lift of land,
> There calls a country that was ours
> And here shall be regained.
>
> Here is a parched and stranger place
> We fight for England free,
> The good our fathers won for her,
> The land they hoped to see.[52]

These verses pose a strange ambiguity. Does Lewis mean that,
with victory, Spain will realize the same democratic blessings
that England enjoyed? I think not, although the verses may
convey this idea. More likely, he was echoing the familiar
belief that Spain offered socialists an opportunity to demonstrate to the world their devotion to "freedom," and that
whatever strides they made in Spain would stimulate the
growth of socialism throughout the world. Looked at from
this angle, England is a foreign country ("a country that was
ours"), insofar as the goals the volunteers support and went
to Spain to defend have not yet been realized at home. They
are the vanguard of a small but growing army of partisans
for "freedom," not necessarily "communist freedom," or more
vaguely, "socialist freedom," although considering Lewis'
sympathies in 1938 we must assume that he meant something
of this sort. But the verses are too vague to support an interpretation this definite. All that is finally certain is a kind of
prophecy of a new integration, no more. This is the main

weakness in the poem, which captures the better side of the volunteer's participation in the war. After hearing their choice defended, we have only a hazy notion of what it is they are fighting for.

Lewis' magnum opus is certainly *The Nabara,* which is based on an episode described in G. L. Steer's *The Tree of Gernika* (1938). It is a long, sustained narrative, written in ten-line stanzas and divided into three phases. The simple yet dramatic quality of the story of the Basque seamen who outwit a rebel cruiser until a freighter loaded with precious ammunition can be safely led into port ideally illustrates the struggle for human freedom. Indeed, the meaning of the event was so well dramatized that the moralistic verses at the beginning and end of the poem, which provide a sort of frame for the story, seem slightly inflated and superfluous. The verses are, however, vehicles of condemnation as well. Lewis contends that freedom is more deeply felt in the hearts and acts of simple men than in the dubious words and transactions of statesmen :

> Freedom is more than a word, more than the base coinage
> Of statesmen, the tyrant's dishonoured cheque, or the
>   dreamer's mad
> Inflated currency. She is mortal, we know, and made
> In the image of simple men who have no taste for carnage
> But sooner kill and are killed than see that image
>   betrayed.[53]

Once the point is made that the adventure is an example of the thesis that "freedom is more than a word," Lewis stops editorializing, except for some comments in the second phase about nonintervention.

The story itself receives the careful attention due a major naval encounter. Lewis names the Basque trawlers that escort the *Galdames,* "with her cargo of nickel and refugees," from Bayonne to Bilbao. He describes the seamen's skill at probing the treacherous seas in a heavy mist and "chill North-Wester." Suddenly the trawlers come face to face with the rebel cruiser *Canarias,* "a giant in metal," which has just seized an Estonian freighter loaded with arms for the Republic. Since the freighter presumably carried arms from Russia, it is a little surprising to find Lewis referring to the senders as "exporters of death," which indeed they were, but at the same time the Republic depended almost completely on Russian supplies for its existence. The second phase of the action describes how one of the Basque trawlers daringly snatches away the freighter while the *Canarias* is busy demanding the surrender of the *Galdames.* But when the ruse is detected, the *Canarias* opens fire on the three little ships that remain. Although considerably outgunned, they return fire, until at day's end only one, the *Nabara,* is still afloat. The third phase recounts the Nabara's refusal to surrender, even when the handful of seamen alive face the prospect of almost certain death. Finally, forced to abandon their burning ship, they take to a "matchwood boat," still attempting to resist capture by hurling hand grenades at a launch that has set out from the *Canarias.*

This somewhat idealized picture of a heroic people fighting for freedom suggests the intense feeling among writers in England for the Spanish people. Their self-sacrifice, their generous devotion to their cause, their role as "underdog," which must have appealed to Lewis, made them an ideal symbol of freedom-loving humanity, although no more moving perhaps than the international volunteers. Lewis made a conscious effort to minimize the part that politics played, or that the merely topical occupied, and focused primarily on the cause of human freedom, which is a timeless and politically neutral literary theme.

Louis MacNeice: A "Tripper's" Return

Although Louis MacNeice was closely associated with both Spender and Auden (with the latter he collaborated on *Letters from Iceland*), he made political anonymity as distinctive a quality of his work as his colleagues made socialism a part of theirs. Before 1936 MacNeice apparently felt no concern over the "injustices" of the capitalistic system, nor any pity for the entrapped workers. Though unpleasant and regrettable, such matters simply failed to interest him. And the fact that it was considered fashionable in certain circles to write about unemployed mill hands and the social revolution only strengthened his determination to avoid social themes altogether. A responsible poet, he felt, should select only that material which interested him personally, not what was merely popular; he "may write about anything provided that that thing matters to him to start with."[54] The value of the work done by Auden and Spender, he believed, went beyond diagnosing society's sickness and recommending remedies. Their verse was important because it represented an attempt to fuse a personal and a public philosophy; it was neither a romantic depiction of the proletarian struggle nor propaganda. Before 1936, however, MacNeice's verse had more in common with the Georgians than with the poets of the Movement. It was the fanciful world of childhood and the pleasures and joys of a life uncomplicated by economic concerns that preoccupied him. Only occasionally did he seem aware of the impermanence of his world :

> For we are obsolete who like the lesser things
> Who play in corners with looking-glasses and beads[55]

The beginning of something akin to a social consciousness in MacNeice's work can be traced to an almost accidental involvement in the Spanish war. In *Autumn Journal* (1938), a rambling, facile commentary on public and private events, he recounts a visit that he and some other "trippers" made to Spain on the eve of the war. Typical tourists, they are half bored with the sights and inclined to find fault with the normal inconveniences of travel. In Seville, the bullfights are clumsy; "Ávila was cold/ And Segovia was picturesque and smelly." They complain about the Spanish cigarettes, the unprofessional character of businessmen, the rainy weather, and blame everything on the low standard of living. The newspapers, "with their party politics and blank invective"—noisy but ominous symptoms of the tensions seething beneath the surface—only amuse them. They fail to perceive the fate awaiting Spain even as they stand, transfixed, watching a mob divest a church "of its images and aura." The terrible prophecy of the desecration eludes them, and they depart ignorant of the role Spain will assume in their lives:

> And next day took the boat
>   For home, forgetting Spain, not realizing
> That Spain would soon denote
>   Our grief, our aspirations;
> Not knowing that our blunt
>   Ideals would find their whetstone, that our spirit
> Would find its frontier on the Spanish front,
>   Its body in a rag-tag army.[56]

As the lines quoted above suggest, the naïveté and indifference of the "trippers" finally vanished, and Spain turned

out to be the "whetstone" of their "blunt ideals." What
happened to MacNeice, according to John Lehmann, was
that he drew closer to the Movement. The observation is
sound, but Lehmann does not clarify the role of the Spanish
war in effecting the change. Was the appeal, in his case, political or humanistic? On what did his interest in the struggle
center? Did it presage, for example, a change in his poetic
views, or perhaps in his political outlook?

Considering the last question first, we can assume that the
war neither strengthened nor weakened MacNeice's political
beliefs, which, as we have seen, hardly affected his poetry, and
can only be considered to have been vaguely left, an observation which MacNeice himself corroborated in an amusing
dialogue with his "Guardian Angel," published in *I Crossed
the Minch* (1938). To a question concerning his principles, he
replied: "My sympathies are, I suppose, Left. . . . On paper
and in the soul. But not in my heart or my guts. On paper—
yes. I would vote Left any day, sign manifestos, answer questionnaires. Ditto, my soul. My soul is all for moving towards
the classless society. But unlike Plato, what my soul says does
not seem to go. There is a lot more to one than soul, you
know." What appeared to keep the soul from realizing its
objectives through him was, quite simply, snobbery, snobbery
of class and snobbery of property. "With my heart and my
guts I lament the passing of class. . . . [and] a man for me is
still largely characterized by what he buys." But can these be
your only occupations? asks the Guardian Angel. "I cannot
say," he answers, "but it seems . . . so likely . . . that I should
be ashamed to join any crusade for the betterment of the
world, knowing . . . that my motives would again be snobbish,
even if the snobbery is inverted."[57] That he was prepared to
let his soul have its say, but at the same time see to it that his
heart and guts retained their superiority was suggested in his

vague reply in *Authors Take Sides,* where a kind of mercenary self-interest collides against political idealism. "I support the Valencia Government in Spain. Normally I would only support a cause because I hoped to get something out of it. Here the reason is stronger; if this cause is lost, nobody with civilized values may be able to get anything out of anything." While the statement indicates MacNeice's determination to remain outside politics and, perhaps, even snugly encased in a comfortable class snobbery, it does nevertheless suggest that he had at least responded to the war. If that response seems to be nonpolitical, was it humanistic?

The answer lies in Part XXIII of *Autumn Journal,* written following a wartime visit to Catalonia, in which the changes the war had produced in Spain are optimistically described. This time there is nothing frivolous or superficial about Mac-Neice's reaction. Barcelona at war, its people worn down but not dispirited by war's heavy demands, has affected the mood of the poet:

> The road ran downhill into Spain,
>   The wind blew fresh on bamboo grasses,
> The white plane-trees were bone-naked
>   And the issues plain:
>
>   .   .   .   .   .
>
> When I reached the town it was dark,
>   No lights in the streets but two and a half millions
> Of people in circulation
>   Condemned like beasts in the ark
> With nothing but water around them:
>
> But still they manage to laugh
>   Though they have no eggs, no milk, no fish, no fruit,
>   no tobacco, no butter
> Though they live upon lentils and sleep in the Metro,

Though the old order is gone and the golden calf
Of Catalan industry shattered :
The human values remain, purged in the fire,
And it appears that every man's desire
Is life rather than victuals,

Life being more, it seems, than merely the bare
Permission to keep alive and receive orders,
Humanity being more than a mechanism
To be oiled and greased and for ever unaware
Of the work it is turning out, of why the wheels keep
turning;
Here at least the soul has found its voice
Though not indeed by choice;[58]

While MacNeice found inspiration in the permanence of human values in the midst of war, his kinship with the Spanish people never went beyond a vague general sympathy. For example, he never supported the Republic in any political sense, probably because he was as aware as Spender was of the hazards of mixing propaganda and poetry. A lie, however useful in politics, he wrote shortly after the war ended, "hampers artistic vision. Systematic propaganda is, therefore, foreign to the artist insofar as it involves the condoning of lies. Thus, in the Spanish Civil War some English poets were torn between writing good propaganda (dishonest poetry) and honest poetry (poor propaganda). I believe firmly that in Spain the balance of right was on the side of the government; propaganda, however, demands either angels or devils. This means that in the long run a poet must choose between being politically ineffectual and poetically false."[59] MacNeice's choice was clearly made on the side of "honest poetry." His interest in Spain centered in the will of the people to maintain, even under the most inhuman conditions, a sense of human dignity, not in the conflict of opposing ideologies, and certainly not in the purely political side of the struggle.

Conclusions

IT IS EVIDENT THAT MOST OF THE BRITISH POETRY OF THE
Spanish Civil War has far more historic value than intrinsic
literary worth. Only a few Spanish war poems can compare
favorably, either technically or thematically, with the best
poems written about the two world wars. Yet their weaknesses
must not dim their importance as a repository—at once exciting, hopeful, and sad—of the social and political attitudes of
a generation of British poets. If we have enough charity to
make allowances for all the verbal pyrotechnics and the technical pretentiousness, as well as for the overt oversimplifying
and romanticizing of the struggle, which are the chief faults
of their work, we can, perhaps, agree that collectively these
poets implemented their belief in the Spanish Republic by
creating a literature that is at least morally earnest if it is not
technically distinguished. Besides intensifying their political
beliefs, the Spanish struggle moved their consciences as men;
it aroused in them a greater concern for humanity. Backing
the Republic transcended just supporting the liberal-demo-
cratic tradition represented by the Azaña government; it
meant being on the side of social justice and progress; it meant
defending civilization itself. As poets, their duty to mankind
was clear, and if it was manifested in ringing challenges to the
conscience of Western humanity, it was not because they had

252

abjured their responsibilities as poets but because they were aware of them.

There is considerable acumen in Spender's assertion that he and his colleagues "may . . . have written, during the Spanish Civil War, the English poetry of a just democratic war against Fascist tyranny." The description is applicable to the work of nearly all the poets mentioned in this study. Most did not even visit Spain. They knew little or nothing about the internecine feuding among the political groups supporting the Republic, and they relied—probably too much—on the announcements of the Popular Front for information about the struggle. Moreover, they probably acceded too readily to the vision that the Republic represented "democracy" (it did, of course, but they accepted it dogmatically, and not after proper reflection), that the choice was between fascism and "democracy," and that their duty was to support the Republic. When duty demanded attending or speaking at Popular Front rallies, or at the "boring meeting," or, as was more often the case, employing their talents to write the "flat ephemeral pamphlet," or verses acclaiming the Republican cause, they responded. Forsaking the traditional privacy of the artist, and perhaps even artistic ambitions for the "democratic" cause was a costly but necessary sacrifice. Among other things, it meant collaborating with political parties and individual politicians more closely than ever before. If acting for the public interest conflicted with the responsibility they felt toward their art, there was at least the consoling and encouraging factor that the right action might help restore democracy in Spain, and deter the Fascist dictators from further aggression.

2.

Now that we can see the Spanish war from the other side in time, and have been forced to view it through the dark prisms of Arthur Koestler and George Orwell, and have heard that Stalin betrayed the Republic and turned Spain into a "convenient killers' lane" for political unreliables, and that after the war he even went so far as to liquidate many of the Russians and Spaniards who presumably knew too much about what had happened in Spain, it is tempting to conclude that these poets were merely docile pawns in a power struggle, that they were duped by cynical politicians, and that their ideals turned out to be ideological chimeras. Whatever truth this conventional literary picture of the Spanish war may possess—and its most recent supporter, Julian Symons, is a most knowledgeable critic of the thirties[2]—it seems to me to fail to take into account two important matters: first, the knowledge that was not available to most people, including the poets, at the time of the war; second, the possibility of retaining a belief in the justice and purity of the Spanish war despite whatever pernicious schemes any political group might have tried to carry out in Spain. Who among these poets, even among the Communists, was perspicacious enough to foresee, in 1936–37, the outcome of the war, or to suspect how much falsehood and distortion existed beneath the surface? And even when a few, such as Auden and Spender, found instances of dishonesty or ruthlessness, their first reaction was to assume that the situation probably made a certain amount of persecution and chicanery unavoidable. Of course they were disturbed, and rebelled against the "deliberate lie," but they also went on supporting the Republic. At least for awhile, even in Spender's case, a few wrongs did not soil the just cause. Condoning what seemed impure was not simple self-deception either. Most of these poets were not completely ingenuous. If war contained the sordid, it also promised to win what was worthwhile, and if the latter had to be achieved partly by ignoble means, then this was only one of many paradoxes of war.

Contributing to the legend that these poets somehow failed to act responsibly during the Spanish war is the belief that in the long run they were ineffective. For all their foresight and concern and sacrifice, the Spanish Republic did lose and six months later the Second World War did begin. Had they, then, expended themselves for a lost, or as it is often called, an illusory cause? It would be going beyond the bounds of this study to go into the reasons for the defeat of the Spanish Republic, except to say that, at bottom, they were mostly political and that the burden of guilt must be shared partly by the democracies and not by Russia alone. But despite the loss of the Republic and the failure of these poets to effect social change, it seems to me completely unfair to dismiss them, ex post facto, as poets who betrayed their functions as poets, or who abjured their responsibilities as men. The lost battle does not lessen the really generous idealism and industry and hope and purpose that they put into it. To scorn their defense of the Republic is to mock their belief in humanity at a time when it was above all needed. To berate their sense of purpose, which was predicated on the belief that the individual could alter the course of events, is to belittle their determination to confront fascism when appeasement was winning applause. Certainly, it can be said that those who fought in Spain did so primarily for political reasons. But they were also conscious of their role as defenders of Europe's spiritual and cultural tradition. In the largest sense, Ralph Fox, Charles Donnelly, John Cornford, Christopher Caudwell, and Julian Bell died

for this tradition. Those who never ventured to the battlefields made fewer and, of course, less important sacrifices, but
they nonetheless responded to the challenge of their time by
sacrificing, in some degree, their artistic hopes for the sake of
mankind. The loss of the Republic reflects no discredit upon
their participation in the struggle to preserve it.

The only illusions a few of these poets had concerned the
morality of politicians and political parties, or their ability to
combine the functions of poet and politician. The point often
overlooked by commentators on the Spanish war is that the
ideals these poets believed in and, in some instances, fought
for, were and are noble ones. In the widest sense, it is of little
importance whether the poet happened to be a Communist or
not. If a Communist, he was most likely a dedicated Marxist,
and consequently not apt to object to the operations of the
NKVD in Spain or to the infiltration of Communists into
military and governmental positions. And above all, he was
under no illusions about respecting the rights of uncooperative
groups like the POUM. If he was a non-Communist, he either
cooperated with Communists, or dissociated himself from
organizations in which Communists were influential and supported the Republic as an individual. As for the claim that the
Soviets betrayed the Spanish Republic—and the claim has
been vigorously supported—it is still a moot question whether
the real betrayer was not the democracies, England, France,
and even the United States, all of whom hid behind nonintervention policies while Russia became the only major nation to
assist the Republic.[3] Furthermore, the Loyalists were able to
fight as long as they did only because Russia sent supplies,
whether or not for Stalin's own benefit. It is not so simple to
contend that the Spanish Civil War produced a crop of dis-
illusioned idealists, for among the Communists there was only
Koestler, and among the socialists and liberals there were only

a few, such as Orwell, who continued to support the Republicans even while he somewhat unreasonably excoriated the Communists. The point is, there were few among these poets who really felt that they had been betrayed, that they had been duped or cheated by the Soviets or anyone else.[4] Those mainly responsible for the belief that Stalin betrayed the intellectuals who supported the Republic are Koestler, who, as a dissident, was interested mostly in justifying his defection, and Orwell, who, by his own admission, was politically naïve when he joined the POUM and who, after all, saw the war only in Catalonia.

3.

But, it might be asked, did not Auden, Spender, and Day Lewis experience something like betrayal when, during the Spanish war, they discovered that the cause they were espousing was being sullied by political chicanery despite their own good intentions? And did they not declare that a philosophy that pursued its ends by the most reprehensible means had become intolerable? And was not this nearly an open condemnation of Marxism, and hence an admission that they had been mistaken, if not actually betrayed? While the answer to each question is yes, there is some doubt about whether their encounter with Marxism really ended with a feeling that they had been betrayed, or whether, during the period of the Spanish war, they had learned not only that war was unpleasant, but that Marxism made unusually heavy demands in a time of crisis, demands that afforded more insight into the movement they had aligned themselves with than they had ever had before. In other words, having been forced into closer relations with Marxists at all levels, did they finally comprehend that there was a difference between professing to be a Marxist and actually being one? If so, was not their experience more like a revelation than a betrayal?

As much as their vociferous colleagues, Auden, Spender, and Day Lewis wanted to be useful, and their contributions to the cause were considerable. Auden went to Spain, at least with the intention of volunteering for ambulance duty, wrote "Spain" and donated the receipts to Spanish Medical Aid. Spender joined the Communist Party, made three trips to Spain, spoke at Popular Front rallies, attended Writers' Conferences, and in a spate of articles published between 1936 and 1939 defended the legitimacy and morality of the Madrid government. He celebrated the heroism of the international volunteers, praised the meticulous care with which the Republic had handled Spain's art masterpieces, and confirmed the agony of Spain which Picasso had epitomized in *Guernica*. In writing alone, Spender did more than either Lewis or Auden to advance the Loyalist cause. Lewis, already a Communist when the war started, performed, until the spring of 1938, innumerable tasks for the party and the Republic, the extent of which can be measured partly by the artistic sacrifices they incurred. Besides these specific duties, they all lent their names to pro-Loyalist groups, appeared at demonstrations sponsored by the Popular Front, signed petitions, and answered questionnaires.

But, ironically, it was this very willingness to sink their individualities in the collective forces of politics that led ultimately to a repudiation of the political life. An event as momentous as the Spanish war was needed to push them into the noisy hurly-burly world of mass demonstrations and expediency. But they nevertheless accepted it all hopefully, although apprehensively, and gave it their full support. How else could they hope to be really effective in the struggle to save civilization from fascism? The sacrifice in terms of time lost to their art was of minimal consequence if collective action worked to deter the enemy. The world of political exigency and intrigue, however, proved to be as disruptive and disconcerting to Lewis, Spender and Auden as the sudden embroilment in warfare had been to Cornford, Bell, and Donnelly. Somewhat at a loss as to how they could make themselves useful, they rather docilely obeyed the whims and crude directives of party leaders, who generally lacked the insight to use them and other intellectuals effectively. Gradually, they lost faith in their abilities as amateur politicians, partly because they objected to the ethics of expediency and the moral duplicity of the propagandists and parties with whom they worked. They became increasingly skeptical of the choice they had made and, finally, they withdrew completely from political life. Auden retired first, in 1937, and Lewis and Spender followed not long afterward. And in each case, the reason for withdrawing was the same: the belief that a worthy goal could be attained without having to resort to cynical and corrupting means, which in the long run could only damage the goal.

It seems evident now that the slogans and rigid ideology and opportunism of the extreme Left, which they had at one time treated with "considerable levity or scepticism,"[5] had finally become too powerful for their separate individualities as writers, and that unless they removed themselves from the political realm quickly they, like Orestes, would be pursued forever "by Furies of Ends and Means, Propaganda and Necessity."[6] Withdrawal was in no sense a surrender, or an admission that fascism could not be contained. It was done partly in the interests of self-defense, to decide how their own beliefs, which had grown firmer as a result of their political experience, might be made more effective. That their retirement from politics in no way signified that they were abandoning the Republican cause both Spender and Lewis confirmed at the time.

All that really happened was that a close-up view of political life had led to shedding some political illusions. Left-wing politics proved to be too potent for them to accept, and they consequently made some revaluations about how social change could best be effected. To say, then, that they were betrayed one has to assume that they had been deliberately hoodwinked, tricked, or misled. That they were mistaken about Marxism there can be no doubt. But when they became aware of their own errors, they readjusted their views, which they could not have done prior to the Spanish war, because it was only during that war that they discovered what political commitment really involved.

If we consider the war as a crucible which tested the charges that Cornford, Caudwell, and Bell made against Auden, Spender, and Day Lewis, we must concede that it verified most of their accusations. As a group, they resisted placing their talents as poets at the disposal of propagandists or political groups; they scrupulously put their art above politics, and it remained, as Caudwell had predicted, bourgeois rather than revolutionary, by which he meant that they would continue to write for a middle-class audience rather than for the "people." Neither did they declass themselves to achieve that amalgamation with the workers which, according to the Marxists, was the talismanic rite that permitted one to write as a true revolutionary. They remained what they had essentially always been: middle-class intellectuals, with a penchant for social change and all that promised improved conditions, whose poetry alternately showed a revolutionary zeal and respect for art, but who stood outside the class struggle and hence maintained that a division between life and art existed.

4.

That Spender, Auden, and Lewis were primarily poets, not politicians, and that they were inspired first of all by the Loyalist cause and not Marxism, their Spanish war poems abundantly show. In verse free from political slogans and cant words, polemics and dialectics, they consciously strove to avoid the pitfalls of the political poem. Nonconformists in both form and content, they insisted, even under the pressure of war, on the artist's inviolate right of choice. And perhaps it is for this reason that their Spanish war poems, generally, lack a feeling of *élan*. Auden's "Spain," despite the poet's efforts to impregnate the struggle with meaning, is at bottom a denial of Marxism. The intellectual vigor, the cosmic sweep, and the vitality of metaphor all help to transform the struggle into something unprecedented and even magnificent. But Auden seemed so painfully aware that, although the balance of justice resided with the Republic, the struggle would demand tremendous sacrifice, and that ideals could not substantially lessen the pain of that sacrifice. At best, "Spain" commented on the historical and social significance of the war, but at the center of the poem exist a vacuity, an emotional void, an absence of commitment, which, paradoxically, helps to explain its partial failure as well as its reputation as a poem considerably above the caliber of most Spanish war verse. Auden shunned the excesses of propagandist verse, but he did not conceal, even under the grand metaphorical layers, an emotional and perhaps even an intellectual inadequacy to deal with the Spanish war. The studied, hypothetical content and elegant form arouse speculation, but the poem never suggests that Auden is doing more than stating an argument. We are intrigued by his brilliant insights, but they leave us unmoved.

Lewis' poems, though decidedly more partisan in feeling than Auden's, are almost politically neutral. They celebrate universal themes suggested by the war : man's irrepressible desire for freedom, the cruelty involved in war, and the idealism that prompts men to volunteer to fight in another country. Even in "The Volunteer," his tribute to the British members of International Brigades, Lewis avoided assigning to them any definite political motives that would explain their presence in Spain. The only certainty is that the volunteers presage a new social integration and greater freedom. *The Nabara* celebrates the same theme : freedom is more than a word, a belief decidedly nonpartisan and timeless.

The exclusion of political ideology from war verse is best illustrated in the case of Spender. For personal reasons, he was perhaps more deeply involved in the Spanish war than either Auden or Lewis, although for him politics counted too. But despite this Spender rigidly omitted from his war poetry all but what was "true to his own experience," which disallowed any overt acclamation of the Republican cause with which he was so closely associated in public life. Most of his poetry, therefore, is an examination of the human predicament, the hopeless confusion of men caught up in the chaos of war and their inability to adapt to it or escape from it. Thus, its negative quality is unmistakable, and its inchoate antiwar sentiment is redolent of Owen and Sassoon. Only the "smaller unheroic truths" of Spender's experience in Spain come through, and too often they are somewhat commonplace thoughts on suffering, fear, and death. In "Fall of a City," the one poem where the ideological meanings of the war emerge, Spender adumbrated the hope that flowered even as the tragedy of defeat overtook the Republicans. But since only this poem and "At Castellon" are ones in which Spender turned away from the "smaller unheroic truths," and since neither does more than suggest the idealistic side of the war, we must conclude that Spender was—quite rightly—asserting his belief in the inviolability of the artist and his art. That is, Spender must have assumed that an examination of ideals or aims, regardless if he happened to agree with them, lay outside his immediate experience and was therefore unsuitable for poetry. Such a view, while it no doubt kept Spender from writing the deliberately propagandistic poem, scarcely allowed him all the materials he needed to write circumspectly about this most idealistic of all wars.

5.

The most conspicuous weakness of the war verse written by poets who remained in England during the conflict is its contemporaneousness. In their opinion, so many and so urgent were the immediate needs—the need to ridicule nonintervention out of existence, the need to warn the world of the spread of fascism—that there was no time left to ponder anything except the most pressing demands of the moment. Eager to function as Cassandras whose prophecies would be heeded, they mistakenly ignored two matters that reduced their influence both as prophets and poets. First, they knew almost nothing about warfare; and second, and more important, they had almost no idea of the complex origins of the Spanish war. As a result, they depended for the content of their verse upon the press, or more often upon experienced propagandists like Charles Duff, Willi Muenzenberg, and H. C. O'Neill. Instead of being the shapers of opinion, they became the ones whom opinion shaped. What the time needed, they felt, was not interpretations or personal reactions to war so much as concise directives about what had to be done to effect a Republican victory in order to prevent world catastrophe. Toward this end, they argued that their verse made a major contribution.

Obviously, they ignored C. Day Lewis' admonition that one must write only about what one experiences first as a man rather than as a poet. And the poems of Gawsworth, Mallalieu, Heinemann, Richardson, Warner, Lindsay, Rickword, and Howard illustrate the difficulty of attempting to fit one's poetic talent into a rigid political movement. Nearly always the result was either verse journalism or rhetoric, which sometimes unashamedly echoed the oratory of Popular Front speakers, or pilfered their slogans and clichés. Almost everything about it was synthetic. Grafting onto a poetic structure the inflexible dogmatism of their outlook on Spain proved disastrous. Seldom were slogans successfully assimilated and transposed into the substance of poetry.

6.

Unlike their colleagues in England, Cornford, Donnelly and, occasionally, even Wintringham expressed some antiwar feeling alongside the expected doctrinaire political pronouncements. When the experience of war became the raw material of their verse, the result was poetry that conveyed an intense and sincere emotion, often in language that was at once simple and lucid and yet capable of suggesting the emotional overtones of the situation. In this sense, at least, there was a unity of word and deed in their best poetry. Cornford and Donnelly, besides showing more technical promise than Wintringham and most of the others, alone seemed capable of transcending the particular and the demands of political orthodoxy and attaining something like universal significance in their verse. As seminal poets they demand attention.

But because the Spanish struggle was not just an ordinary

war for the Marxist poets, they felt the need to reinforce its peculiar meanings. They believed they had to explain not only their part in the war. But, more importantly, they believed they had to justify its tremendous cost. To this end, they often turned their verse into a platform for a political ideology, and it was when they tried to vindicate or sanctify the Republican cause, which they regarded as embodying the goals of communism, that their poetry was in danger of becoming a treatise. For supporting a conflict by ideological reasons meant subsuming its meaner aspects in favor of its supposedly more positive ones. It meant distorting an ugly experience so that it became something wholesome and even heroic. While Wintringham's attempts to use ideology to justify the pain of war degenerated into misrepresentation and patent falsehood, the similar efforts of Cornford and Donnelly benefited from at least being rendered more poetically. Wintringham saw the war first as a political commissar; Cornford and Donnelly were more apt to view it as poets. The doctrinaire elements in their exhortative stanzas, although less bulky and pronounced, nonetheless seriously damage the over-all effect of their poems. The conclusions of Cornford's "As Our Might Lessens" and "Full Moon at Tierz," for example, illustrate the compulsion he felt to include certain ideological pronouncements. This is not to say that Marxism was incapable of generating poetry. Rather, it was too often a case of the ideology being unimaginatively rendered, as dogma rather than poetry, as theory rather than thought which was the result of an intensification process involving the poet and the ideas.

As for the remainder of the volunteer-poets, little needs to be said. Being participants, they were naturally closer to the heat of the struggle than most, which no doubt made any concentrated creative work exceedingly difficult. In attempting to reproduce the effect which the war made upon them, or more simply, to document as realistically as possible their own observations, they lapsed into a pretentiousness of style which, in turn, either created unnecessary confusion or blurred the overall effect of their poetry. As art their verses scarcely count. But taken as somewhat ingenuous yet serious attempts to record the impression of a powerful social event, these slight verses reveal the fugacity of political ideology. What Hyndman, Lepper, Birch, Branson, and Marshall recorded bespoke a lot less about their devotion to a political ideal than their disgust with the entire experience of war.

7.

Proof that the war could appeal to poets for reasons besides its immediate political and social importance is found in the poems by three poets who had only tenuous connections with the Left. Barker, Read, and MacNeice sympathized with the Republic, but their main concern was not a Loyalistic victory. It was something more personal and, in a sense, more significant than victory. Barker's three poems, especially *Calamiterror,* form a study in self-integration, which culminated in "Elegy on Spain." The theme is the poet's development, his turning away from excessive self-interest toward greater compassion and oneness with humanity, and it was the Spanish war which embodied these qualities that helped to effect his integration. Barker's steady advance toward greater social responsibility unify these poems.

The engaging idealism of the Spanish anarchists appealed to Read's rather exalted concept of anarchism. Although it could be argued that his interests were basically social, it is apparent that his belief in anarchism necessitated seeing it as apolitical and as a philosophy of life based on organic change and freedom. His espousal of anarchism, therefore, differed from the emotional sort of homage most Leftists paid to the Republican cause. Where the verses of the latter bayed the slogans of the Popular Front, Read managed to convey the essence of anarchism in spare yet impressive images.

Roy Campbell and Louis MacNeice had at least one thing in common. Prior to the outbreak of the Spanish war, both remained well outside the realm of politics. The political currents stirred up by the war impressed both poets, particularly Campbell. However, his embroilment in the struggle came about primarily because of a wish to defend the Catholic faith and to castigate his literary enemies, rather than from any desire to propound the merits of fascism. Since the disposition of friends and foes on the Republican and Nationalist sides coincided so completely with his likes and dislikes, the urge to condemn or extol proved far stronger than the need to see and feel the misfortunes of war. Except in a few short verses, Campbell used his Spanish war poems as convenient and, at times, devastating sounding boards for his long pent-up grudges. And when he stopped venting his spleen, he marveled at his own prescience, or expounded on the wondrous nature of the Church. MacNeice's political involvement in the Spanish war was even less complete than Campbell's; in fact, it is a moot question whether MacNeice felt any political commitment at all. Like Campbell, who was inspired by the courageous Carmelite priests at Toledo, MacNeice felt that the resurgence of human values in war-weary Barcelona was a moving and awesome testament of man's goodness. His whole concern was with the sense of human dignity that had somehow managed to assert itself even in the midst of war.

8.

Although the matter of writing "poetry for the people" has been mentioned in various places, the subject should be amplified a bit more here, for the reason that many believed the Spanish war might effect a closer relationship between poet and public. David Daiches, for example, writing shortly after the war had ended, noted that the Spanish war had given the "first real impetus to this [unification] movement," and prophesied that "the struggle for Spain against the fascist invader" would "one day be seen to have meant more for English poetry than the Greek struggle for independence meant for the Romantics of the early nineteenth century."[7] Communists like Cornford, Caudwell, and Fox had expounded upon the need for a "people's literature" long before the outbreak of war in Spain. But the possibility of a truly formidable proletariat literature seemed immeasurably greater once the war had begun. Of course, not all who sympathized with the Spanish workers would consent to write for the masses. But many felt that the struggle in Spain was symptomatic of some sort of new integration of the classes, which would affect the nature of literature.

The strongest agitators for integration of poet and public turned out to be the amateur poets who published *Poetry and the People,* the repository for most of the verse written by members of the Poets' Groups formed by the Left Book Club. Their objectives were to "stimulate and encourage the poet to write out of his experience, to reflect the life and feelings of his fellowmen, to arouse an interest in such poetry among the people, and bring the poet and the people into as close a contact as possible for their mutual understanding and enjoyment." Appeals went out from *Poetry and the People* for verse that was "vivid, real, alive," that "appealed to people on the basis of their own real life experience."[8] The response, though large, was hardly aesthetically satisfying. Beginners had no idea of how to go about writing a poem, and their first efforts were embarrassing imitations of school verse on which had been grafted some revolutionary material. No matter how bad the verse was, the editors, themselves poets, felt that a start had been made toward reaching a mass audience. What Jack Lindsay, Janet Watson, Miles Carpenter, Julius Lipton and other more or less professional poets on the staff of *Poetry and the People* learned, however, was that most workers could be made to listen to a poem, providing it was easily understood, but that they were unable to write a decent line.

To say, however, that this work presaged the fusion of the literary world with the world at large, or with the laboring classes, necessitates asking the related question of why the movement, once started, failed to continue. One answer, no doubt an obvious one, is that it became increasingly difficult for poets to find new "mass" themes once the focus and stimulus provided by the war had ceased to exist. As Julian Symons noted in his evaluation of the period, the end of the war meant the end of Spain as a "symbol of hope, pride, and reproach." Moreover, it terminated "a whole way of life." A few months after the fall of Madrid—and after the Nazi-Soviet pact—"the great tide of left-wing feeling had receded beyond the bounds of vision, and the land it had covered was as smooth, almost, as though the tide had never been."[9] The retreat from large social themes to more subjective material was the inevitable result.

9.

The poetry of the Spanish Civil War marks, then, not only the climax but also the end of a phase of British poetry. At no time during the decade had so many poets written so much about a single social event. Never before had they been so closely identified with a popular movement that embraced so many disparate elements. Never before had verse been forced to bear so many extraliterary functions. But despite all the sincerity and moral integrity that lay behind this poetry, it reinforces the lesson that good crusaders do not necessarily become good poets. The majority of them, with the note-worthy exceptions of Auden, Spender, Lewis, Barker, Read, and MacNeice, turned their verse into a tool with which to cajole, coerce, badger, and threaten their countrymen into supporting the Spanish Republic. Instead of interpreting their times, they sought to transform them. This is perhaps the worst result of the generally unhappy relationship between poetry and politics.

Perhaps the best that can be said for their work is that it is a fascinating and invaluable mirror of an era, reflecting what Elizabeth Bowen has called the Romantic Movement of our century. The comparison is not inappropriate. Just as the first and second generation Romantics of the last century imbibed the spirit of revolutionary ideals from France, Spain, and Greece and envisaged the dawn of a new world, so the British poets of the Spanish war thrilled to the prospect of turning ideals into realities. Their generous idealism and compassion and purpose were exhausted on behalf of a cause which, despite all the political distortions it has undergone, embodied as much truth and nobility as any which excited Byron, Shelley, or Wordsworth. And the majority of British poets have never lost faith in this cause. They have perhaps become suspicious of ideology. But they have not stopped believing that the Republican cause stood for. tolerance, freedom, and human dignity.

As the most recent historian of the Spanish Civil War has pointed out,[10] the Spanish war was the last in a series of liberal European revolutions. But it was also the precursor of the social revolutions which have flared up on all continents since the end of the Second World War. Its position as perhaps a turning point in European history can be suggested for still another reason. And that is, that the issues about which the war was fought are the very issues which continue to divide the world today. It is unnecessary to say more than that these issues remain unresolved, and that, therefore, in an important sense the Spanish Civil War is not yet finished. Perhaps it is also unnecessary to remind the reader at this point that among those who first saw the need to resolve such issues were the socially conscious poets of the 1930's.

Notes

Introduction

1. Michael Roberts (ed.), *New Signatures* (London, 1932), p. 19.
2. C. Day Lewis, *The Buried Day* (London, 1960), p. 218.
3. C. Day Lewis, *A Hope for Poetry* (Oxford, 1945), p. 49.
4. *Ibid.,* p. 55.
5. See Chapter 5, ft. 6.
6. John Sommerfield, *Volunteer in Spain* (New York, 1937), p. 96.
7. R. A. Scott-James, "Editorial," *London Mercury,* 25 (Feb., 1937), p. 353.
8. Hilaire Belloc, "The Issue in Spain," *Spain,* No. 44 (July, 1938), 100.
9. Robert Graves and Alan Hodge, *The Long Week-End* (London, 1939), p. 337.

Chapter 1

1. John Lehmann, *The Whispering Gallery* (London, 1955), pp. 216–17.
2. W. H. Auden, *The Dance of Death* (London, 1933), p. 7.
3. The Popular Front consisted of the following groups: Republican Left, Republican Union, Left Republican Party of Catalonia, Socialist Party, Communist Party, Workers Party of Marxist Unity (POUM), National Confederation of Labor, and Iberian Anarchists Federation. Rightists often claimed that this election was illegal. For example, see Arnold Lunn, *Spain and the Christian Front* (New York, n.d.), p. 6.
4. For a complete account of the lawlessness, see Arnold Toynbee, *Survey of International Affairs,* 1937: Vol. II (London, 1938), pp. 21 ff.
5. Salvador de Madariaga, *Spain* (New York, 1958), p. 455.
6. E. Alison Peers, *The Spanish Tragedy* (New York, 1936), p. 205.
7. Quoted in Peers, p. 208.
8. Nearly all commentators agree on this point. See Madariaga, p. 460; Charles Foltz, Jr., *Masquerade in Spain* (Boston, 1948), pp. 40–41; H. Edward Knoblaugh, *Correspondent in Spain* (London, 1937), p. 29.

For a highly dramatic account of the murders, see John Langdon-Davies, *Behind the Spanish Barricades* (London, 1936), p. 86.

9. This view is supported by the following: Foltz, Madariaga, Langdon-Davies, Peers, Ruiz Vilaplana, *Burgos Justice* (New York, 1938), J. Alvarez del Vayo, *Freedom's Battle* (New York, 1940), and Herbert L. Matthews, *Two Wars and More to Come* (New York, 1938), and many others.

10. That Hitler and Mussolini were instigators was maintained by the then American Ambassador to Spain, Claude Bowers. See *My Mission to Spain* (New York, 1954), p. 290. Cf. Louis Fischer, *Why Spain Fights On* (London, 1938). Fischer claimed Germany and Italy were instigators but were not involved in an organized plot to overthrow the Spanish government. A. L. Strong, *Spain in Arms* (New York, 1937). Strong wrote that "documents unearthed in the raid on German Nazi centers in Barcelona and later in Madrid make it plain that the connecting network between German Nazi agents and the reactionary Spanish generals existed long before the revolt." (77) The documents Strong referred to were published as *The Nazi Conspiracy in Spain* (London, 1937). R. W. Seton-Watson, *Britain and the Dictators* (New York, 1937). Seton-Watson contended that the dictators promised help before the revolt. (368–69, 388). See also G. T. Garratt, *Mussolini's Roman Empire* (New York, 1938), pp. 164 ff.

11. During the war, Insurgents maintained they were ridding Spain of Communist conspirators. And pro-Francoists abroad usually blamed the Communists for forcing the generals to act. See, for example, F. Yeats-Brown, *European Jungle* (Philadelphia, 1939), pp. 298–299. Arthur Koestler, who was a member of the Communist Party during the period of the Spanish war, has since denied that Communists were planning a revolution in Spain in 1936. "In England and France, Franco relied on the hoary story that the insurrection had started just in time to forestall a Communist rising. . . . As we (Communists) were openly advocating revolution, we had no reason to wax indignant, except on the technical grounds that we had not been planning a revolution in that particular country at that particular time." *The Invisible Writing* (New York, 1954), pp. 334–335. Cf. Madariaga, pp. 482 ff; G. M. Godden, *Communism in Spain, 1931–1936* (New York, 1937); Gil Robles, *Spain in Chains* (New York, 1937); Arnold Lunn, *Spanish Rehearsal* (London, 1937).

12. The army was soon commanded by General Franco, whose flight from the Canaries to Morocco was arranged by Douglas Jerrold, who described the arrangements in *Georgian Adventure* (New York, 1938).

13. The figures, which most commentators support, are based on those quoted by Álvarez del Vayo and Madariaga. Hugh Thomas, however, reduces the number of officers that remained loyal to the Republic to "200 regular officers . . . including 13 generals." *The Spanish Civil War* (London, 1961), p. 200.

14. Spanish novelist Pío Baroja, speaking for an older generation of Spanish writers, wrote: "We sympathize neither with the Right nor with the Left. At the present time (1937) independent people are not acceptable. One must be either Fascist or a Communist. The lack of compromise,

united to the plebeian and rancorous background of Spanish politicians, engenders hatred." *Spanish Liberals Speak on the Counter-Revolution in Spain* (San Francisco, 1937), p. 28.

15. William L. Shirer, *Berlin Diary* (New York, 1941), p. 31.

16. Koestler, *Invisible Writing*, pp. 319–320.

17. William L. Shirer, *The Rise and Fall of the Third Reich* (New York, 1960), pp. 297–301.

18. See Álvarez del Vayo, pp. 51–54; Madariaga, pp. 506–507; David Cattell, *Communism and the Spanish Civil War* (Berkeley, Calif., 1955), p. 82; Henry Blythe, *Spain over Britain* (London, 1937), p. 22.

19. Winston Churchill, *Step by Step* (New York, 1939), p. 37.

20. In recognition of Attlee's support, the No. I Company of the British Battalion was named the Major Attlee Company.

21. Malraux has told his own story of the Spanish war in *Man's Hope* (New York, 1938).

22. The most comprehensive account of the complex history of the Nonintervention Committee is found in Toynbee.

23. Trade unionists and collectivized peasants were assessed one half of one percent of one month's pay for the Spanish workers' cause. The amount collected supposedly amounted to $4,000,000, which was sent to Spain in the form of cash and food supplies. "Intervention in Spain," *Round Table*, 27 (1937), 276.

24. Franz Borkenau, *European Communism* (London, 1953), p. 169.

25. W. G. Krivitsky, *In Stalin's Secret Service* (New York, 1939), p. 126.

26. David Cattell, *Soviet Diplomacy and the Spanish Civil War* (Berkeley, Calif., 1957), chapter 4.

27. For details of the amount of gold dispatched to Russia and of the rather bizarre procedures that attended its arrival in Odessa, see Thomas, pp. 309–310, 331–332.

28. Hugh Thomas, "The International Brigades in Spain," *History Today*, II (May, 1961), 318.

29. Fischer was Moscow correspondent for *Nation*. In October, 1936, he went to Spain where, a few weeks later, he enlisted in the International Brigades. He now claims to be the first American enlister. See Fischer's autobiography, *Men and Politics* (New York, 1941), pp. 386 ff.

30. Cattell, *Communism*, pp. 114 ff. See Thomas, pp. 296–304. Besides the abovementioned, the roster of Comintern officials involved in the work of the International Brigades included Ulbricht, Gottwald, Tito, Thorez, Aragon, Konev, Pavlov, Rokossovsky.

31. Matthews, *Two Wars*, p. 182.

32. Regler described the war in a novel, *The Great Crusade* (London, 1940), and more recently in his autobiography, *The Owl of Minerva* (New York, 1959). Romilly recalled his three month adventure with the Thaelmann Battalion in *Boadilla* (London, 1937).

33. Fischer, *Politics*, p. 393.

34. Regler, *Owl*, p. 283.

35. Matthews, *Two Wars*, p. 181. See also Robert Colodny, *The*

Struggle for Madrid: The Central Epic of the Spanish Conflict (New York, 1958).

36. Cattell, *Communism,* chapter 9.

37. For accounts of the anarchists' position, see V. Richards, *Lessons of the Spanish Revolution* (London, 1953), George Orwell, *Homage to Catalonia* (New York, 1952), and John Dos Passos, *The Villages Are the Heart of Spain* (Chicago, 1937), *Journeys Between Wars* (New York, 1938), *The Theme Is Freedom* (New York, 1956).

38. See G. L. Steer, "Guernica," *London Mercury,* 36 (Aug., 1937), 330; Philip Robinson, "Guernica," *National Review,* 109 (Aug., 1937), 253. The best documentation is G. L. Steer, *Tree of Gernika* (London, 1938).

39. Thomas, p. 428.

40. Despite many assertions that the Communists engineered the liquidation of the POUM, the disorderliness of the entire episode strongly suggests it was not planned by either side. This is not to say, however, that the Communists hesitated to take full advantage of what was happening. Some of the charges and countercharges follow. According to Fenner Brockway, the POUM only "participated when the resistance began, and then ordered its members not to fire a shot unless attacked." *Inside the Left* (London, 1942), p. 302. Brockway's Independent Labour Party was the British counterpart of the POUM. Brockway went to Spain to try to temper some of the POUMist doctrines. When he failed and the organization was liquidated, Brockway defended its actions. See *The Truth about Barcelona* (London, 1937). Cf. Augustin Souchy, *The Tragic Week in May* (n.p., 1937). The communist version was elaborately presented by George Soria, *Trotskyism in the Service of Franco* (New York, n.d.). See also, Lambda, *The Truth about the Barcelona Events* (New York, n.d.); William Krehm, *Spain: Revolution and Counter-Revolution* (Toronto, n.d.); Pasionaria, *People's Tribune of Spain* (New York, 1938). Perhaps the most vivid account of the episode is by George Orwell, who had been a member of a POUM militia. See *Homage,* p. 123 ff.

41. Madariaga, pp. 528–529.

42. See Segismundo Casado, *Last Days of Madrid* (London, 1939); Álvarez del Vayo, pp. 307 ff.

Chapter 2

1. *Daily Mail* (July 19, 1937).

2. Reproduced in Winston Churchill, *The Gathering Storm* (Boston, 1948), p. 265. A complete account of Eden's resignation appears in the second volume of his memoirs, *Facing the Dictators* (Boston, 1962), pp. 666 ff.

3. *News of Spain* (April 6, 1938).

4. Robert Graves and Alan Hodge, *The Long Week-End* (London, 1955), p. 411.

5.   Philip Gibbs, *Ordeal in England* (New York, 1937), p. 262.

6.   Churchill, *Step by Step*, p. 51. In November, 1937, Churchill admitted that nonintervention had been disappointing and that belligerent rights perhaps should have been granted to both sides. By April, 1938, he began wondering if England would run less risk if the Republic won. See pp. 163, 275.

7.   Graves and Hodge, *Week-End*, p. 416. The notion that Franco would not tolerate continued foreign involvement after the end of the war had historical precedents. Conservatives continuously pointed out that the proud, sensitive Spaniards had always greeted foreign interference with an outburst of xenophobia, and, besides, there was growing evidence that considerable enmity had already arisen between Spaniards and Italians. This reasoning apparently did not apply to British assets in Spain. Most Conservatives believed that Franco would be more receptive to a plan to preserve British investments than a left-wing Popular Front government would be.

8.   *Manchester Guardian* (Sept. 10, 1937).

9.   See William Rust, *Britons in Spain: The History of the British Battalion of the XVth International Brigade* (London, 1939), pp. 100–101.

10.   Fenner Brockway, *Inside the Left* (London, 1942), p. 323.

11.   *Ibid.*, p. 344.

12.   Charles L. Mowat, *Britain Between the Wars, 1918–1940* (London, 1955), p. 584.

13.   Gibbs, *Ordeal,* p. 161.

14.   Rex Warner, "Education," in *The Mind in Chains,* edited by C. Day Lewis (London, 1937), p. 24.

15.   Charlotte Haldane, *Truth Will Out* (London, 1949), p. 90.

16.   Koestler has written that the Committee for War Relief for Republican Spain, with a Spanish Milk Fund added to it, was a "philanthropic cover for political operations. The Committee of Inquiry into Foreign Intervention in the Spanish War as well as the others were hatched by Willi Muenzenberg, head of Comintern's West-European AGITPROP Dept." *Invisible Writing,* p. 314. The Spanish Medical Aid Committee, however, was formed by non-Communists and was an entirely voluntary project. It was created in August, 1936, and remained in existence until 1939. See Arthur Peacock, *Yours Fraternally* (London, 1954), p.98.

17.   Harry Pollitt, *Selected Articles and Speeches,* vol. II (London, 1954), p. 22.

18.   *Ibid.,* p. 14.

19.   *Ibid.*

20.   Rust, *Britons in Spain,* p. vi.

21.   Haldane, *Truth Will Out,* p. 87.

22.   *Ibid.,* p. 93.

23.   Volunteers usually received £3 and a weekend ticket to Paris from the C.P.G.B. No passport was required for short visits to the French capital.

24. Haldane, *Truth Will Out*, p. 114. That the majority of volunteers were laborers has been confirmed by all the former members of the International Brigade with whom I have spoken.

25. Rust, *Britons in Spain*, pp. 13–14. Miles Tomalin, whose middle-class background and Cambridge education distinguished him from most of his comrades, told me that he was watched closely by his laboring class comrades until they had satisfied themselves that he had not come to Spain for adventure, and then they tended to respect him as someone whose words were of more than ordinary value. (Interview: London, March, 1961.)

26. Graves and Hodge, *Week-End*, p. 269.

27. Mowat, *Britain Between the Wars*, p. 542.

28. *Ibid.*

29. *Ibid.*, p. 538.

30. Graves and Hodge, *Week-End,* p. 329. Perhaps more influential was B. Nichols' *Cry Havoc!*, which was based on emotional rather than rational arguments against war.

31. C. E. Black and E. C. Helmreich, *Twentieth Century Europe* (New York, 1959), p. 496.

32. George Orwell, "Looking Back on the Spanish War," *Such, Such Were the Joys* (New York, 1945), p. 131.

33. Philip Gibbs, *Across the Frontiers* (New York, 1938), p. 269.

34. *Ibid.*, pp. 269–270.

35. As editor of an anthology of pacifist writings published in 1935, Julian Bell, then a pacifist himself, predicted that his generation had learned too much from its enemy to try to prevent war by peaceful means only. "I believe that the war-resistance movements of my generation will in the end succeed in putting down war — by force if necessary." See *We Did Not Fight* (London, 1935), p. xix.

36. C. E. M. Joad, "What Is Happening to the Peace Movement?," *New Statesman and Nation*, 13 (May 15, 1937), 802.

37. A. W. H. James, "Background to Franco," *Spectator*, 162 (March 3, 1939), 348.

38. Julian Huxley, "Spanish News: A Quantitative Analysis," (letter) *New Statesman and Nation*, 12 (Aug. 8, 1936), 187.

39. James, *Background to Franco*, 348. For the Nationalist view, see Joseph F. Thorning, *Why the Press Failed on Spain* (New York, n.d.).

40. James, *Background to Franco*, 348.

41. *Times* (Aug. 27, 1936).

42. No doubt the *News Chronicle*'s policy was influenced by its correspondents in Spain, William Forrest and Arthur Koestler, both of whom belonged to the Communist Party. See Koestler, *Invisible Writing*, p. 335.

43. "Editorial," *Saturday Review*, 162 (Aug. 15, 1936), 161.

44. F. H. Mellor, "Spain's Holy War," *Saturday Review*, 162 (Oct. 31, 1936), 554.

45. C. H., "Bolshevist Spain and After, A Lost Opportunity," *Saturday Review*, 162 (Aug. 5, 1936), 198.

46.   Meriel Buchanan, "Red Terror in Spain," *Saturday Review,* 162 (Aug. 1, 1936), 136.

47.   "Editorial," *Spectator,* 157 (Oct. 13, 1936), 665.

48.   Several small publications began on a weekly or monthly basis soon after the war started, such as *Spain,* a lavish weekly financed by the Nationalists, *Spain and the World,* a fortnightly containing reports and editorials by Herbert Read, Ethel Mannin and J. Cowper Powys, and *The War in Spain* (after January 1938 *Voice of Spain*), a weekly edited by Charles Duff, who also published the monthly *Spain at War.* Duff was the chief assembler and distributor of Loyalist propaganda in England. During the war he maintained contacts with Spaniards on both sides, news from Nationalist territory being transmitted by means of a code previously arranged with him. After the demise of *Voice of Spain* and *Spain at War,* Duff published *Spanish News Letter,* devoted to developments in Francoist Spain, which lasted until February 1948.

49.   Louis Fischer, "The War in Spain," *New Statesman and Nation,* 16 (Aug. 20, 1938), 272.

50.   "Editorial," *New Statesman and Nation,* 16 (Sept. 12, 1938), 367.

51.   Typical of the attacks on nonintervention was Louis Fischer's: "The international device which denies them (Loyalists) these defensive weapons is one of the major atrocities of a cruel age. Hands very far from this city have the blood of innocents upon them." "Peace on Earth, Good Will to Men," *New Statesman and Nation,* 16 (Dec. 10, 1938), 953. See also, Geoffrey Brereton, "Air Raid," *New Statesman and Nation,* 15 (Jan. 1, 1938), 15, and G. T. Garratt, "Home Thoughts from Madrid," *New Statesman and Nation,* 16 (Sept. 24, 1938), 449.

52.   In the first number Grigson wrote: "It (*New Verse*) favours only its time, belonging to no literary or political-literary cabal." *New Verse,* 1 (Jan., 1933), 2. And in the second number, he added: "If there must be attitudes, a reasoned attitude of toryism is welcomed no less than a communist attitude." *New Verse,* 1 (March, 1933), 3.

53.   To find out how the poets it printed stood politically, *New Verse* asked them the following question: "Do you stand with any political-economic party or creed?" The replies ranged from Herbert Read's terse "No" to Hugh MacDiarmid's admission, "I am a member of the Communist Party." *New Verse,* 1 (Oct., 1934), 10, 18.

54.   "Contributors Conference," *Left Review,* 1 (June, 1935), 366.

55.   "Labour and Reaction," *Left Review,* 1 (Aug., 1936), 537.

56.   "Editorial," *Left Review,* 3 (May, 1938), 960. The information in this paragraph is based on this author's conversations with Randall Swingler. Before *Left Review* ceased publication, Victor Gollancz was asked if he wanted to take on *Left Review.* He declined, presumably wary of taking on a publication with such slight chances of being financially successful. The demise of the *Left Review* left the Party without a literary outlet, and even the *Daily Worker* was suppressed the following year. However, in 1940, the Party gained control of *Poetry and the People* and turned it into *Our Time.* Later it also got control of *Seven.*

57.   "Editorial," *The Left News,* (June, 1937), 384.

58. *The Left News,* (Oct., 1938), 1014.

59. *Ibid.,* (July, 1938), 901.

60. *Ibid.,* (March, 1937), 249.

61. "Spain," *The Left News,* (Jan., 1938), 637.

62. John Strachey, "The Road to Victory," *Left Book News,* No. 7 (Nov., 1936), 138.

63. "Editorial," *The Left News,* (May, 1938), 788.

64. John Lehmann, "Manifesto," *New Writing,* I (Spring, 1936).

65. Lehmann, *Gallery,* p. 232, 236.

66. *Ibid.,* p. 279.

Chapter 3

1. See below, pp. 204–205.

2. Meynell's statement appears in Julian Symons, *The Thirties* (London, 1960), p. 119.

3. Cyril Connelly, *The Condemned Playground* (London, 1945), p. 180.

4. Priestley's statement appears in Symons, *Thirties,* p. 119.

5. *Authors Take Sides* (London, 1937). The idea of polling British writers on their attitude toward the Spanish war first occurred to Nancy Cunard around June, 1937. A few names quickly multiplied into a fairly long list, and questionnaires, sometimes accompanied by a personal note or letter, began reaching the authors within a few weeks. As replies came back, Miss Cunard classified, edited and typed them. In two months the work was completed, but efforts to place it with three London publishers failed. As a last resort, Miss Cunard sent it to Randall Swingler at *Left Review,* who accepted it immediately, collected a few more statements, including Shaw's, added a list of prominent sponsors, and brought out a printing of 3,000, at 6*d* a copy. In April, 1938, the League of American Writers published a similar survey called *Writers Take Sides.*

Besides editing *Authors Take Sides,* Miss Cunard edited and published six numbers of *Les Poétes du Monde Défendent le Peuple Espagnol,* which contained poems about the Spanish war by Tristan Tzara, Langston Hughes, Cedric Dover, Rafael Alberti, Auden, Nicolas Guillén, Brian Howard, Swingler, Pablo Neruda, and Raùl Tuñon. Miss Cunard's own poems on the Spanish war appeared in *New Statesman and Nation, Voice of Spain, Life and Letters To-day,* and *Left Review.* In addition, Miss Cunard made valuable contributions of time and money to the Republic. Her articles for the *Manchester Guardian,* written in 1939, are lucid and vivid accounts of the final days of the Republic. Her concern for the Spanish refugees interned in southern France helped to focus attention on their conditions. Perhaps more than any other Republican supporter, she has continued to aid the exiled Spanish Loyalists and to foster their cause in numerous ways.

6. Lewis, *Hope,* p. 55.

7. Edward Upward, "A Marxist Interpretation of Literature," *The Mind in Chains* (London, 1937), p. 46.

8. Ralph Fox, *The Novel and the People* (London, 1937), p. 118 ff. Extracts from Fox's letters, together with several tributes by friends and some excerpts from his writings, were collected in *Ralph Fox, A Writer in Arms,* edited by John Lehmann, T. A. Jackson, C. Day Lewis (London, 1937).

9. John Lehmann, "Should Writers Keep to Their Art?", *Left Review,* 2 (Jan., 1937), 881–84.

10. C. Day Lewis, "Labour and Fascism: the Writer's Task," *Left Review,* 2 (Nov., 1936), 731.

11. Stephen Spender, *Life and the Poet* (London, 1942), pp. 7–8.

Chapter 4

1. Robert Graves, "A Life Bang-Full of Kicks and Shocks," *New York Times Book Review* (Jan. 5, 1958), 6.

2. Churchill, *Step by Step,* p. 95. Inge's statement appears in Tom Wintringham, *English Captain* (London, 1939), p. 329.

3. *Poems for Spain,* edited by Stephen Spender and John Lehmann (London, 1939), p. 31. Laurie Lee, *The Sun My Monument* (London, 1944), pp. 9–10.

4. Dozens of protests signed by a host of well-known literary figures were published regularly, but probably made only a fraction of the impression that Picasso's *Guernica* created in 1937. Of decidedly less importance, however, was a poem by the artist, entitled "Dreams and Lies of General Franco," which was included in an exhibition of his paintings in London, in November, 1938.

> Fandago of shivering owls. Souse of swords of evil-omened polyps scouring brush of hairs from priests' tonsures standing naked in the middle of the fryingpan.

5. *Poems for Spain,* pp. 31–33. For a description of Marshall in Spain, see Keith Scott-Watson, *Single to Spain* (London, 1938), p. 37.

6. Dennis Birch, "Incident 1938," *Voice of Spain,* No. 6 (Sept., 1938), 212–213.

7. Jarama was the first battle for the XVth International Brigade,. of which the first battalion was composed chiefly of British. So devastating was the fight that of the 600-odd members of the British battalion only 225 were alive when it ended, and not more than 80 were left unwounded. For accounts of the Jarama battle, see Wintringham, *Captain,* pp. 151 ff; *Book of the XVth International Brigade* (Madrid, 1939), pp. 35 ff; Fred Copeman, *Reason in Revolt* (London, 1948), pp. 86 ff. Alex McDade, a veteran of the battle, captured the feelings of many survivors in his cynical ballad set to the tune of *Red River Valley:*

> There's a valley in Spain called Jarama,
> That's a place that we all know so well,

For 'tis there that we wasted our manhood
And most of our old age as well.

From this valley they tell us we're leaving,
But don't hasten to bid us adieu,
For e'en though we make our departure,
We'll be back in an hour or two.

Oh, we're proud of our British Battalion,
And the marathon record it's made,
Please do us this little favour,
And take this last word to Brigade:

You will never be happy with strangers,
They would not understand you as we,
So remember the Jarama Valley
And the old men who wait patiently.

8. *Poems for Spain*, pp. 33–34. Jarama was probably the setting of the author's short story, "Conscience Is a Funny Thing," which appeared in *New Writing*, New Series III (Christmas, 1939), p. 255.

9. *Poems for Spain*, p.40. See below, pp. 221–222.

10. Clive Branson, "San Pedro," *New Writing*, New Series (Spring, 1939), p. 53. Branson, who was killed while on active duty in World War II, was better known as an artist than as a poet. See James Boswell, "Clive Branson, A Tribute," *Our Time*, 4 (Nov., 1944), 6. ·

11. Wintringham, *Captain*, pp. 204–205. Wintringham began his studies at Balliol College, Oxford, in 1914, interrupted his schooling to join the Royal Flying Corps, and returned to Oxford following the armistice. In 1923 he joined the Communist Party.

12. Wintringham, "Barcelona Nerves," *Volunteer for Liberty*, 1 (Nov. 15, 1937), 7; "Granen," *Volunteer for Liberty*, 1 (Nov. 17, 1937), 3. Both poems also appeared in *Poems for Spain*.

13. Wintringham, "Monument: A Poem from the Spanish Front," *Volunteer for Liberty*, 2 (Nov. 7, 1938), 18. This was the final issue of the *Volunteer for Liberty*, the official organ of the English-speaking battalions of the International Brigades. Started in Madrid in May, 1937, it printed 63 issues, had three editors—Ralph Bates, Edwin Rolfe, and John Tisa—and published articles by nearly every politically active American and British writer who visited Spain.

14. Only Caudwell, whose name was actually Christopher St. John Sprigg, was not a university student. In 1933, with numerous articles already to his credit, he became a free-lance writer, publishing eight mysteries and five aviation books, besides considerable poetry, in the next few years. Absorbed by Marxism after 1934, he joined the Communist Party in 1935. Both Julian Bell and John Cornford were students at Cambridge. The son of pacifists Clive and Vanessa Bell, Julian frequently commented on his heritage in his writings. Cornford, the son of Francis MacDonald Cornford, Laurence Professor of Ancient Philosophy at Cambridge, and Francis Cornford, the poet, was the driving force behind

the socialist movement at British universities. Though the bulk of his work was polemical, Cornford's poetic output was impressive. See Christopher Caudwell, *Poems,* with biographical notes by Richard Church (London, 1939); Pat Sloan (ed.), *John Cornford: A Memoir* (London, 1938); Quentin Bell (ed.), *Julian Bell. Essays, Poems, and Letters* (London, 1938).

15.   Bell's letters appear in Quentin Bell, *Julian Bell,* pp. 156–157, 183, 192.

16.   Among other British intellectuals who went to Spain soon after hostilities began were Ralph Fox, Esmond and Giles Romilly, nephews of Winston Churchill, Lorimer Birch, a young Cambridge scientist, and David Guest.

17.   Wintringham, *Captain,* p. 50.

18.   John Sommerfield, the novelist who accompanied Cornford to Spain, dedicated his Spanish war book, *Volunteer in Spain,* to Cornford. In a final note he paid homage to his friend: ". . . because of those whom I honour without being able to pay them tribute here, I have dedicated this book to John Cornford. I did not see him dead; I can only remember him alive and laughing, strong, resolute, and reliable. . . . To me he is the type and symbol of the youth of today whose conscious task it is to change the world, and who are strong enough to carry out that task. I remember him for that, and for a friend, for a personality that enriched everyone with whom he came into contact." (p. 155).

19.   Edwin Rolfe, *The Lincoln Battalion* (New York, 1939), p. 73.

20.   *Poems for Spain,* pp. 26–29.

21.   Wintringham, *Captain,* p. 46.

22.   Both poems appeared in *New Writing,* IV (Autumn, 1937), pp. 36–39.

23.   See below, pp. 159–161.

24.   Miss Heinemann's reaction to Cornford's death is found in her poem, "Grieve in a New Way for New Losses."

25.   Spender, *Poems for Spain,* p. 12.

26.   Montagu Slater, "Charles Donnelly," *Left Review,* 3 (July, 1937), 318.

27.   Donnelly's poem appeared in *Romancero de los Voluntarios de la Libertad* (Madrid, 1937), pp. 67–68.

28.   *Poems for Spain,* pp. 50–51.

29.   Ewart Milne, *Letter from Ireland* (Dublin, 1940), pp. 27–29.

30.   Milne, "The Hour Glass," *Letter,* p. 34.

Chapter 5

1.   Jack Lindsay, *Fanfrolico and After* (London, 1962), p. 264.

2.   Lewis, *Day,* p. 218.

3.   Gawsworth's poem appeared in *Voice of Spain,* No. 2 (Feb., 1939), 68–69. John Gawsworth is a pseudonym. The poet's name is Terence Armstrong.

4. *Poems for Spain,* pp. 84–85.

5. Miss Raine's poem appeared in *The Year's Poetry,* compiled by Denys K. Roberts and Geoffrey Grigson (London, 1937), pp. 91–95. J. K. Raine, in 1937, was Mrs. Charles Madge.

6. Rex Warner, "The Tourist Looks at Spain," *Poems for Spain,* pp. 65–69.

7. Mallalieu's poem appeared in *Left Review,* 2 (Oct. 1936), 33,

8. *Poems for Spain,* p. 34.

9. *Ibid.,* pp. 59–60.

10. *Ibid.,* pp. 24–25.

11. *Ibid.,* p. 88. The Calpe hunt brought British officers and Spanish aristocrats together once a year. Richardson, a Cambridge graduate, was in Spain when war broke out. Soon afterwards, he returned to England to work for the Spanish government. In writing of Richardson's death in a bombing raid on London, on March 8, 1941, Charles Duff called him a "'practical humanitarian." *Voice of Spain,* No. 103 (March 22, 1941), 408.

12. *Poems for Spain,* pp. 25–26.

13. Lindsay, *Fanfrolico,* p. 264.

14. *Poems for Spain,* pp. 60–64.

15. *Left Book News,* No. 27 (July, 1938), 901. Lindsay himself prepared detailed directions for its production. See "Directions for 'On Guard for Spain!' ", *Left Poets News Sheet,* 2–3 (April, 1938).

16. Jack Lindsay, "A Plea for Mass Declamation," *Left Review,* 3 (Oct., 1937), 511.

17. Lindsay's poem appeared in *Left Review,* 3 (March, 1937), 79–86.

18. *Poems for Spain,* pp. 74–77.

19. *Ibid.,* pp. 77–78.

20. Sagittarius' poem appeared in the *New Statesman and Nation,* 17 (May 13, 1939), 734. Sagittarius was the pen name of Mrs. Hugh Miller.

21. Richardson's poem appeared in *Voice of Spain,* No. 3 (June, 1938), 112.

22. Miss Cluer's poem appeared in the *New Statesman and Nation,* 17 (April 8, 1939), 536.

23. Peader O'Donnell, *Salud!* (London, 1937), p. 247. O'Donnell reported that Franco received in the neighborhood of £32,000 from Ireland.

24. W. B. Yeats supported O'Duffy as one who would keep the rebellious peasants down and defend ancestral houses. Yeats' "Three Songs to the Same Tune" was adapted as their marching song, with the following refrain:

> Down the fanatic, down the clown
> Down, down, hammer them down,
> Down to the tune of O'Donnell Abu,
> When nations are empty up there at the top,
> When order has weakened and faction is strong,

Time for us all, boys, to hit on a tune, boys,
Take to the roads and go marching along.

25. See O'Donnell, *Salud!*, pp. 250–251. Cf. Eoin O'Duffy, *Crusade in Spain* (Dublin, 1938), pp. 116–117.

26. See O'Duffy, *Crusade in Spain,* pp. 236–239.

27. Macalastair's ballad appeared in O'Donnell, *Salud!*, p. 251. Somhairle Macalasṭair is a pseudonym. The author's name is Desmond Fitzgerald. During the Spanish war, Sean Nolan, Dublin bookseller and printer, published one of Fitzgerald's ballads almost weekly.

28. Macalastair's ballad appeared in *Left Review*, 2 (Dec., 1936), 817–818. Ballyseedy, in Kerry, was the scene of a massacre of Republicans by Free State soldiers.

29. To make a more direct appeal to the people, several Spanish poets revived the old medieval form of the romance which, according to Rolfe Humphries and others, enjoyed considerable popularity at the time. See Humphries' anthology of Spanish songs and ballads, *And Spain Sings* (New York, 1937), and his article, "The Balladry of the Civil War," *International Literature,* No. 3 (March, 1937), 31–39.

30. In an article on Spanish literature, F. V. Kelyin wrote: "The name of the real hero of Spain is—the people of Spain." See "Heroism in Spanish Literature," *International Literature,* No. 10 (Oct., 1936), 72.

31. One of Pasionaria's more affectionate admirers was A. L. Strong, who once wrote: "Not by intellect nor by education but by her tremendous depth of feeling she has become a great leader, more worshipped by wide masses than perhaps any other person in Spain. Passionate love for human beings, passionate indignation over the wrongs they suffer, turn in her with a pure intensity akin to genius. . . . By gesture and tone she diffuses around her an atmosphere of deeply concerned love—love for plain, ordinary people." See A. L. Strong, *Spain in Arms,* pp. 23–24. Cf. Hemingway's portrait of Pasionaria in *For Whom the Bell Tolls,* where she is satirized. Today, at 68, Pasionaria lives alone some seventy miles from Moscow. Recently, she published her autobiography, *Memoirs of a Revolutionary Woman.*

32. See Rolfe's poem, "City of Anguish," in *First Love and Other Poems* (Los Angeles, 1951).

33. Miss Haldane's poem appeared in *Left Review*, 3 (April, 1938), 926.

34. *Poems for Spain,* pp. 95–96. *Left Review* had editorialized that Lorca, Fox, and Cornford had "re-established with their blood that unity between the creators of beauty and the masses of the people, for lack of which culture had become a petty play-word in the mouths of an isolated sect." *Left Review*, 3 (March, 1937), 65.

35. *Poems for Spain,* pp. 64–65.

36. Roy Campbell, *Lorca, An Appreciation of his Poetry* (New Haven, 1952), p. 7.

37. Arturo Barea, *Lorca, the Poet and his People* (London, 1944), p. 11. Barea described his participation in the Spanish war in his autobiography, *The Forging of a Rebel* (New York, 1946).

38. Urrutia, "Romancero a la Muerto de Garcia Lorca," *Poems for Spain,* pp. 105–108.

39. *Poems for Spain,* pp. 103–104.

40. *Poems for Spain,* pp. 104–105.

41. See Rust, *Britons in Spain.*

42. L. Kendall, "To the Heroes of the International Brigades in Spain," *Poetry and the People* (Oct., 1938), 7.

43. R. Gardner, "International Brigade," *Poetry and the People* (Jan., 1939), 4.

44. Miles Carpenter, "Ballad of a Volunteer," *Poetry and the People* (Feb., 1939), 5.

45. *New Lyrical Ballads,* edited by Jack Lindsay *et al.* (London, 1945), pp. 104–110.

46. *British Battalion XV International Brigade* (Memorial Souvenir) (London, 1939), pp. 7–9.

47. T. E. Nicholas, "In Remembrance of a Son of Wales," *Voice of Spain,* No. 5 (Aug., 1938), 178.

48. Hugh MacDiarmid, *Speaking for Scotland* (Baltimore, 1946), p. 29.

49. *Ibid.*

50. Hugh MacDiarmid, "To the Spanish Republican Army." MacDiarmid sent this poem to Miss Edith T. Aney. It is included in her dissertation, *British Poetry of Social Protest in the 1930's* (Unpubl. diss., University of Pennsylvania, 1954), p. 307.

Chapter 6

1. *New Verse,* 1 (Oct., 1934), 3.

2. Herbert Read, *Poetry and Anarchism* (London, 1938), pp.82, 87.

3. *Ibid.,* p. 97.

4. *Ibid.,* p. 14.

5. *Ibid.,* pp. 15, 20.

6. *Ibid.,* pp. 14–15.

7. Read defined the syndicalist as "the anarchist in his practical rather than his theoretical activity." In other words, the syndicalist was more interested in practical results than ideas, and hence sought to organize the workers as a revolutionary force. It might be said that Sorel was the philosophical poet of anarchism and Durruti its practitioner.

8. Read, *Poetry and Anarchism,* p. 67.

9. Herbert Read, *Thirty-Five Poems* (London, 1940), p. 41.

10. *Ibid.,* p. 11.

11. *Poems for Spain,* pp. 39–40.

12. *Authors Take Sides.*

13. Herbert Read, *The Philosophy of Anarchism* (London, 1940), pp. 32–33.

14. Barker replied to the query from *New Verse*, "Do you stand with any political or political-economic party or creed?", with a terse, "I do not." *New Verse*, 1 (Oct., 1934).

15. *Authors Take Sides.*

16. George Barker, *Collected Poems* (London, 1957), p. 58.

17. *Poems for Spain*, p. 59.

18. Barker, *Collected Poems*, p. 98.

19. *Ibid.*, p. 101.

Chapter 7

1. Roy Campbell, *Light on a Dark Horse* (London, 1951), p. 184.

2. *Ibid.*

3. *Ibid.*, p. 249.

4. *Ibid.*, p. 317.

5. *Ibid.*, pp. 346–347.

6. Roy Campbell, *Flowering Rifle, Collected Poems*, II (London, 1957), p. 139. Henceforth abbreviated *FR*.

7. *Ibid.*, p. 138.

8. Campbell, "The Carmelites of Toledo," *Collected Poems*, p. 30. See also *FR*, p. 192.

9. *FR*, p. 160.

10. Campbell, "A Letter from the San Mateo Front," *Collected Poems*, pp. 53–54.

11. Campbell, "Author's Note Added to Proofs in Sept. 1938," *Collected Poems*, p. 138.

12. *FR*, p. 148.

13. "Letter," p. 45.

14. Campbell, "The Hoopoe," *Collected Poems*, p. 35.

15. See *Light*, p. 185.

16. "Hoopoe," p. 37.

17. Campbell, "Note to Flowering Rifle," *Collected Poems*, p. 137. Campbell's claim has been matched by Jack Lindsay, whose poem, "Warning of the End," published in February, 1936, in *The Eye*, trade journal of the then newly formed Lawrence and Wishart publishing house, the author believes was probably the first on the Spanish war.

18. "Letter," (footnote 1), p. 48.

19. Campbell, "Dedication to Mary Campbell," *Collected Poems of Roy Campbell* London, 1949), p. 178.

20. "Hoopoe," pp. 36–37.

21. "Letter," pp. 47–48.

22. *Ibid.*, p. 40.

23. *FR*, p. 186, pp. 166–168; see also, pp. 216, 250.

24. Campbell, "Talking Bronco," *Collected Poems*, pp. 92–93.

25. *FR*, pp. 145, 147, 160, 221.

26. "Letter," p. 46.

27. *FR*, pp. 160, 181, 238–239.

28. "Letter," p. 40.

29. *FR,* p. 152.

30. "Bronco," p. 85.

31. For example, see *FR,* pp. 167–168, 250.

32. "Letter," pp. 39, 44, 49.

33. "Bronco," pp. 87, 89.

34. In reply to Spender's review of *Flowering Rifle,* Campbell wrote: "It is by now an axiom that whatever Stephen Spender and his colleagues support, even if it were the pyramids themselves, would collapse like rotten, worm-eaten cheeses within a few hours of the manifestation of their sympathy. This happened in the case of Azaña's, Caballero's, and finally Negrín's Government which collapsed on the day of the joint manifestation of the British poets with their *Poems for Spain.* The form of collective bedroom palmistry which they mistake for poetry can be guaranteed to work out inversely and reversely to a hair." Letter to *New Statesman and Nation,* 17 (April 8, 1939), 540–541. The Spanish Nationalists published two anthologies of war poetry; *The Lyre of War* (Valladolid, 1939), and *The Verses of the Fighter* (Burgos, 1938).

35. "Bronco," p. 88.

36. *Ibid.,* p. 93.

37. *FR,* p. 224.

38. *Ibid.,* p. 235.

39. Robert Graves, "A Life Bang-Full of Kicks and Shocks," *New York Times Book Review* (Jan. 5, 1958), 6. Campbell served as war correspondent for the *Tablet* (London) for a brief period.

40. Accompanying some poems he sent to the *Right Review,* Campbell sent the following letter: "Dear Count Potocki—Sorry your letter followed me to Madrid front and only caught me up here nearly two months after you sent it to Faber. I like your Right Review very much except that as a Catholic soldier of Spain, I regard either anti-Christianity or pornography as red activities and too unsoldierly for a Real Right Review." *Right Review,* (April 1939). A reviewer of *Flowering Rifle* wrote: "Roy Campbell . . . writes from the ranks in a battle where he may yet lay down his life. . . ." *Spain,* No. 72 (Feb. 16, 1939), 139. Another contributor to *Spain* added: "Roy Campbell had lived for some years in Toledo engaged in horse-breeding. He was witness to all the horror of the city in the hands of the hordes. He fought in Franco's forces from the day of the Relief." J. Arteaga de Leon, "Roy Campbell Through Spanish Eyes," *Spain,* No. 85 (May 18, 1939), 140.

41. Robert C. Elliott, *The Power of Satire: Magic, Ritual, Art* (Princeton, N.J., 1960), p. 252.

42. Campbell, *Collected Poems,* p. 32.

43. Campbell, *Collected Poems,* p. 43.

44. Campbell, *Collected Poems,* p. 68.

Chapter 8

1. Michael Roberts (ed.), *New Country* (London, 1933), p. 19.

2. Roberts (ed.), *New Signatures,* p. 19.

3. Roberts (ed.), *New Country,* pp. 18, 21.

4. See Q. Bell, *Julian Bell,* pp. 309, 313.

5. See Sloan, *John Cornford,* p. 131.

6. Christopher Caudwell, *Illusion and Reality* (London, 1937), pp. 319–322.

7. Stephen Spender, *World Within World* (London, 1951), p. 247. The poem was also published by Nancy Cunard in the first of a series of booklets devoted to Spanish war poetry called *Les Poétes du Monde Défendent le Peuple Espagnol.*

8. *Ibid.* Spender told this author that although he learned no more from Auden about his visit than what he had written in *World Within World,* he felt certain that Auden's visit had strongly influenced the content of "Spain." (Interview: London, May, 1961). Charles Duff, who was with Auden in Valencia in January, 1937, told me that Auden seemed impatient to leave Spain as soon as he could and that he badgered Duff and others for information about the Republican cause. (Interview: London, May, 1961).

To this author, Auden wrote: "I did not wish to talk about Spain when I returned because I was upset by many things I saw or heard about. Some of them were described better than I could ever have done by George Orwell, in *Homage to Catalonia.* Others were what I learned about the treatment of priests." (Letter to author: November 29, 1962).

9. It would be a mistake to assume that "Spain" suddenly dropped the curtain on all his political involvement. As his statement in *I Believe* (1940) revealed, he still held what appeared to be rather vague socialist views.

> I do not see how in politics one can decide *a priori* what conduct is moral, or what degree of tolerance there should be. One can only decide which party in one's private judgment has the best view of what society ought to be, and to support it; and remember that, since all coercion is a moral evil, we should view with extreme suspicion those who welcome it. Thus I cannot see how a socialist country could tolerate the existence of a Fascist party any more than a Fascist country could tolerate the existence of a socialist party. I judge them differently because I think that the Socialists are right and the Fascists are wrong in their view of society. (It is always wrong in an absolute sense to kill, but all killing is not equally bad; it does matter who is killed.)
>
> It is idle to lament that the world is becoming divided into hostile ideological camps; the division is a fact. No policy of isolation is possible. *I Believe* (London, 1940), p. 30.

10. W. H. Auden, "Spain" (London, 1938). All excerpts come from this edition of the poem.

11. George Orwell objected to the use of the phrase "necessary murder," declaring that it could only have been written by one who was removed from the realities of war, including murder. He believed that Auden could not have comprehended the total meaning of "necessary murder," and that by using the phrase he revealed his inexperience as well as his distance from the war. It was the sort of leftist war talk carried on by people who knew they were immune. "Inside the Whale," *Such, Such Were the Joys,* pp. 184–185.

12. American Communist Joseph North registered the Marxist reaction to defeat. ". . . a just war is never lost and no life given in it is ever lost: those who died offered tomorrows up in their image. If Republican Spain would go down, the precepts of the dead would inspire multitudes to enlist in a just and timeless cause. . . . The Spanish people will rise again as they have always risen before tyranny.

The dead do not need to rise. They are part of the earth now and the earth can never be conquered. For the earth endureth forever. It will outlive all systems of tyranny." *No Men Are Strangers* (New York, 1958), pp. 146–147.

13. W. H. Auden and John Garrett (eds.). *The Poet's Tongue* (London, 1935), ix.

14. Spender, *World,* p. 191.

15. Stephen Spender, *Forward from Liberalism* (London, 1937), p. 27, pp. 185–186, 189 ff.

16. Stephen Spender, in *The God That Failed,* edited by R. Crossman (New York, 1952), p. 250.

Though there is some doubt about what transpired at this meeting, it has been reported that Pollitt advised the poet that the best way he could help the Party was "to go and get killed, comrade, we need a Byron in the movement." (Thomas, p. 348.) That this may be aprocryphal, I would suggest for several reasons. First, Spender wrote nothing about such a request either in *World Within World* or in *The God That Failed,* where detailed accounts of this meeting appear. Second, if Pollitt really wanted a Byron, he had only to choose one from several poets who were already in Spain, such as John Cornford or Charles Donnelly. Third, in an interview with this author, Spender could not recall that Pollitt had made such a request of him. In any event, Byron himself seemed to fulfill most of the Party's needs. He almost literally became the bard of the Republic. See references to Byron in *Ralph Fox: A Writer in Arms,* by Pollitt; in *Spain at War,* No. 8, by Charles Duff; and in *Truth Will Out,* by Charlotte Haldane. In addition, Alvarez del Vayo, Herbert Matthews, and Charles Foltz either quote from Byron's works or use him as a synonym for protest. Cf. Anatoly Lunacharshy, "Byron and Byronism," *International Literature,* No. 1 (Jan., 1938), 71.

17. Spender, *World,* p. 211.

18. Spender, *God,* p. 248.

19. Spender, *World,* pp. 216–218.

20. *Ibid.,* p.223; *God,* p. 252.

21. Spender, *God,* p. 253.

22. *Ibid.,* p. 257. Naturally such divergent views came to the attention of the Party leaders. At a meeting of several Communist writers, Spender was asked to explain his attitude toward the Party and Spain. He replied that he supported the Spanish Republic completely and that he was prepared to support the Party as well since it "had done so much for Spain." But he asked the committee if they were willing to take responsibility for certain "injustices" he had witnessed in Spain. When he recounted what they were, one member chided him that one of his informers was not a "reliable witness." Spender's unorthodox views had undoubtedly begun to annoy the Party. See *Life and the Poet,* p. 16. Some of the information in this note was given this author by Randall Swingler, who attended the meeting.

23. Spender, *World,* p. 212. Younger is actually T. A. R. Hyndman. His single poem about Spain, "Jarama Front," was published in *Poems for Spain.* See above, pp. 106–107.

24. *Ibid.,* pp. 214, 228

25. *Ibid.,* pp. 240–241, 247. Compare, however, Spender's more positive report of the Congress in the *London Mercury.* The Congress, he wrote, "was as emphatic an assertion as could be made of our conviction that the creation of literature to-day is inseparable from the struggle for a world in which the standards of culture are not destroyed by Fascism." "International Writers' Congress, a Communication," *London Mercury,* 36 (Aug., 1937), 373. See Symon's comments on Spender's contrasting versions of the Congress in *The Thirties,* pp. 126–128.

The British contingent to the Congress was kept small due to the refusal of the British Foreign Office to issue visas to those who wished to attend. Besides Spender, those who got to Spain, presumably without visas, were Edgell Rickword, Sylvia T. Warner, and Valentine Ackland. British and Irish writers already in Spain who attended included Claud Cockburn and Ralph Bates. See Spender, *World,* p. 243, for a revealing glimpse of Bates as a political commissar.

26. Spender, *God,* p. 247; *World,* pp. 252, 254.

27. Stephen Spender, "Spain Invites the World's Writers," *New Writing,* IV (Autumn, 1937), 250.

28. Stephen Spender, *The Still Centre* (London, 1939), p. 10.

29. Spender, *Centre,* p. 72.

30. See Stephen Spender, *The Destructive Element* (Philadelphia, 1953), pp. 219 ff.

31. Spender, *Centre,* p. 58. Cf. *World,* p. 230.

32. Spender, *World,* pp. 223–224.

33. Spender, *Centre,* p. 60.

34. *Ibid.,* p. 55. See Spender's observations in *World,* p. 223.

35. See Thomas, pp. 376–377. This author has been told by former members of the XV Battalion that in the interests of maintaining discipline under fire a certain number of men belonging to the battalion were shot.

36. Spender, *Centre,* p. 56.

37. *Ibid.,* p. 45.

38. *Ibid.,* pp. 62–63.

39.   *Ibid.,* p. 67.

40.   *Ibid.,* pp. 65–66.

41.   Spender, *Poems for Spain,* pp. 7, 10, 11.

42.   Lewis, *Day,* p. 223.

43.   *Ibid.,* p. 218.

44.   C. Day Lewis, "Letter to a Young Revolutionary," *New Country,* p. 29.

45.   C. Day Lewis, *The Starting Point* (London, 1938). In this novel the character of Anthony Neale has much in common with the author.

46.   Lewis, *Day,* p. 209.

47.   *Ibid.,* pp. 209–211. Some of the information above was the result of an interview this author had with the poet. (Interview: London, June, 1961.)

48.   *Ibid.,* pp. 213, 219, 221.

49.   *Ibid.,* p. 213.

50.   *Ibid.,* pp. 211–212.

51.   C. Day Lewis, *Overtures to Death and Other Poems* (London, 1938), p. 15.

52.   *Ibid.,* p. 40.

53.   *Ibid.,* p. 41.

54.   Louis MacNeice, *Modern Poetry* (London, 1938), p. 6.

55.   Louis MacNeice, "Turf-Stacks," *Poems* (London, 1935), p. 30.

56.   Louis MacNeice, *Autumn Journal* (London, 1939), pp. 27–29.

57.   Louis MacNeice, *I Crossed the Minch* (London, 1938), pp. 125–129.

58.   MacNeice, *Journal,* pp. 89–90.

59.   Louis MacNeice, "The Poet in England Today," *New Republic,* 102 (March 25, 1940), 412–413.

Conclusions

1.   Stephen Spender, *Poetry Since 1939* (London, 1946), p. 29.

2.   Julian Symons, "The Betrayed Idealists," *Sunday Times Magazine Section* (London) (July 23, 1961), 21.

3.   Two commentators have recently noted that the failure of the democracies to take sides in the Spanish war worked to the disadvantage of the Republic. See Allen Guttmann, *The Wound in the Heart* (New York, 1962), p. 210, and Hugh Thomas, pp. 611 ff.

4.   Discussions with Spender, Day Lewis, Lindsay, Swingler, Rickword, Nancy Cunard, Leslie Daiken, Miles Tomalin, and others have confirmed this.

5.   Lewis, *Day,* p. 218.

6.   Spender, *Life and the Poet,* p. 21.

7,   David Daiches, *Poetry and the Modern World* (Chicago, 1940), p. 241.

8.   "Editorial," *Poetry and the People* (October, 1938), 2.

9.   Symons, *Thirties,* pp. 166, 170.

10.   Hugh Thomas, *The Spanish Civil War* (London, 1961).

A Selected Bibliography

WITH THE EXCEPTION OF THE BOOKS LISTED IN SECTIONS TWO, three, and seven, the bibliography contains only primary sources. The exceptions are books which have been published since 1939 and which have a special interest for students of the Spanish Civil War.

I have relied mainly upon British sources. However, certain books by non-British writers, and a few periodicals published in the United States have been indispensable to me, and therefore I have included them in this listing.

A few months ago, Hugh Thomas pointed out in a review of a book about the Spanish war that, since around 3,000 books have been written on the subject, "any historian of the civil war will be able to present an enormous if largely useless bibliography at the back of his book and thus gain a quick reputation for learning." It is this author's hope that the bibliography that follows will seem neither enormous nor useless.

Abbreviations

In section five of the bibliography, the following abbreviations have been used :

International Literature	*IL*
Labour Monthly	*LM*
Left Book News	*LBN*
Left News	*LN*

Left Review	*LR*
Life and Letters Today	*L&LT*
New Republic	*NR*
New Statesman and Nation	*NS&N*
Saturday Review	*SR*
Spain	*S*
Spectator	*SP*
Volunteer for Liberty	*VFL*

I. Contemporary Accounts

Acier, Marcel (ed.). *From Spanish Trenches.* New York, 1937.

Atholl, Katherine Duchess of. *Searchlight on Spain.* London, 1938.

Ballou, Jenny. *Spanish Prelude.* London, 1937.

Bernanos, George. *A Diary of My Times.* London, 1938.

Bessie, Alvah. *Men in Battle.* New York, 1939.

Blasquez, Jose. *I Helped to Build an Army.* London, 1939.

Blythe, Henry. *Spain over Britain.* London, 1937.

Book of the XVth International Brigade. Madrid, 1939.

Borkenau, Franz. *The Spanish Cockpit.* London, 1937.

Brereton, G. *Inside Spain.* London, 1938.

Cardozo, H. G. *March of a Nation.* London, 1937.

Casado, S. *Last Days of Madrid.* London, 1939.

Clerisse, Henry. *Espagne 36–37.* Paris, 1937.

Conze, Edward. *Spain Today.* London, 1936.

Cox, Geoffrey. *Defence of Madrid.* London, 1937.

Dzelepy, E. N. *The Spanish Plot.* London, 1938.

Forrest, William. *It Happened in Spain.* London, 1937.

Gerahty, Cecil. *The Road to Madrid.* London, 1937.

———, and Foss, William. *The Spanish Arena.* London, 1938.

Jellineck, Frank. *The Civil War in Spain.* London, 1938.

Knickerbocker, H. R. *The Siege of Alcazar.* London, 1937.

Koestler, Arthur. *Spanish Testament.* London, 1937.

Langdon-Davies, John. *Behind the Spanish Barricades*. London, 1936.

Low, Mary, and Brea, Juan. *Red Spanish Notebook*. London, 1937.

Matthews, Herbert. *Two Wars and More to Come*. New York, 1938.

Medio, Justo. *Three Pictures of the Spanish Civil War*. London, 1937.

Memorial Book: British Battalion XVth International Brigade. London, 1939.

Mitchell, Sir Peter Chalmers. *My House in Malaga*. London, 1938.

Nazi Conspiracy in Spain. London, 1937.

O'Donnell, Peadar. *Salud!* London, 1937.

O'Duffy, Eoin. *Crusade in Spain*. Dublin, 1938.

One Year of War. New York, 1937.

Orwell, George. *Homage to Catalonia*. New York, 1938.

Osborne, E. A. (ed.). *In Letters of Red*. London, 1938.

Paul, E. *The Life and Death of a Spanish Town*. New York, 1937.

Pitcairn, Frank (Claud Cockburn). *Reporter in Spain*. London, 1936.

Prieto Carlos (Charles Duff). *Spanish Front*. London, 1936.

Rolfe, Edwin. *The Lincoln Battalion*. New York, 1939.

Romilly, Esmond. *Boadilla*. London, 1937.

Rust, William. *Britons in Spain*. London, 1939.

Scott-Watson, K. *Single to Spain*. London, 1937.

Sender, Ramon. *The War in Spain*. London, 1937.

Sommerfield, John. *Volunteer in Spain*. London, 1937.

Steer, G. L. *Tree of Gernika*. London, 1938.

Strong, A. L. *Spain in Arms*. New York, 1937.

Tinker, F. G. *Some Still Live*. London, 1938.

Vilaplana, Ruiz. *Burgos Justice*. New York, 1938.

White, F. *War in Spain*. London, 1937.

Woolsey, Gamel. *Death's Other Kingdom*. London, 1939.

Worsley, T. C. *Behind the Battle*. London, 1939.

Yeats-Brown, F. *European Jungle*. Philadelphia, 1939.

II. Histories of the Spanish Civil War and Later Accounts

Álvarez del Vayo, Julio. *Freedom's Battle*. New York, 1940.

Barea, Arturo. *The Forging of a Rebel*. New York, 1946.

Bolloten, Burnett. *The Grand Camouflage*. London, 1961.

Bowers, Claude. *My Mission to Spain*. New York, 1954.

Buckley, Henry. *Life and Death of the Spanish Republic*. London, 1940.

Cattell, David. *Communism and the Spanish Civil War*. Berkeley, 1955.

———. *Soviet Diplomacy and the Spanish Civil War*. Berkeley, 1957.

Cockburn, Claud. *In Time of Trouble*. London, 1956.

Colodny, Robert. *The Struggle for Madrid: The Central Epic of the Spanish Conflict*. New York, 1958.

Copeman, Fred. *Reason in Revolt*. London, 1948.

Cowles, V. *Looking for Trouble*. London, 1941.

Diaz, Jose. *Lessons of the Spanish War*. London, 1940.

Duff, Charles. *Key to Victory: Spain*. London, 1940.

Feis, Herbert. *The Spanish Story*. New York, 1948.

Foltz, Charles. *The Masquerade in Spain*. Boston, 1948.

Haldane, Charlotte. *Truth Will Out*. London, 1949.

Hanighen, Frank. *Nothing but Danger*. London, 1940.

Hughes, Emmet. *Report from Spain*. New York, 1947.

Kemp, Peter. *Mine Were of Trouble*. London, 1957.

Krivitsky, W. G. *In Stalin's Secret Service*. New York, 1939.

Matthews, Herbert. *The Yoke and the Arrows*. New York, 1957.

Nelson, Steve. *The Volunteers*. Berlin, 1958.

North, Joseph. *No Men Are Strangers*. New York, 1958.

Payne, Robert (ed.). *The Civil War in Spain*. New York, 1962.

Peers, E. A. *Spain in Eclipse*. London, 1943.

Regler, Gustav. *The Owl of Minerva*. New York, 1960.

Richards, V. *Lessons of the Spanish Revolution*. London, 1953.

Thomas, Hugh. *The Spanish Civil War*. London, 1961.

Toynbee, Arnold (with V. M. Boulter and Katherine Duff). *Survey of International Affairs, 1937:* Vol. II; and *1938:* Vol. I. Oxford, 1938, 1948.

Watkins, K. W. *Britain Divided*. London, 1963.

Ydeville, Charles. *Interlude in Spain*. London, 1945.

III. General Works

Black, C. E. and Helmreich, E. C. *Twentieth Century Europe*. New York, 1959.

Borkenau, Franz. *European Communism*. London, 1953.

Brenan, Gerald. *The Spanish Labyrinth*. New York, 1943.

———. *The Face of Spain*. London, 1950.

Brockway, Fenner. *Inside the Left*. London, 1942.

Calder-Marshall, A. *The Changing Scene*. London, 1937.

Castillejo, J. *Wars of Ideas in Spain*. London, 1937.

Churchill, Winston. *Step by Step*. New York, 1939.

———. *The Gathering Storm*. Boston, 1948.

Cole, G. D. H. *A History of the Labour Party from 1914*. London, 1948.

———. *Socialism and Fascism, 1931–1939*. London, 1960.

———, and Postgate, Raymond. *The Common People*. London, 1938.

Connelly, Cyril. *The Condemned Playground*. London, 1945.

Dos Passos, John. *Journeys Between Wars*. New York, 1938.

———. *The Theme Is Freedom*. New York, 1956.

Eden, Anthony. *Facing the Dictators*. New York, 1962.

Fischer, Louis. *Men and Politics*. London, 1941.

Garratt, G. T. *Gibraltar and the Mediterranean*. New York, 1939.

Gibbs, Philip. *Ordeal in England*. New York, 1937.

———. *Across the Frontiers*. New York, 1938.

Goldring, Douglas. *The Nineteen Twenties*. London, 1945.

Gollancz, Victor. *The Betrayal of the Left*. London, 1941.

Graves, Robert, and Hodge, Alan. *The Long Week-End*. London, 1939.

Harrison, S. *Good to be Alive, The Story of Jack Brent*. London, 1954.

I Believe. London, 1940.

Jerrold, Douglas. *Georgian Adventure*. New York, 1938.

Koestler, Arthur. *The Invisible Writing*. London, 1954.

Madariaga, Salvador de. *Spain: A Modern History*. New York, 1958.

Mirsky, Dmitri. *The Intelligentsia of Great Britain*. New York, 1935.

Montagu, Ivor. *The Traitor Class*. London, 1940.

Mowat, Charles L. *Britain Between the Wars,* 1918–1940. London, 1955.

Muggeridge, Malcolm. *The Thirties*. London, 1940.

Peacock, Arthur. *Yours Fraternally*. London, 1945.

Peers, E. A. *The Spanish Tragedy*. New York, 1936.

Pollitt, Harry. *Selected Articles and Speeches,* Vol. II. London, 1954.

Rayner, Robert M. *The Twenty Year's Truce*. London, 1943.

Rubinstein, Alvin. *The Foreign Policy of the Soviet Union*. New York, 1960.

Schapiro, Leonard. *The Communist Party of the Soviet Union*. New York, 1960.

Schuman, F. L. *Europe on the Eve, the Crisis of Diplomacy*. New York, 1939.

Seton-Watson, R. W. *Britain and the Dictators*. New York, 1938.

Shirer, William L. *Berlin Diary*. New York, 1941.

———. *The Rise and Fall of the Third Reich*. New York, 1960.

Willis, Jerome, *Restless Quest*. London, 1938.

Wintringham, Tom. *New Ways of War*. London, 1940.

Wolfers, Arnold. *Britain and France Between Two Wars*. New York, 1940.

Wood, Neal. *Communism and British Intellectuals*. London, 1959.

Writers Take Sides. New York, 1938.

IV. Contemporary Pamphlets

Bahamonde, Antonio. *Memoirs of a Spanish Nationalist*. London, 1939.

Barea, A. *The Struggle for the Spanish Soul*. London, 1938.

Bartlett, Vernon. *I Accuse*. London, 1937.

Britain in Spain, by the Unknown Diplomat. London, 1939.

Brockway, Fenner. *The Truth about Barcelona*. London, 1937.

Cripps, Stafford, *et al. The Unity Campaign*. London, 1937.

Cunard, Nancy. *Authors Take Sides*. London, 1937.

Diaz, G. *Spain's Struggle Against Anarchism and Communism*. New York, n.d.

Dimitrov, Georgi. *Spain's Year of War*. New York, 1937.

Dzelepy, E. N. *The Spanish Plot*. London, 1937.

Fischer, Louis. *The War in Spain*. New York, 1937.

———. *Why Spain Fights On*. London, 1938.

Five on Revolutionary Art. London, 1936.

Foreign Intervention in Spain. London, 1937.

Franco in Barcelona. London, 1939.

Franco's Rule. London, 1938.

George, Right Honorable David L. *Spain and Britain*. London, 1937.

Gifford, John. *Arms for Red Spain*. London, 1939.

Greaves, H. R. G., and Thomson, David. *The Truth about Spain*. London, 1938.

Gurrea, J. M. *A Catholic Looks at Spain*. London, 1937.

Hispanicus. *Badajoz*. London, 1937.

Huntz, Jack. *Spotlight on Spain*. London, 1936.

In Spain with the International Brigade. London, 1938.

Italian Air Force in Spain. London, 1938.

It's Up to Us. London, 1936.

Journalist. *Foreign Journalists under Franco's Terror.* London, n.d.

Krehm, William. *Spain: Revolution and Counter-Revolution.* Toronto, n.d.

Lambda, R. *The Truth about the Barcelona Events.* New York, n.d.

Langdon-Davies, J. *The Case for the Government.* New York, 1938.

———. *The Spanish Church and Politics.* New York, 1938.

Lewis, C. Day. *We're Not Going to do Nothing.* London, 1936.

Lunn, Sir Arnold. *Spain and the Christian Front.* New York, n.d.

McGovern, John. *Terror in Spain.* London, 1938.

MacKee, Seumas. *I Was a Franco Soldier.* London, 1938.

Matteo, Johan. *Democracy or Revolution in Spain?* London, 1937.

Nazi Germany and Fascist Italy Have Invaded Spain. London, 1938.

Negrín, Juan. *The Will to Victory.* London, 1938.

Oliveira, A. R. *The Drama of Spain.* London, n.d.

Pasionaria, *People's Tribune of Spain.* New York, 1938.

Pollitt, Harry. *Spain and the TUC.* London, 1936.

———. *Arms for Spain.* London, 1936.

Pollitt Visits Spain. London, 1938.

Robles, Gil. *Spain in Chains.* New York, 1937.

Rocafull, Jose. *Crusade or Class War?* London, 1937.

Spain Against the Invaders. London, 1938.

Spain and Us. London, 1936.

Spain at War. London, 1937.

Story of the British Medical Aid Unit in Spain. London, 1936.

Thorning, Joseph F. *Why the Press Failed on Spain.* New York, n.d.

Three Years of Struggle in Spain. London, 1939.

Trotsky, Leon. *The Lesson of Spain, the Last Warning.* London, 1938.

Visit of an All-Party Group of Members of Parliament to Spain. London, 1937.

Wertheim, Barbara. *The Lost British Policy*. London, 1937.

Zamora, Niceto Alcala, *et al. Spanish Liberals Speak on the Counter-Revolution in Spain*. San Francisco, 1937.

V. Articles

Abrams, S. H. "International Brigade," *Canadian Forum,* 19 (August, 1939), 157.

Álvarez del Vayo, J. "Organizing for Victory," *LN,* No. 20 (December, 1937), 598; No. 21 (January, 1938), 647.

———. "The Last Phase of Spain," *NS&N,* 17 (March 18, 1939), 413.

Araquistain, Luis. "Communism and the War in Spain," *S,* No. 8 (July 6, 1939), 4.

"Arriba España," *S,* No. 42 (July 18, 1938), 50.

Arteaga de Leon, J. "Spain Replies to the Duchess of Atholl and Her Book," *S,* No. 49 (September 6, 1938), 193.

———. "Roy Campbell Through Spanish Eyes," *S,* No. 85 (May 18, 1939), 140.

Attlee, C. R. "What I Learnt in Spain," *LN,* No. 21 (January, 1938), 645.

Auden, W. H. "Sermon by an Armament Manufacturer," *L&LT,* 10 (May, 1934), 164.

Barker, George. "Funeral Eulogy on Garcia Lorca," *L&LT,* 21 (October, 1939), 61.

Baroja, Pio. "What Underlies Marxism," *S,* No. 18 (February 1, 1938), 1.

Bates, Ralph. "Castilian Drama," *NR,* 92 (October 20, 1937), 210; 92 (October 27, 1937), 333.

———. "Spanish Improvisation," *London Mercury,* 35 (November, 1936), 23.

———. "Of Legendary Time," *Virginia Quarterly Review,* 15 (January, 1939), 21.

Bates, Winifred. "British Nurse in Spain," *Spain at War,* No. 7 (October, 1938), 244.

Beals, Carleton. "The Spanish War of Words," *NR,* 91 (June 2, 1937), 94.

Beeching, Jack. "Edgell Rickword," *Our Time,* 7 (March, 1948), 144.

Bell, J. "No Quiet in Spain," *English Review,* 62 (May, 1936), 558.

Belloc, H. "The Issue in Spain," *S.* No. 44 (July, 1938), 100.

Bennett, Richard. "Portrait of a Killer," *NS&N,* 62 (March 24, 1961), 471.

Beste, R. V. "On Mass Declamations," *Our Time,* 2 (May, 1943), 3.

"Birthday of the International Brigades," *LR,* (November, 1937), 575.

Boswell, James. "Clive Branson : A Tribute," *Our Time,* 4 (November, 1944), 6.

Branting, George. "The Situation in Spain," *LM,* 18 (October, 1936), 600.

Bray, Norman. "Spain Betrayed by Russia," *S,* No. 15 (January 8, 1938), 1.

Braybrooke, N. "W. H. Auden : the Road from Marx," *America,* 88 (March 21, 1953), 680.

Brent, J. "International Brigade Association," *NS&N,* 22 (September 13, 1941), 255.

Brown, Ernest. "No Quiet on the Spanish Front," *LM,* 21 (September, 1939), 527.

Buchanan, Meriel. "Red Terror in Spain," *SR,* 162 (August 1, 1936), 136.

————. "How Moscow Helps the Spanish Reds," *SR,* 162 (October 17, 1936), 492.

Burns, Emile, "Further Stages in the Spanish Struggle," *LN,* No. 8 (December, 1936), 179.

Campbell, Roy. "The Rise of Roy Campbell," *The Poetry Journal,* 1 (April, 1937), 9.

C. H. "Bolshevist Spain and After, A Lost Opportunity," *SR,* 162 (August 15, 1936), 198.

Cohen, J. M. "Since the Civil War," *Encounter,* 12 (February, 1959), 44.

Connolly, C. "The Future in Spain," *NS&N,* 12 (December 26, 1936), 1052.

————. "Spanish Diary," *NS&N,* 13 (February 20, 1937), 278.

Cornford, John. "John Cornford," *LR,* 3 (March, 1937), 67.

Cowley, M. "Spender, Auden and After," *NR,* 107 (October 5, 1942), 418.

Cripps, Sir S. "The British Public and Spain," *LN,* No. 20 (December, 1937), 594.

Cunard, Nancy, "Three Negro Poets," *LR,* 3 (October, 1937), 529.

————. "A Message from South-West France," *Our Time,* 5 (August, 1945), 4.

"Defence of Democracy," *SP,* 157 (September 4, 1936), 382.

Donnelly, Charles. "Portrait of a Revolution," *LR,* 2 (October, 1935), 1.

Dourec, M. J. "How the International Brigaders Are Forced to Fight," *S,* No. 33 (May 17, 1938), 18.

"Drive for United Party Spreads," *VFL,* 1 (August 29, 1937), 1.

Drummond, John. "The Mind of W. H. Auden," *Townsman,* 1 (July, 1938), 23.

Duncan, Ronald. "Epitaph on the Illiterate Left," *Townsman,* 3 (February, 1940), 9.

Dutt, R. Palme. "Britain and Spain," *LM,* 18 (September, 1936), 523.

————. "In Memory of Ralph Fox," *LM,* 19 (March, 1937), 169.

Ehrenburg, Ilya. "Spain's Tempering," *IL,* No. 3 (March, 1938), 61.

————. "Volunteers for Murder," *Living Age,* 354 (August, 1938), 491.

Elwell-Sutton, R. "Days in Spain," *Blackwood's Magazine,* 248 (September, 1940), 259.

Fenby, C. "British Public Opinion on Spain," *Political Quarterly,* 7 (October, 1936), 537.

"The XV International Brigade," *S*, No. 67 (January 12, 1939), 24.

Fischer, Louis. "Back to the Wall in Spain," *NS&N*, 15 (April 9, 1938), 599.

———. "The War in Spain," *NS&N*, 16 (August 20, 1938), 272.

———. "Peace on Earth, Good Will toward Men," *NS&N*, 16 (December 10, 1938), 953.

"For Culture Against Fascism," *LR*, 3 (March, 1937), 65.

Ford, Walter. "Poetry and Who Cares Anyway," *Poetry and the People*, No. 8 (February, 1939), 13.

Fox, Ralph. "Ralph Fox," *LR*, 3 (February, 1937), 1.

Franco, R. "They Fight for Spain," *SR*, 162 (November 28, 1936), 682.

Franford, J. A. "Trotskyist Traitors," *VFL*, 1 (September 13, 1937), 9.

Fraser, G. S. "Poetry and Civilization," *London Mercury*, 26 (September, 1937), 440.

Fuller, J. F. C. "The Soviet War in Spain," *S*, No. 13 (July 1, 1937), 2.

———. "Rag-Picking on the Spanish Battlefield," *S*, No. 35 (May 31, 1938), 1.

Fyfe, H. "The Press and the People's Front," *LR*, 2 (December, 1936), 807.

Ganthorne-Hardy, G. M. "The Spanish Situation Reviewed," *International Affairs*, 16 (May, 1937), 403.

Garratt, G. T. "Home Thoughts from Madrid," *NS&N*, 16 (September 24, 1938), 449.

Gillett, Eric. "Roy Campbell and Some Others," *National and English Review*, 138 (July, 1952), 37.

Glicksberg, Charles I. "Poetry and Marxism," *University of Toronto Quarterly*, 6 (April, 1937), 309.

———. "Poetry and the Social Revolution," *Dalhousie Review*, 17 (April, 1937), 493.

Gollancz, V. "The Left Book Club, the People's Front, and Communism," *LN*, No. 15 (July, 1937), 420.

———. "Spain," *LN*, No. 21 (January, 1938), 636.

Goodman, R. "Poisoned Peace," *LM,* 19 (August, 1937), 473.

Graves, Robert. "A Life Bang-Full of Kicks and Shocks," *New York Times Book Review,* (January 5, 1958), 6.

Haldane, J. B. S. "Can London Learn from Barcelona?", *NS&N,* 16 (July 9, 1938), 66.

Hart, Liddell. "Lessons of the Spanish War," *National Review,* 109 (November, 1937), 606.

Hausermann, H. W. "Left-Wing Poetry, a Note," *English Studies,* 21 (October, 1939), 13.

Hemingway, Ernest. "The Spanish War," *Fact,* No. 16 (July, 1938), 7.

Humphries, Rolfe. "The Balladry of the Civil War," *IL,* No. 3 (March, 1937), 31.

Huxley, J. S. "The Spanish News : A Quantitative Analysis," *NS&N,* 12 (August 8, 1936), 1871.

"International Brigades," *NS&N,* 22 (September 27, 1941), 300.

"Intervention in Spain," *Round Table,* 27 (1937), 276.

"The Ishmaels of Europe," *S,* No. 19 (February 8, 1938).

Jackson, F. "No Munich for Spain," *LM,* 20 (November, 1938), 699.

James, A. W. H. "Background to Franco," *SP,* 162 (March 3, 1939), 348.

Jerrold, D. "The Re-Birth of Spain," *S,* No. 4 (October 23, 1937), 14.

———. "Spain : Impressions and Reflections," *Nineteenth Century and After,* 121 (April, 1937), 470.

———. "The Issues in Spain," *The American Review,* 9 (April, 1937), 1.

Joad, C. E. M. "What is Happening to the Peace Movement?", *NS&N,* 13 (May 15, 1937), 802.

Johnson, H. "Special for Spain," *LN,* No. 29 (September, 1938), 958.

Kelyin, F. V. "Heroism in Spanish Literature," *IL,* No. 10 (October, 1936), 72.

———. "Fascist Kultur in Spain," *IL,* No. 11 (November, 1936), 90.

———."Recent Spanish Literature," *IL*, No. 2 (February, 1937), 80.

Kemp, Peter, "People's Army," *Nineteenth Century*, 123 (March, 1938), 365.

———. "Lessons of the Spanish War," *National War*, 112 (February, 1939), 175.

———. "Spain and the Myth that Survives," *Daily Telegraph and Morning Post* (April 27, 1961).

Kim. "Rout of the Reds," *SR*, 162 (October 24, 1936), 518.

Kirk, R. "The Last of the Scalds," *Sewanee Review*, 64 (1956), 164.

Knoblaugh, H. E. "Loyalist Propaganda Machine," *Catholic World*, 146 (January, 1938), 479.

Koltsov, Michael. "Spanish Diary," *IL*, No. 7 (July, 1938), 41; No. 8 (August, 1938), 41.

Krivitsky, W. G. "Stalin's Hand in Spain," *Saturday Evening Post*, 212 (April 15, 1939), 5.

Langdon-Davies, John. "The Struggle for Anti-Fascist Unity in Spain," *LM*, 19 (October, 1937), 609.

———. "Bombs over Barcelona," *Living Age*, 355 (September, 1938), 58.

Laski, H. J. "The Labour Party and the Left Book Club," *LN*, No. 16 (August, 1937), 456.

Lehmann, John. "Some Revolutionary Trends in English Poetry," *IL*, No. 4 (April, 1936), 60.

———. "Should Writers Keep to Their Art?", *LR*, 2 (January, 1937), 881.

Lehmann, Rosamund. "My Husband Went to War in Spain," *Reynolds News* (August 8, 1937), 5.

Leslie, Shane. "The Heart of Spain," *S*, 7 (July 20, 1939), 41.

Lewis C. Day. "Revolutionaries and Poetry," *LR*, 1 (July, 1935), 397.

———. "English Writers and a People's Front," *LR*, 2 (October, 1936), 671.

———. "Labour and Fascism, the Writer's Task," *LR*, 2 (November, 1936), 731.

————. "Sword and Pen," *LR,* 2 (December, 1936), 794.

————. "Poetry To-Day," *LR,* 2 (January, 1937), 899.

Lindsay, Jack. "A Plea for Mass Declamation," *LR,* 3 (October, 1937), 511.

————. "The Broadsheet Tradition," *Left Poets News Sheet* March, 1938).

————. "Directions for On Guard for Spain!", *Left Poets News Sheet* (April, 1938).

————. "A Plea for Broadsheet and Ballad," *Left Poets News Sheet* (January, 1938).

Lipton, Julius. "A Few Remarks about Proletarian Poetry," *Poetry and the People,* No. 3 (September, 1938), 12.

Lloyd, A. L. "Lorca : Poet of Spain," *LR,* 3 (March, 1937), 71.

"The Long Run," *NS&N,* 16 (December 17, 1938), 971.

Lore, Ludwig. "Has Britain Betrayed Spain?", *NR,* 90 (March 3, 1937), 99.

Loveday, A. F. "The B.B.C. and Spain," *SR,* 162 (August 29, 1936), 275.

Lunacharsky, Anatoly. "Byron and Byronism," *IL,* No. 1 (January, 1938), 71.

Macaulay, R. "Marginal Comments," *S,* 159 (July 23, 1937), 141.

MacNeice, Louis. "Comment on Poetry," *New Verse,* No. 11 (October, 1934), 7.

————. "Letter to W. H. Auden," *New Verse,* No. 26–27 (November, 1937), 11.

————. "Today in Barcelona," *SP,* 162 (January 20, 1939), 84.

Malraux, André. "Men in Spain," *NR,* 96 (October 12, 1938), 261.

Mann, H. "Spain and Culture," *L&LT,* 17 (Autumn, 1937), 9.

Mann, T. "Epilogue to Spain," *L&LT,* 16 (Summer, 1937), 68.

Maranon, M. G. "Surveying the Spanish War," *Revue de Paris,* 24 (December 15, 1937), 7.

Mazarani, C. A. "Volunteers," *SP,* 158 (February 12, 1937), 264.

Mellor, F. H. "Spain, Land of Terror," *SR,* 162 (October 17, 1936), 490.

Mirsky, D. "About Stephen Spender and C. Day Lewis," *IL,* No. 10 (October, 1936), 80.

Moody, V. A. "Spain in Revolt," *Social Forces,* 15 (1936), 563.

Moroney, Brendan. "Twenty Months in the International Brigade," *S,* No. 43 (July 26, 1938), 86.

Muggeridge, M. "Exploding Bombs and Poets," *Time and Tide,* 42 (May 11, 1961), 785.

N.B. (Nicholas Breakespeare). "The New Statesman and Spain," *Arena,* 1 (July, 1937), 114.

Neruda, Pablo, "Federico Garcia Lorca," *IL,* No. 8 (August, 1937), 100.

O'Donnell, Paedar. "Irishmen in Spain," *Nineteenth Century,* 120 (December, 1936), 698.

Oliver, James. "Don Quixote and John Bull," *Colosseum,* 3 (September, 1937), 149.

Ortega, Juan. "Quixotism in the Spanish Revolution," *Colosseum,* 3 (September, 1937), 130.

Orwell, George, "The Spanish War," *Adelphi,* 16 (1939), 125.

―――. "Looking Back on the Spanish War," *Such, Such Were the Joys* (New York, 1945), p. 131.

"Our Dangerous Bunglers," *SR,* 162 (November 29, 1936), 676.

Peers, E. A. "General Franco's New Spain," *Dublin Review,* 200 (April, 1937), 221.

―――. "Evolution of the New Spain," *Dublin Review,* 202 (January, 1938), 1.

Peman, Jose M. "The Intellectuals Support Franco," *S,* No. 24 (March 15, 1938), 1.

Pitcairn, Frank. "On the Firing Line in Defense of Madrid," *Travel,* 68 (February, 1937), 18.

"Poetry, the Voice of the New Spain," *S,* No. 15 (January 8, 1938), 20.

"The Poetry of the Nationalist Movement," *S,* 7 (April 20, 1939), 60.

"The Policy of British Imperialism," *VFL,* 1 (June 15, 1937), 1.

Pollitt, Harry. "Building the People's Front," *LR,* 2 (December, 1936), 797.

Pritchett, V. S. "Spain and the Future," *SP,* 157 (September 4, 1936), 371.

———. "Ebb and Flow in Spain," *SP,* 158 (May 21, 1937), 939.

"The Pulpit and the Press," *SR,* 162 (August 22, 1936), 230.

Read, Herbert. "Poetry in My Time," *Texas Quarterly,* 1 (February, 1958), 87.

Rickword, Edgell. "Art and Propaganda," *LR,* 1 (November, 1934), 44.

———. "Stephen Spender," *LR,* 1 (August, 1935), 479.

———. "In Defence of Culture," *LR,* 3 (August, 1937), 381.

———. "Writers in Spain," *LR,* 3 (September, 1937), 446.

———. "Auden and Politics," *New Verse,* 26–27 (November, 1937), 21.

———. "Poetry and Two Wars," *Our Time,* 1 (April, 1941), 1.

Roberts, Michael. "Aspects of English Poetry," *Poetry,* 49 (January, 1937), 210.

Robinson, P. "Guernica," *National Review,* 109 (August, 1937), 253.

Rust, W. "The Spanish People's Army," *LM,* 20 (August, 1938), 508.

Ryan, William G. "International Brigadier Confesses," *S,* 7 (August 24, 1939), 154.

———. "Men Against Machines," *Catholic World,* 153 (June, 1941), 249.

Ryerson, B. "A Foreign Volunteer in Spain," *NR,* 90 (April 21, 1937), 317.

Savage, D. S. "Poetry Politics in London," *Poetry,* 53 (January, 1939), 200.

Sender, Ramon. "The First Steel Battalion," *IL,* No. 7 (July, 1937), 35.

Slater, Montagu. "The Purpose of the Left Review," *LR,* 1 (June, 1935), 359.

Slater, Montagu. "Charles Donnelly," *LR,* 3 (July, 1937), 318.

Sommerfield, John. "From a Spanish Diary," *LR,* 3 (March, 1937), 75.

"Spain and China Are Our Affair," *LR,* 3 (December, 1937), 637.

"The Spanish Shambles," *NS&N,* 12 (August 21, 1936), 167.

"The Spanish Shambles," *SP,* 157 (August 21, 1936), 296.

Spender, S. "The Problems of Poet and Public," *SP,* 143 (August 3, 1929), 132.

———. "Writers and Manifestoes," *LR,* 1 (February, 1935), 145.

———. "An Open Letter to Aldous Huxley on His Case for Constructive Peace," *LR,* 2 (August, 1936), 539.

———. "Tangiers and Gibraltar Now," *LR,* 3 (February, 1937), 17.

———. "Heroes in Spain," *NS&N,* 13 (May 1, 1937), 714.

———. "Poetry," *Fact,* No. 4 (July, 1937), 18.

———. "Pictures in Spain," *SP,* 159 (July 30, 1937), 199.

———. "A Communication," *London Mercury,* 37 (August, 1937), 373.

———. "Oxford to Communism," *New Verse,* 26–27 (November, 1937), 9.

———. "Spain Invites the World's Writers," *New Writing,* I (Autumn, 1937), 12.

———. "Poetry and Mass Observation," *NS&N,* 15 (March 19, 1938), 477.

———. "Picasso's Guernica," *NS&N,* 16 (October 15, 1938), 567.

———. "Left-Wing Orthodoxy," *New Verse,* 31–32 (Autumn, 1938), 10.

———. "Importance of W. H. Auden," *London Mercury,* 39 (April, 1939), 613.

———. "Lessons of Poetry, 1943," *Horizon,* 9 (March, 1944), 207.

Steer, George. "Spanish Profile," *London Mercury,* 35 (March, 1937), 467.

———. "The Future in Spain," *SP,* 159 (July 3, 1937), 7.

———. "Guernica," *London Mercury,* 36 (August, 1937), 330.

Strachey, John. "A People's Front for Britain?", *LBN,* No. 4 (August, 1936), 61.

———. "The Civil War in Spain," *LBN,* No. 6 (October, 1936), 116.

———. "The Road to Victory," *LBN*, No. 7 (November, 1936), 138.

———. "The Fascist World Offensive," *LN*, No. 8 (December, 1936), 171.

———. "The Left Book Club and the Future of the British Labour Movement," *LN*, No. 14 (June, 1937), 401.

———. "Visit to Teruel," *LN*, No. 23 (March, 1938), 721.

Swingler, R. "Spender's Approach to Communism," *LR*, 3 (February, 1937), 110.

Symons, Julian. "The Betrayed Idealists," *Sunday Times*, 21 (July 23, 1961).

Thomas, Hugh. "The International Brigades in Spain," *History Today*, 11 (May, 1961), 316.

Toller, E. "Madrid-Washington," *NS&N*, 15 (October 8, 1938), 521.

Torr, Dona, "Ralph Fox and Our Cultural Heritage," *LR*, 3 (February, 1937), 5.

"Towards the United Front in Britain," *VFL*, 1 (October 25, 1937), 5.

Traversi, D. A. "Marxism and English Poetry," *Arena*, 1 (October–December, 1937), 199.

"Trenches Across Europe," *NS&N*, 12 (August 1, 1936), 147.

Trevor, D. "Poets of the Spanish War," *LR*, 3 (September, 1937), 455.

"Truce in Spain," *SP*, 158 (May 28, 1937), 981.

Turner, David. "Children of Spain," *LR*, 3 (January, 1938), 703.

U. R. P. "Spain Fights for Democracy," *LM*, 18 (September, 1936), 533.

———. "Spain and the People's Front," *LM*, 19 (March, 1937), 169.

Wall, B. "W. H. Auden and Spanish Civilization," *Colosseum*, 3 (September, 1937), 142.

Warner, Rex. "Modern English Poetry," *IL*, No. 7 (July, 1939), 80.

Warner, S. T. "Barcelona," *LR*, 2 (December, 1936), 812.

———. "The Drought Breaks," *L&LT*, 16 (Summer, 1937), 68.

Whitridge, Arnold, "English Poetry and the Spanish Civil War," *Dalhousie Review,* 19 (January, 1940), 456.

Whittock, M. "The Old Man Died," *LR,* 3 (September, 1937), 461.

Wintringham, Tom. "The Road to Caporetto," *LR,* 2 (November, 1935), 63.

———. "War Is Also an Art," *LR,* 2 (February, 1936), 194.

———. "Across the Languages," *L&LT,* 21 (May, 1939), 90.

———. "How to Reform the Army," *Fact,* 5 (1939), 15.

"With the International Brigades," *Nation,* 144 (May 8, 1937), 531.

Worsley, T. C. "The Flight from Malaga," *LR,* 3 (April, 1937), 137.

———. "Propaganda and Spain," *L&LT,* 17 (Autumn, 1937), 14.

"Writers-in-Arms, with the Spanish Republican Forces," *IL,* No. 12 (December, 1937), 88.

Young, G. M. "Forty Years of Verse," *London Mercury,* 35 (December, 1936), 112.

Zabel, Morton D. "The Poetry of Unrest," *Poetry,* 50 (May, 1937), 90.

VI. Poems, Novels, Memoirs

Auden, W. H. *Dance of Death.* London, 1933.

———. *Spain.* London, 1938.

———. *Collected Poetry.* New York, 1954.

Barker, George. *Elegy on Spain.* London, 1939.

———. *Collected Poems.* London, 1957.

Bell, Julian (ed.). *We Did Not Fight.* London, 1935.

Bell, Quentin (èd.). *Julian Bell: Essays, Poems, and Letters.* London, 1938.

Bessie, Alvah (ed.). *The Heart of Spain.* New York, 1952.

Campbell, Roy. *Flowering Rifle.* London, 1939.

———. *Collected Poems.* London, 1957.

————. *Light on a Dark Horse*. London, 1951.

Carpenter, Maurice *et al. New Lyrical Ballads*. London, 1945.

Caudwell, Christopher. *Poems*. London, 1939.

(Cornford, John) Sloan, Pat (ed.). *John Cornford, a Memoir*. London, 1938.

Cunard, Nancy. *Nous Gens D'Espagne*. Perpignan, 1949.

(Fox, Ralph) Lehmann, John *et al.* Ralph Fox : *A Writer in Arms*. London, 1937.

Grigson, Geoffrey. *The Crest on the Silver*. London, 1950.

————, and Roberts, Denys K. (eds.). *The Year's Poetry*. London, 1937.

Hewett, Peter (ed.). *Poets of Tomorrow*. London, 1939.

Lee, Laurie. *The Sun My Monument*. London, 1944.

Lehmann, John. *The Whispering Gallery*. New York, 1955.

————. *I Am My Brother*. New York, 1960.

————. (ed.). *Poems from New Writing, 1936–1946*. London, 1946.

Lewis, C. Day. *Noah and the Waters*. London, 1936.

————. *Overtures to Death and Other Poems*. London, 1938.

————. *Starting Point*. London, 1938.

————. *Child of Misfortune*. London, 1939.

————. *The Buried Day*. London, 1960.

Lindsay, Jack. *Fanfrolico and After*. London, 1962.

MacDiarmid, Hugh. *Speaking for Scotland*. Baltimore, 1946.

————. *The Battle Continues*. Edinburgh, 1957.

————. *Collected Poems*. New York, 1962.

MacNeice, Louis. *Poems*. London, 1935.

————. *I Crossed the Minch*. London, 1938.

————. *Autumn Journal*. London, 1939.

Milne, Ewart. *Letter from Ireland*. Dublin, 1940.

————. *Listen Mangan*. Dublin, 1941.

Pollitt, Harry. *Serving My Time*. London, 1940.

Read, Herbert. *Thirty-Five Poems*. London, 1940.

Roberts, Michael (ed.). *New Signatures*. London, 1932.

————. *New Country*. London, 1933.

Romancero de los Voluntarios de la Libertad. Madrid, 1937.

Spender, Stephen. *The Burning Cactus.* London, 1936.

―――. *Forward from Liberalism.* London, 1937.

―――. *The Still Centre.* London, 1939.

―――. *World Within World.* London, 1951.

―――, and Lehmann, John (eds.). *Poems for Spain.* London, 1939.

―――. *The God That Failed,* edited by Richard Crossman. New York, 1950.

Swingler, Randall. *Spain.* London, 1936. (Unpublished).

Warner, Rex. *Poems.* New York, 1938.

―――. *Return of the Traveller.* New York, 1944.

Wintringham, Tom. *English Captain.* London, 1939.

Woodcock, George. *The Centre Cannot Hold.* London, 1943.

VII. Critical Books

Baker, Denys Val. (ed.). *Little Reviews,* 1914–1943. London, 1943.

―――. *Modern British Writing.* New York, 1947.

Barea, Arturo. *Lorca, the Poet and his People.* London, 1944.

Berry, F. *Herbert Read.* London, 1953.

Campbell, Roy. *Lorca, An Appreciation of his Poetry.* New Haven, 1952.

Caudwell, Christopher. *Illusion and Reality.* London, 1937.

Connelly, Cyril. *Enemies of Promise.* London, 1938.

Daiches, David. *Poetry and the Modern World.* Chicago, 1940.

―――. *The Present Age.* London, 1958.

Dyment, Clifford. *C. Day Lewis.* London, 1955.

Elliott, Robert C. *The Power of Satire: Magic, Ritual, Art.* Princeton, 1960.

Fox, Ralph. *The Novel and the People.* London, 1937.

Grigson, G. *The Arts Today.* London, 1935.

―――― (ed.). *Poetry and the Present.* London, 1949.

Guttmann, Allen. *The Wound in the Heart: America and the Spanish Civil War.* New York, 1962.

Hart, Henry (ed.). *The Writer in a Changing World.* New York, 1937.

Henderson, Philip. *The Poet and Society.* London, 1939.

Jameson, Storm. *The Writer's Situation and Other Essays.* London, 1950.

Kemp, Harry, and Riding, Laura, *et al. The Left Heresy in Literature and Life.* London, 1939.

Lehmann, John. *New Writing in Europe.* London, 1940.

———. *The Open Night.* New York, 1952.

Lewis, C. Day. *Revolution in Writing.* London, 1935.

———. *A Hope for Poetry.* Oxford, 1945.

———. *The Poetic Image.* London, 1947.

——— (ed.). *The Mind in Chains.* London, 1937.

Lewis, Wyndham. *The Writer and the Absolute.* London, 1952.

Lindsay, Jack. *After the 'Thirties.* London, 1956.

MacNeice, Louis. *Modern Poetry.* London, 1935.

Mander, John. *The Writer and Commitment.* London, 1961.

Read, Herbert. *Poetry and Anarchism.* London, 1938.

———. *The Philosophy of Anarchism.* London, 1940.

Savage, D. S. *The Personal Principle.* London, 1944.

Scarfe, Francis. *W. H. Auden.* Monaco, 1949.

———. *Auden and After.* London, 1942.

Spender, Stephen. *The New Realism.* London, 1939.

———. *Life and the Poet.* London, 1942.

———. *Poetry Since 1939.* London, 1946.

———. *The Destructive Element.* Philadelphia, 1953.

———. *The Creative Element.* New York, 1954.

Stanford, Derek. *The Freedom of Poetry.* London, 1947.

Symons, Julian. *The Thirties.* London, 1960.

Tindall, William. *Forces in Modern British Literature.* New York, 1956.

Treece, Henry (ed.). *Herbert Read: An Introduction to his Work by Various Hands.* London, 1945.

West, Alick. *Crisis and Criticism.* London, 1937.

Wilder, Amos. *The Spiritual Aspects of the New Poetry*. New York, 1940.

Woodcock, George. *The Writer and Politics*. London, 1947.

VIII. Leading Periodicals

Among Friends
Arena
Colosseum
Dublin Review
English Review
Fact
Fight
Freedom
Horizon
International Literature
Irish Front (Freedom)
Labour Monthly
Left News
Left Poets News Sheet
Left Review
Life and Letters Today
Living Age
London Mercury
Nation
National Review
New Masses
New Republic

New Times and Ethiopia News
New Verse
New Writing
News of Spain
New Statesman and Nation
Our Time
Poetry
Poetry and the People
Right Review
Saturday Review
Spain
Spain and the Revolution
Spain at War
Spain Today
Spanish News Letter
Spectator
Time and Tide
Townsman
Voice of Spain
Volunteer for Liberty
War in Spain

Index

317